LANDMARK VISITORS GUIDE

Somerset

Richard Sale

Published By
Landmark Publishing Ltd
Waterloo House, 12 Compton, Ashbourne,
Derbyshire DE6 1DA England

A research scientist before concentrating on writing and photography. Richards titles for Landmark include the Cotswolds, Dorset, Italian Lakes, Madeira and Provence.

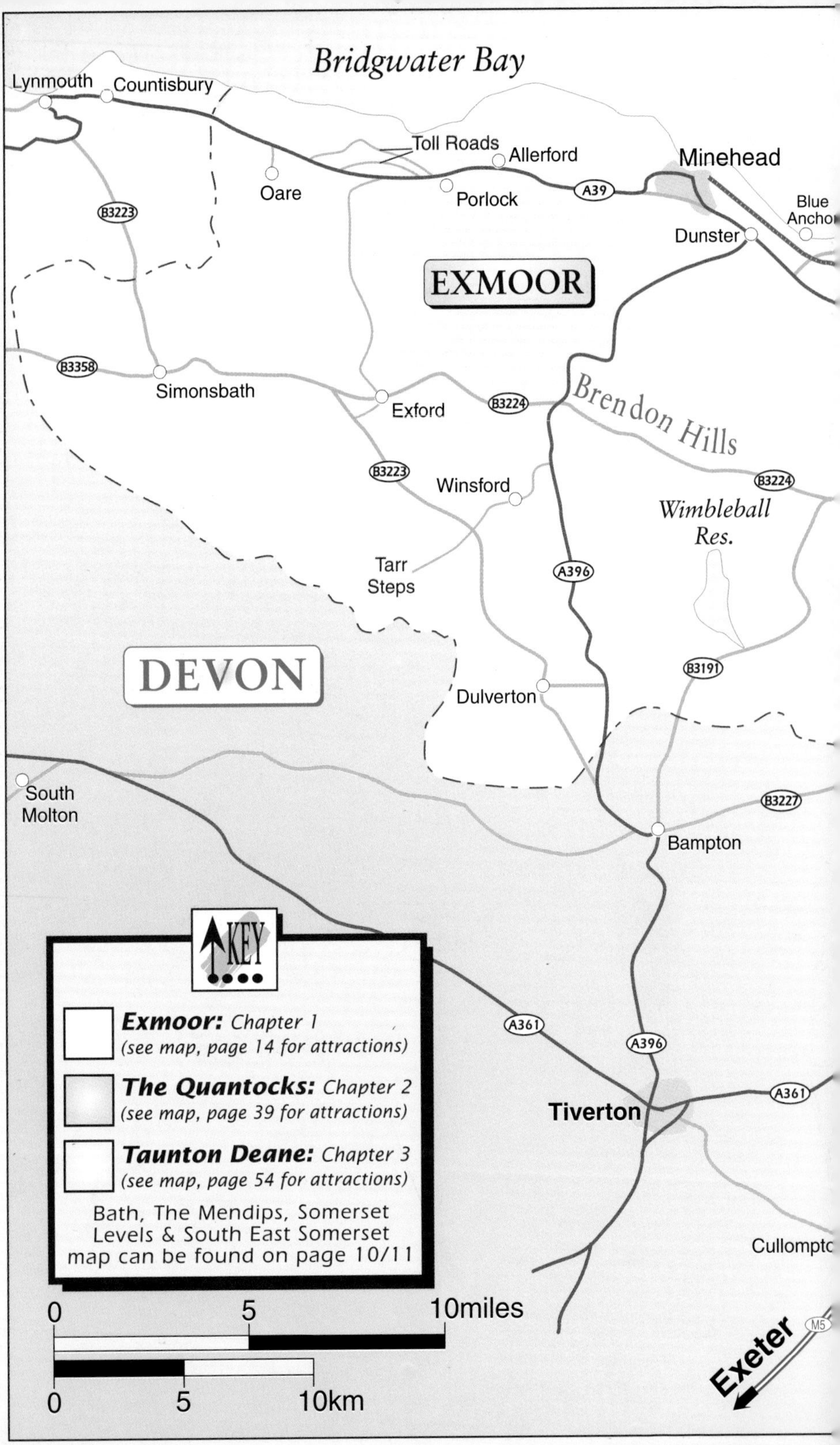

Bridgwater Bay
Lynmouth
Countisbury
Toll Roads
Allerford
Minehead
Oare
Porlock
A39
Blue Ancho
B3223
Dunster
EXMOOR
B3358
Simonsbath
Exford
B3224
Brendon Hills
B3223
Winsford
B3224
Wimbleball Res.
Tarr Steps
A396
DEVON
B3191
Dulverton
South Molton
B3227
Bampton
KEY
Exmoor: Chapter 1 (see map, page 14 for attractions)
The Quantocks: Chapter 2 (see map, page 39 for attractions)
Taunton Deane: Chapter 3 (see map, page 54 for attractions)
Bath, The Mendips, Somerset Levels & South East Somerset map can be found on page 10/11
A361
A396
A361
Tiverton
Cullompto
0
5
10miles
0
5
10km
Exeter
M5

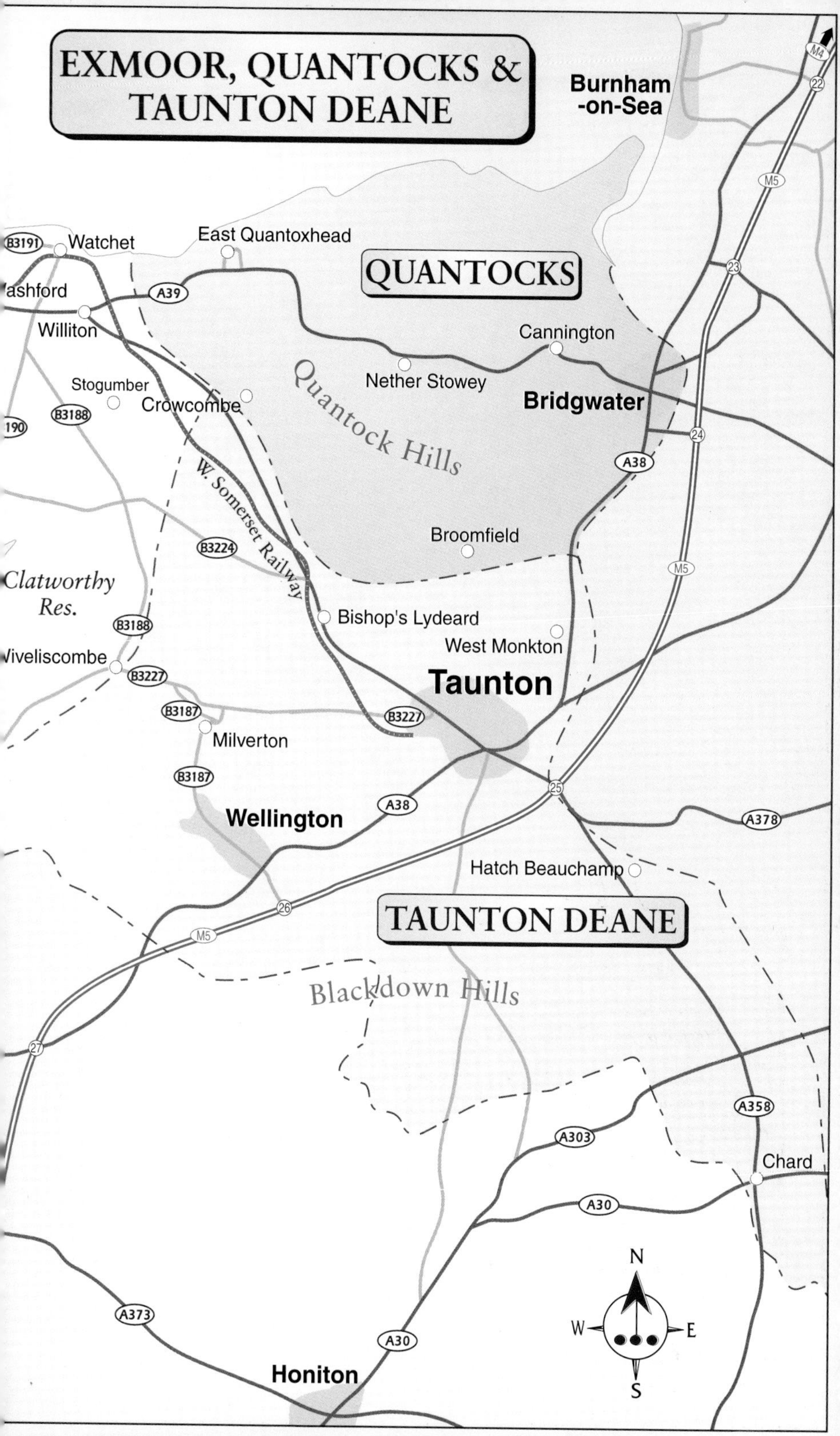
EXMOOR, QUANTOCKS & TAUNTON DEANE
Burnham -on-Sea
M4
22
M5
B3191
Watchet
East Quantoxhead
QUANTOCKS
23
'ashford
A39
Williton
Cannington
Nether Stowey
Stogumber
Crowcombe
Quantock Hills
Bridgwater
190
B3188
24
A38
W. Somerset Railway
B3224
Broomfield
M5
Clatworthy Res.
B3188
Bishop's Lydeard
West Monkton
'iveliscombe
B3227
Taunton
B3187
B3227
Milverton
B3187
25
A38
A378
Wellington
Hatch Beauchamp
26
TAUNTON DEANE
M5
Blackdown Hills
27
A358
A303
Chard
A30
N
W
E
S
A373
A30
Honiton

• Contents •

Introduction

The abbey at Glastonbury

Somerset, the country where smock-clad rustics lean on farmyard gates, taking large gulps from pints of scrumpy – pausing only to exchange views in an incomprehensible dialect liberally punctuated with 'ooh arr'.

As with all such clichéd identities, there is an element of fact about this one, but what is equally true about such generalisations is that it can obscure real truths. And the real truth of Somerset is that it is a wonderful county, with a diversity of scenery and interests that make it one of the finest of English counties for the visitor.

But before listing the delights Somerset has to offer the visitor, it is necessary to define what we mean by the county. Until 1974 this was a nonsensical question, but in that year the redrawing of county boundaries created the county of Avon. At a stroke northern Somerset was lost to the old county, the loss including not only fine country at the base of the Mendip Hills, but Bath and Weston-super-Mare and that most wonderfully named of all English places – Nempnett Thrubwell.

Avon is gone now. Its demise was lamented by almost no one, not least because national commentators could never pronounce it correctly, preferring the A-Von beloved of cosmetic sellers rather than the A-ven the locals knew to be correct. But the death of Avon did not return Somerset's lost lands to it. Somerset remained the decapitated county it had become, with two new districts being created. But they took the county's name, making it clear where their allegiance lay. Here we maintain the old allegiance, exploring an area that extends northwards to the River Avon – just as the real Somerset did.

Topography

The greater part of the Exmoor National Park lies within Somerset's borders, that part including the moor's highest top – Dunkery Beacon. The moor is famous for its heather, which provides brilliant purple covering when it flowers, but it also has excellent wooded valleys – particularly those of Horner Water and the River Barle.

The National Park also includes a section of coast, and though Somerset cannot boast the rugged coastal scenery of Cornwall or Devon, the section followed by the South-West Peninsula National Trail (which has a terminal point in Minehead) is as isolated as anywhere on the path. Walkers on the Trail from Foreland Point (just over the Devon border) to Porlock Weir are likely to be alone with their thoughts and the wild splendour of the coast.

In addition to the National Park, Somerset also has two Areas of Outstanding Natural Beauty (AONB) and a part share in a third. The Quantocks are one of England's smallest AONBs – a fit walker can traverse the long axis in a day – but are renowned for their wooded combes and long views which have long attracted artists. Wordsworth and Coleridge walked here, the latter finding local inspiration for his most famous works – *The Rime of the Ancient Mariner* and the 'lost' masterpiece of *Kubla Khan*.

The Mendip Hills AONB is also wholly contained within the county. The hills are formed of a limestone that supports a very individual flora, and which dissolves in rainwater so that it is honeycombed with caves. Some of Britain's best show caves are found beneath the Mendips.

Somerset claims only a slice of the AONB which encompasses the Blackdown Hills, but that slice includes the best of the range. Here there are deeply wooded valleys and ridges, the Blackdown edge offering viewpoints that overlook Taunton Deane and the county of south Somerset.

And, as if these areas were not enough diversity, Somerset also has the Levels: only East Anglia can boast a larger area of fenland in Britain than Somerset. The Levels have been protected from the encroaching sea and drained for agriculture, but enough remains to form one of Britain's most important wetland wildlife habitats.

History

Some of the oldest remains of human habitation in Britain have been found in Somerset, the caves of Mendip yielding the remains of Palaeolithic (Old Stone Age) man who shared the land with mammoths, hyenas and cave bears. Dating from a time thousands of years later, the oldest path to have been found, so far, in Europe was uncovered on the Somerset Levels. Known as the Sweet Track, the pathway was of woven hazel and willow sticks and allowed the Levels' dwellers of 6,000 years ago to cross marshland in search of good fishing and wildfowl.

The Neolithic hunters who built the Levels' tracks also raised the long barrow at Stoney Littleton, one of very few such barrows to be found in the county. Have others been eroded into extinction or did New Stone Age man prefer the Levels to the firmer grounds to the north and south? If it was the latter, the view of Bronze Age man was different, his burial chambers – round barrows – being found in numbers on Exmoor and the Mendips. Bronze Age man is also famous for megalithic sites. The word megalith means 'large stone' and no better description could be found: at Stanton Drew the collection of stone circles and standing stones is among the most interesting and evocative in Britain.

Iron Age (Celtic) folk are best known for their hill forts, and there are several fine examples in Somerset, including that on Dolebury Warren (on the Mendips) which is one of the largest in Britain. Later Bronze Age/early Iron Age folk were also responsible for the lake villages which have been excavated on the Somerset Levels. Despite the name these were not villages on platforms and piles actually in (or on) the lakes, but were built at the lake shore, the villagers using crude boats to hunt the marshland.

When the Romans came they exploited the hot springs at Bath, the baths at their town of *Aquae Sulis* being one of the most complete to have been found anywhere. The Romans also exploited the lead deposits of the Mendips, exporting the metal along Fosse Way which runs through the heart of the county.

When the Romans abandoned Britain the Celts they had defeated were

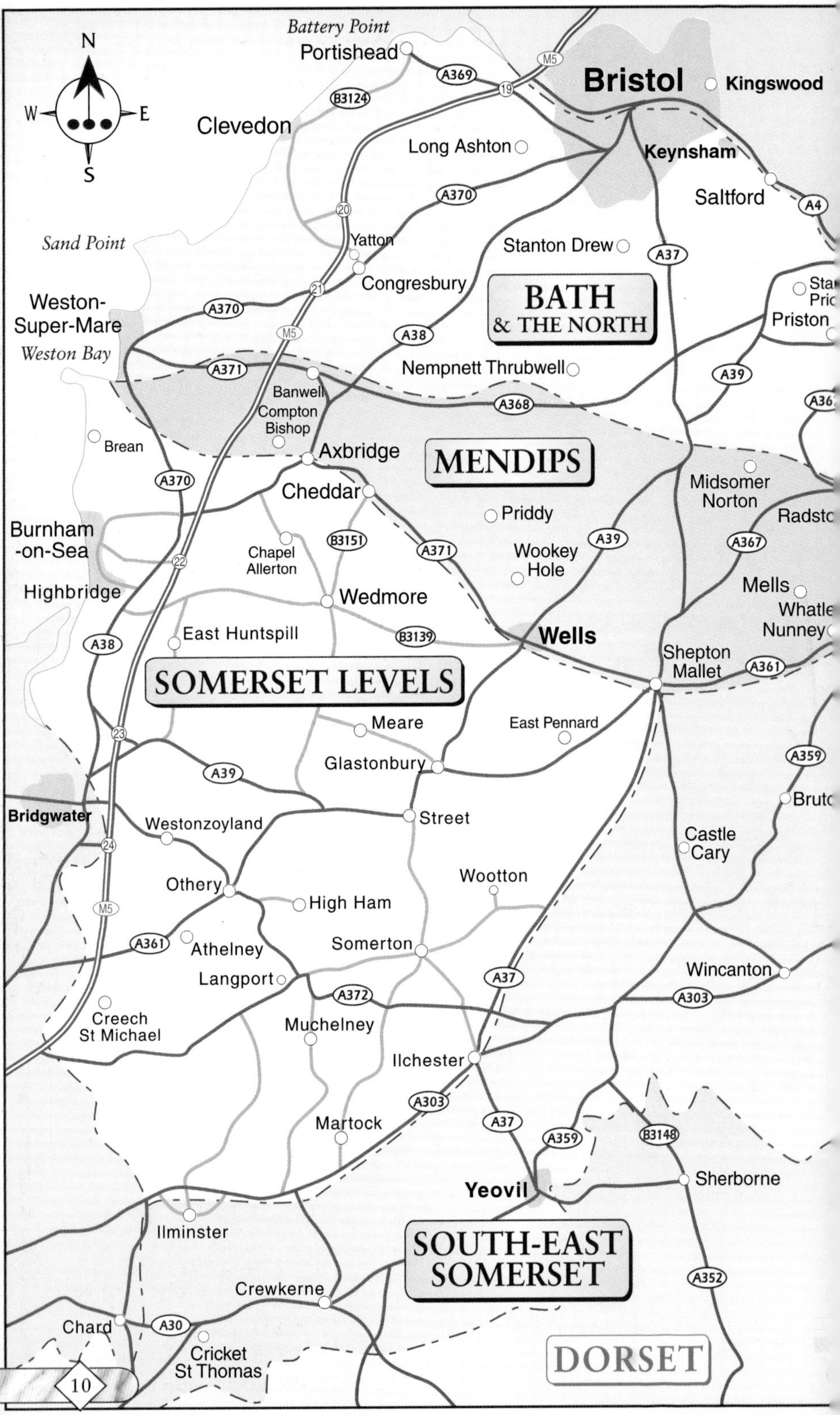
N
W
E
S
Battery Point
Portishead
Clevedon
Bristol
Kingswood
Long Ashton
Keynsham
Saltford
Sand Point
Yatton
Stanton Drew
Congresbury
BATH & THE NORTH
Weston-Super-Mare
Weston Bay
Priston
Nempnett Thrubwell
Banwell
Compton Bishop
Brean
Axbridge
MENDIPS
Cheddar
Midsomer Norton
Priddy
Burnham-on-Sea
Chapel Allerton
Wookey Hole
Highbridge
Wedmore
Mells
East Huntspill
Wells
Shepton Mallet
SOMERSET LEVELS
Meare
East Pennard
Glastonbury
Bridgwater
Westonzoyland
Street
Castle Cary
Othery
Wootton
High Ham
Athelney
Somerton
Langport
Wincanton
Creech St Michael
Muchelney
Ilchester
Martock
Yeovil
Sherborne
Ilminster
SOUTH-EAST SOMERSET
Crewkerne
Chard
Cricket St Thomas
DORSET
M5
A369
B3124
A370
A37
A4
A38
A371
A368
A39
A367
B3151
B3139
A361
A359
A372
A303
A352
B3148
A30

BATH, MENDIPS, SOMERSET LEVELS & SOUTH EAST SOMERSET

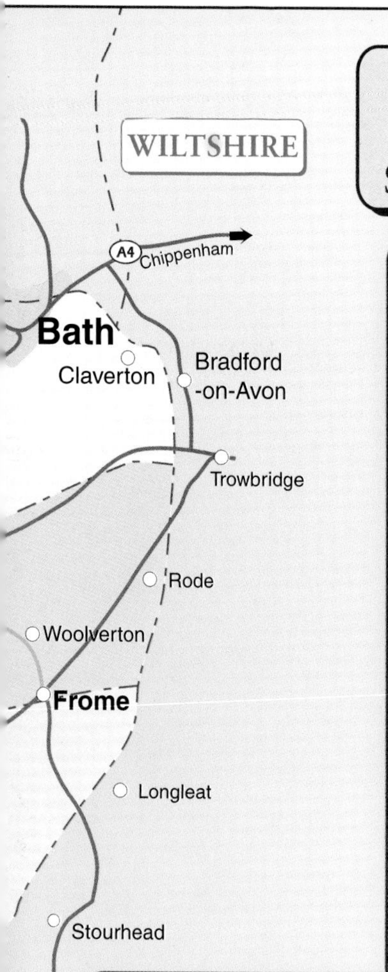

Above: In the garden at Barrington Court Left: The Saturday market outside the entrance to the Bishop's Palace, Wells

KEY

S.E. Somerset: *Chapter 4*
(see map, page 75 for attractions)

S Levels: *Chapter 5*
(see map, page 110 for attractions)

Mendips: *Chapter 6*
(see map, page 146 for attractions)

Bath: *Chapter 7*
(see map, page 146 for attractions)

left vulnerable to attacks from mainland Europe. The Saxons landed in Kent and over generations fought their way westwards. In about 500AD their advance was halted by the victories of a Celtic warlord, Arthur. Here in Somerset, the real and mythical Arthur coincide, for the real warlord may have had his headquarters (his Camelot) at South Cadbury, while the Arthur of legend, fatally wounded in his final battle, was taken for healing to Avalon which, the New Age believers claim, was centred at Glastonbury.

After a decisive victory at Dyrham, just north of Bristol, the Saxons split the Celtic kingdom in two and rapidly occupied Somerset. On the Somerset Levels they built villages where folk took the canes of pollarded willows and wove them into baskets and hurdles for enclosing domestic animals. The Saxons called the willows *salh* (which gives us sallow, an alternative name for the tree): the men who wove the canes acquired the name Sale, the ancestors of the author.

Somerset was part of the Saxon kingdom of Wessex, and it was to the impenetrable land of the Somerset Levels that the Wessex king, Alfred, fled when Vikings threatened from the north. At Athelney Alfred famously burnt the cakes, but he also formed an army that soon advanced from the Levels stronghold to defeat the Vikings. The king built an abbey at Athelney in thanksgiving for the victory. It was the first of many, some founded by the Saxons, some by the conquering Normans. The greatest of the abbeys was Glastonbury, still a spiritual home of Christian worship.

The Normans built churches too, many of them with wonderful towers. Such a feature of the county were the towers that they form a specific architectural class, making almost any Somerset village worth a visit for its church tower. The Normans brought peace and stability to Somerset (and England), though there were still spasmodic threats to each.

The Civil War was fought more bitterly elsewhere, though Somerset did not go untouched, and then in 1685 the last battle fought on English soil took place on Sedgemoor, near Westonzoyland, when the rebellion of the Duke of Monmouth ended. The battle cost hundreds of lives, but its aftermath, the infamous Bloody Assizes, was almost as devastating.

Happier times followed, Somerset's towns enjoying prosperity generated by the wool trade. But the greatest prosperity had nothing to do with wool, Bath becoming the social centre of Georgian England. Later, Weston-super-Mare thrived on the new-found enthusiasm for seaside holidays.

This guide explores all aspects of Somerset in a series of seven chapters, each dealing with a well-defined area of the county.

• Highlights of Somerset •

Somerset's scenery and history, as briefly outlined in the Introduction, are enough to tempt many to the county. But though such broad brushes paint a positive picture, they do not pick out all the individual highlights. Consider this list of just some of those highlights:

Bath – (see page 179) Britain's finest Georgian city, with the superb remains of the Roman baths, the magnificent Abbey and a series of museums of international quality.

Wells – (see page 148) One of Britain's greatest cathedrals and its finest Bishop's Palace.

Glastonbury – (see page 113) The mystical capital of Britain. Here, legend has it, Joseph of Arimathea brought the Holy Thorn and the Holy Grail. Earth Magic believers see the zodiac imprinted on the landscape and a maze circling the famous Tor.

Cheddar – (see page 155) The Gorge, with its vast, sheer limestone cliffs is one of the natural wonders of Britain. The village is also the original home of one of the world's best-known cheeses. The visitor can still buy Cheddar cheese at Cheddar.

Wookey Hole – (see page 153) Cheddar has excellent show caves too, but arguably the finest in Britain are to be found at Wookey Hole, near Wells.

Lovely villages – Somerset has not only some of England's loveliest villages and small towns – Selworthy and Winsford, Castle Cary and Bruton, Mells and Nunney – but some of the most romantically named of any in the country. Many Somerset village names have two words, merely adding to their appeal. Who could not fall in love with Huish Champflower, Brympton D'evercy and Compton Pauncefoot? And that list does not include the finest of all – surely the best-named village in Britain – Nempnett Thrubwell.

Seaside resorts – The Somerset coast may be limited in extent, but it still has the marvellous 'old-fashioned' resorts of Weston-super-Mare and Minehead.

Excellent visitor sites – Somerset has many, including some of the finest of their kind in Britain the Fleet Air Arm Museum at Yeovilton, the Haynes Motor Museum and the Cricket St Thomas Wildlife Park. There are superb National Trust properties – Montacute House, Lytes Cary and Clevedon Court. Chard even claims to be the home of powered flight.

Cider – Finally we return to the most famous Somerset image of all, that of the pint of scrumpy. It is no fallacy that Somerset folk like their cider and visiting the cider farms is one of the joys of a stay.

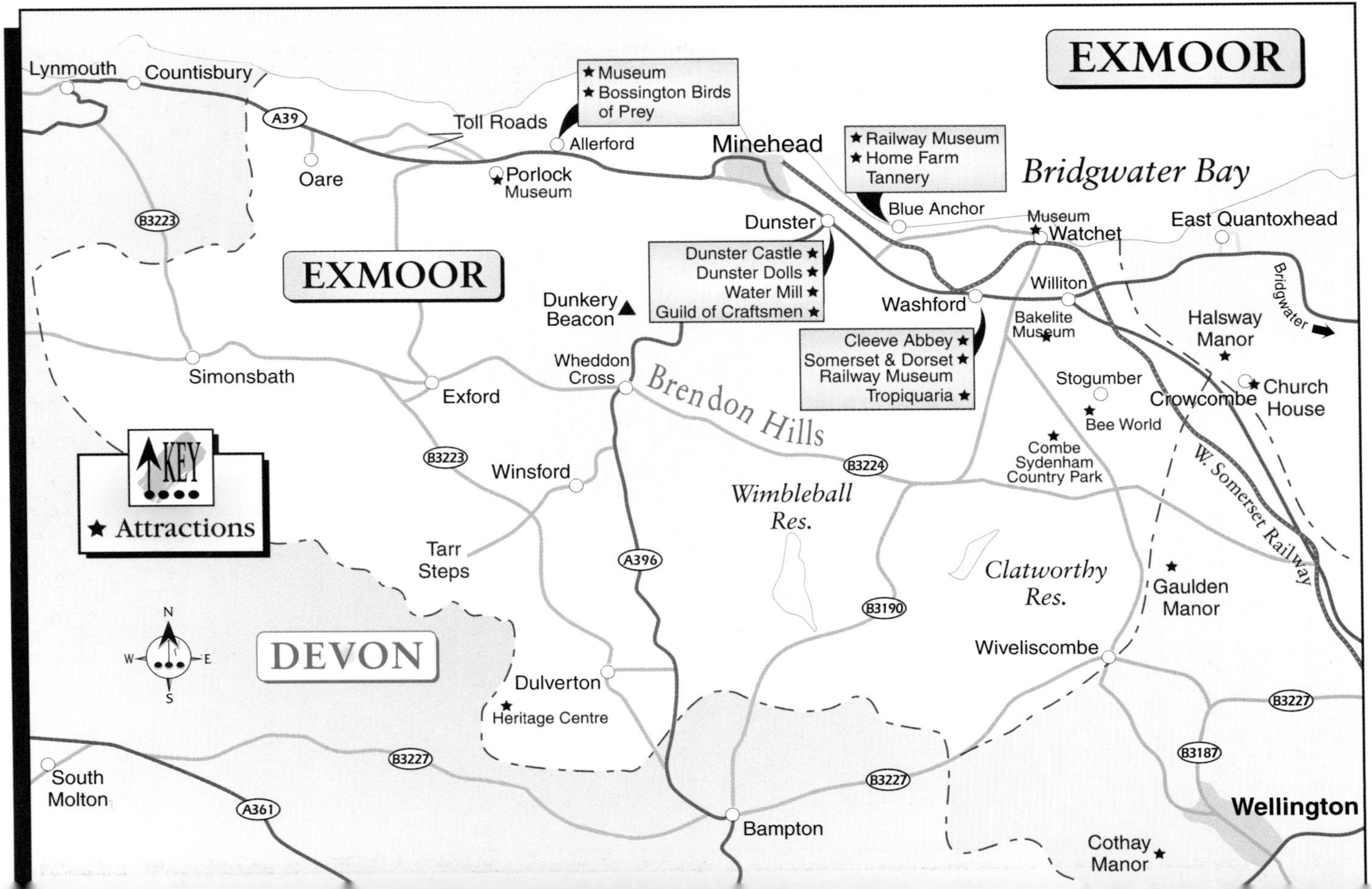
EXMOOR
Bridgwater Bay
Lynmouth
Countisbury
A39
Toll Roads
★ Museum
★ Bossington Birds of Prey
Allerford
Oare
Porlock
Museum
Minehead
★ Railway Museum
★ Home Farm Tannery
Blue Anchor
Museum
Watchet
East Quantoxhead
Dunster
Dunster Castle ★
Dunster Dolls ★
Water Mill ★
Guild of Craftsmen ★
B3223
EXMOOR
Dunkery Beacon
Washford
Williton
Bridgwater
Bakelite Museum
Cleeve Abbey ★
Somerset & Dorset Railway Museum ★
Tropiquaria ★
Halsway Manor
Church House
Crowcombe
Stogumber
Bee World
Simonsbath
Exford
Wheddon Cross
Brendon Hills
Combe Sydenham Country Park
W. Somerset Railway
KEY
★ Attractions
B3223
Winsford
B3224
Wimbleball Res.
Tarr Steps
A396
Clatworthy Res.
Gaulden Manor
B3190
N
W
E
S
DEVON
Wiveliscombe
Dulverton
Heritage Centre
B3227
South Molton
B3227
B3187
A361
B3227
Wellington
Bampton
Cothay Manor

1 Exmoor

Porlock Weir

In this first chapter we explore that part of the Exmoor National Park which lies in Somerset, together with that section of the north Somerset coast which links the National Park to the Quantocks Area of Outstanding Natural Beauty.

The Exmoor National Park

Of all the National Parks of England and Wales, Exmoor has the greatest range of natural scenery. While it has none of the rugged grandeur of the mountains of Snowdonia or the Lake District, the bleak upland moors of Dartmoor or such an extent or range of sea cliff as the Pembrokeshire Coast National Park, Exmoor has a little of all of them and a bit more besides.

The Park's upland is divided into two sections by the River Exe, which gives the moor its name, and by its tributary, the Quarme. The Brendon Hills (not to be confused with Brendon Common, which is in Doone country to the west) lie to the east and the main Exmoor plateau to the west. On its north-eastern edge Exmoor falls into gentle, wooded country studded with beautiful villages such as Selworthy and Dunster.

Underlying Exmoor are rocks of the Devonian era, sandstones and grits. These hard, resistant rocks yield a poor, acidic soil that drains badly and supports a very limited vegetation. In the valleys formed by rivers draining down from the moor the soil is a little better and overlies a subsoil that is more clayey. This better drained, more nutrient-rich soil supports a greater range and growth of vegetation, making the river valleys, themselves more sheltered to give a better growing environment, greener and more lush, a real delight to the eye. In the valleys oaks are the predominant tree, but there are also stands of beech and ash as well as other, less numerous, species.

Wildlife of the Moor

On the high moor the vegetation is chiefly heather – ling and bell heather – with clumps of bilberry (known locally as whortleberry). The former offers a glorious purple show when it blossoms.

On the high moor the animal life is limited: a few Exmoor ponies and, but rarely, deer. The latter, the native red deer together with introduced herds of roe, fallow and sika are mainly encountered in the wooded valleys. Moorland birds are not abundant, despite the fact that over 200 species have been noted within the park's boundaries, but the buzzard is frequently seen, working the thermals of the up-slopes searching for a meal. The bird-watcher will choose the wooded valleys rather than the moor if he is after variety, and he will doubtless travel north to the coast to complete his survey. There, with the moor still visible behind him, he can add razorbills to a list that may also include stonechat, dipper and kingfisher.

County Gate to Minehead: the Exmoor Coast

The Exmoor National Park Visitor Centre at **County Gate** stands on the border between Somerset and Devon. West from here Countisbury Hill – the partner to Porlock Hill, the two famous steep hills on to the Exmoor plateau – drops to Lynmouth. Devon's first town Lynmouth was the scene of a devastating flood in August 1952 which killed 34 people. The town is a centre for visits to Watersmeet and the Valley of the Rocks which few visitors to Exmoor will fail to enjoy.

Eastwards from County Gate, heading along the A39, a turn left is soon reached for **Oare**. The road down to the hamlet is steep and narrow, but a visit is essential for lovers of *Lorna Doone* and scenic beauty. The Domesday Book refers to Oare (as Are) but it is not known whether there was a church here before the present building was constructed in the 14th century. The tower is later, having been built in the mid-19th century when the church was also extended – a fact that helps the Lorna Doone story.

Within the church, most visitors are looking for the window through which Lorna was shot and it is dutifully marked with a card. But the book does not actually specify that Lorna was shot through a window. If Carver Doone had shot her along the length of the church he would probably have walked away, such was his reputation. Nevertheless, the fact that the church has been extended means that where the altar would have been in the 17th century would have left a bride visible from the moor's edge through the southern window. The church also has a fine memorial tablet to R D Blackmore.

Headless Saint

Look, too, for the piscina. It is in the shape of a head held by a pair of hands, a representation of the final act of the Celtic St Decuman who sailed across the Bristol Channel from South Wales accompanied only by a cow. Landing at Watchet he set up a hermit's cell but was beheaded by a thief. The saint picked up the severed head and took it to a holy well to wash it. The piscina represents that final carry.

Of the places that occur in the book many can be identified. Lorna Doone Farm is the residence of Nicholas Snowe, the (real) churchwarden: parts of the building are believed to be over 1000 years old. Opposite the church is Oare House, almost certainly the model for John Ridd's Plover's Barrows Farm. Further along the Oare Water valley, Robber's Bridge, where John Ridd's father was murdered, not only exists but retains the name.

Badgworthy Water is the book's Bagworthy Water, where the young John went fishing. The locals pronounce the stream's name 'badgery' which explains the spelling change. The water-slide (it is definitely more a slide than a falls, despite the exaggerations of several films of the book) is at the entrance to Lank

Heather in bloom on Exmoor

Combe, and the valley contains the ruins of medieval cottages, the old homes of Sir Ensor and Carver Doone.

To reach **Badgworthy Water** the footpath beside the church is followed to Cloud Farm. Beyond the farm, turn left beside the stream, passing a memorial stone to R D Blackmore and continuing to Lank Combe, to the right, and the Doone Valley, also to the right.

Further east along the A39, lying north of the road and best reached on foot – it lies on the Coastal Path – is **Culbone Church** which has the curious distinction of being noted in both the Domesday Book and the Guinness Book of Records. The former is a measure of the church's antiquity, for although the exact date of construction is unknown it was clearly Saxon. The Guinness entry records Culbone as England's smallest parish church. The church is just over 10m (35ft) long, the nave not quite 4m (13ft) wide, and is exquisitely sited on a wooded hillside.

Continue eastwards, either descending the steep hairpins of Porlock Hill or taking the toll road – which has marvellous views of the coast – to reach **Porlock**, an attractive village despite the main road that bisects it. It is known that Vikings landed here in 914 – they were beaten off, their ships later being wrecked on Steep Holm where the warriors starved to death – and that a Saxon army landed in 1052, so clearly the village was a major port in Saxon times.

Today it lies 1km (over half a mile) from the sea as a result of the silting of Porlock Bay. The **Doverhay Manor Museum** in the High Street explores the village's history. The house is late 15th century, but seems never to have been the manor house, despite the name. The name, too, is disputed – is it Dovery as the county authorities would have you believe, or Doverhay as the locals have it?

To the west from the village is **Porlock Weir**, a picturesque small harbour. The poets Coleridge and Robert Southey sheltered from the

The Man of Porlock and Kubla Khan

In the summer of 1797 Samuel Taylor Coleridge, at that time living on the Quantocks, took a cottage above the sea near Culbone in an attempt to shake off ill health. The exact site of the cottage is disputed, but most experts favour the now-demolished Withycombe Farm.

Coleridge is already known to have been taking laudanum and may also have taken other drugs to alleviate his symptoms. Whatever the cause he fell into a deep sleep while reading a book on Kubla Khan and awoke after about three hours with his poem on the great Mongol leader fully formed in his head. He immediately began to transcribe the poem, but when he had completed only 54 lines there was a knock at the door. It was the 'Man of Porlock' who had come on some trivial matter. Neither the man's name nor his errand are known, but he spent an hour with the increasingly frustrated poet. By the time he had left Coleridge had forgotten the verse and so lost the thread that the poem was unfinished. It remains a 54-line masterpiece.

Watersmeet, just over the county boundary near Lynmouth

rain in the Ship Inn, and countless others have also enjoyed its hospitality.

Southwards from Porlock a difficult road rises to **Stoke Pero** where, at 309m (1,013ft), stands the highest church on Exmoor. It is also the most remote – all the more so now that the little village it once served has been reduced from its maximum of about 20 cottages to the solitary Church Farm. One tale, probably apocryphal, recounts a visitor asking at Porlock for the best way to Stoke Pero and being told that there was no best way. By the late 19th century the church was ruinous but the Acland family of Holnicote Estate (see below) paid for its restoration. This was carried out in 1896-97: roofing timber had to be brought from Porlock and was carried by a donkey called Zulu who made the trip twice daily for months. As a reward Zulu has his portrait hanging inside the church which, if not unique, is certainly unusual.

To the north of Porlock is **Bossington**, a very attractive little village. Our journey continues eastwards, soon reaching a turn on the right for **West Luccombe**, where there is a lovely packhorse bridge, Horner and Luccombe, another attractive village, here with a fine 13th-century church. **Horner** is a beautiful, if somewhat overcrowded in summer, little village lying in the wooded valley of Horner Water.

The village is associated with the Acland family who rose from humble beginnings in the 15th century to owning so much land that it was said they could ride from Porlock to

The Great Porlock Rescue

On 12 January 1899 the *Forest Hall* got into difficulties in Porlock Bay and a call went out to launch the Lynmouth lifeboat. Unfortunately the sea was swamping the slipway and launching was impossible, but the coxswain, Jack Crocombe, decided to haul the boat to Porlock for launching there. Helped by his crew, a team of horses and most of the population of Lynton and Lynmouth, Jack hauled the three and a half-ton boat – a ten-oared boat called *Louisa* – up Countisbury Hill on its wheeled launcher carriage. At the top they found a section of moorland road to be too narrow for the carriage, so the boat was taken off and hauled through on skids while the carriage went through fields to the lane's end.

The journey of 15 miles to Porlock, which also required a section of wall beside the road to be dismantled, was completed in about 13 hours, overnight, in appalling weather. The boat was launched immediately, at 7am, and successfully reached the *Forest Hall*. Each of the men on the *Louisa*'s crew, one of whom was only sixteen years old, received a silver watch as a memento. A replica of the *Louisa* can be seen at Lynmouth.

Exeter without ever going over one of their own boundaries.

The family is credited (if credited is the appropriate word) with having re-invented or popularised stag-hunting, but deserve greater appreciation for the magnificent gesture of Sir Richard Acland in 1944 when he gave 12,400 acres of the Holnicote Estate to the National Trust.

Next on the main road – or, rather, just off it – is **Allerford.** It is easy in this part of Somerset to run out of superlatives for the little villages – just what can one say about Allerford and nearby Selworthy to emphasise how beautiful they are? The well-photographed packhorse bridge and stone cottages of Allerford hardly do justice to its attractiveness – it really must be seen. In the Old School, a fine thatched building that was the village school from 1821 to 1981, there is a museum which explores village life over the last 100 years, including a Victorian schoolroom and items on local crafts. On the road from Allerford to Bossington, **Bossington Farm** has rare breed farm animals – young lambs can be bottle fed – a pets' corner and a collection of birds of prey (owls and falcons). There are frequent flying displays with the birds.

Selworthy is a village of white-washed, thatched cottages, largely built by Sir Thomas Acland for workers on his Holnicote Estate, and now owned by the National Trust which, thankfully, has retained its essential character, rejecting over-commercialisation. The village church is also white-washed, giving it a curious, fairy-tale quality which merely adds to the dream-like, timelessness of the village.

Reality is re-established a short distance east of Selworthy at Minehead.

Minehead

The town's curious name derives from the Celtic *mynydd* – hill – referring to the ridge of Exmoor that runs into the sea on the west side of the shallow bay which the town backs. That ridge sheltered the harbour that was the source of the town's early prosperity, Minehead playing a major part in the medieval trade with Ireland. The harbour, and the old thatched cottages in nearby Quay Street are still one of the town's most attractive areas.

"The South West Coastal Path, Britain's longest National Trail, starts (or ends) at the harbour."

Another attractive area of town lies close to St Michael's Church, also on the hilly, western side of town. The church is a fine building with a good tower and some interesting monuments, including a 15th-century brass. Close to the church are Church Steps, a steep, stepped street of lovely old cottages. Closer to the centre of the present town, in Market House Lane, are the Quirkes Almshouses, dating from 1630.

The hillside 'village' around the church is old Minehead, the newer town at the hill base developing rapidly with the vogue for seaside holidays, particularly after the railway reached the town in 1874. The promenade was built in about 1900 and in 1901 a 210m (700ft) pier was added, though this was dismantled in 1939.

Minehead was always the largest resort on Somerset's Exmoor coast, but the national profile of the town increased dramatically in 1962 when Butlin's opened a holiday camp to the east of the town centre. The site, renamed **Somerset World**, is still there, its facilities also available to day visitors. It lies beyond the terminal station of the West Somerset Railway.

In addition, the town has a large assortment of amusements, a permanent funfair and a swimming pool with water slides. Yet despite the overt commercialism which is a requirement of a successful British seaside resort at the end of the millennium, Minehead retains its character, not only in its hillside village and old port, but in its 'Somerset-town' heart, a fact that is reinforced by its being the only county town which celebrates May-day morning with a hobby horse.

Above: Minehead
Below: The White Horse Hotel, Exford

Simonsbath to Wheddon Cross: High Exmoor

Simonsbath lies to the south of Lynmouth, from which it is reached by a scenic road that crosses the moor close to the Doone Valley. It is Somerset's westernmost village and a well-known centre for walkers on the moor. To the south-east, and reached by a fine walk beside the River Barle, is Cow Castle, a tiny

Famous Visitors

R D Blackmore wrote part of *Lorna Doone* in the Royal Oak Inn at Withypool and Gen Dwight Eisenhower came, by horseback it is said, for a pint after visiting American troops who were training on Exmoor.

• Tarr Steps •

In 1968 the Post Office issued a set of commemorative stamps: the 4 old penny stamp (letter post) bore the image of Tarr Steps and the bold title 'prehistoric'. It is difficult to find a reference to the causeway before, or immediately after, that date that does not offer this view as though it were fact, but the truth is that no one knows how old Tarr Steps are.

In form the Steps are a very long version of the clapper bridges more usually found on Dartmoor. In fact this is the longest clapper bridge in Britain, over 36m (120ft) long and comprising 17 slabs, the biggest of which weighs several tons. The slabs average just over 2m (about 7ft) long and 1.5m (4ft) wide and are held about a metre (3ft) above the water by piers placed on the stream bed.

For all its size the bridge is oddly sited: the River Barle can be successfully forded close to it for most of the year, and just a kilometre southward is another crossing known to have been in use in the mid-12th century. This latter fact lends weight to the argument that Tarr Steps are 13th or 14th century. The name, too, seems to suggest a similarity with Dartmoor – Tarr from tor, the exposed slabs of rock found on moorland summits. However, some have suggested that Tarr is from *tochar*, the Celtic word for a causeway. If the Iron Age Celts had named the bridge then a Bronze Age construction becomes more likely. Overall, the weight of evidence suggests Tarr Steps are a medieval pack-horse bridge, but with just enough doubt to maintain interest.

In one sense the age of the bridge could be classified as 'recent' for severe flooding has required its rebuilding several times. The flood of 1952 that destroyed Lynmouth tore 16 of the bridge's 17 spans away. One stone, weighing over a ton, was moved nearly 50m (164ft) downstream. The restoration was as perfect as could be achieved and, using the best of modern equipment, difficult, merely adding to the wonder of the original construction.

One curious folk story also suggests a very early construction date. The bridge, it says, was a ritual crossing rather than a real one – the ford serving that purpose – and there was an annual animal sacrifice (usually of a cat), the poor creature being thrown across the river and killed on the far side before crossings were allowed. Another Exmoor legend suggests that the Devil built Tarr Steps so he could sunbathe near the river.

Tarr Steps, Exmoor

Dunkery Beacon

The name Dunkery is said to derive from the Celtic *dun creagh*, a rocky hill, which is about as inappropriate a name as could be imagined. It is almost easier to believe the story of the Devil creating the hill with the shovelful of earth he removed from the Punchbowl to the south near Winsford. The 'Beacon' was added after successive signal fires, the earliest of which could perhaps go back to very ancient times. Of late, beacon fires have been built here to commemorate the Queen's Coronation and Jubilee, Royal weddings and to celebrate the centenary of the publication of *Lorna Doone*.

The summit is crowned with a huge cairn, a trig point and a toposcope pointing out details of the view. On a good day this takes in the Mendips to the north-east, the Brecon Beacons to the north, and Dartmoor and Bodmin Moor to the south, as well as the Brendons and the Quantocks, the sea and, of course, the superb local scenery, most especially the valley of Horner Water and Horner Wood.

The local high moor here is usually associated with the purple of ling, but in fact it is surprisingly prolific in wildflowers. The list includes not only bell heather, bilberry and gorse, as might be expected, but also tormentil, blue heather speedwell, heath spotted orchid, bog pimpernel and milkwort.

The ridge of moor of which Dunkery is the highest point was almost certainly a trackway in ancient times and the burial mounds along it indicate its importance in the Bronze Age. Two nearby Bronze Age burial mounds, Robin How and Joaney How, derive their second names from the Norse word for a barrow. The first names are harder to pin down, but it is speculated that they may be from Robin Hood and Little John who are often associated with such places. It may seem a long way from Sherwood Forest, but there is another, and distinct, use of the outlaw's name near Taunton.

hillfort set above a bend of the river. From Simonsbath the B3223 heads east through marvellous moorland scenery to **Exford**, for many the 'capital' of Exmoor. There is little here – a few houses around a large green and a church with a fine rood screen – but Exmoor travellers, particularly walkers, love it. To the south are Withypool and Tarr Steps.

It is thought that under the Normans the tiny village of **Withypool** was the 'capital' of Exmoor. The Normans built a church but very little of this remains after substantial rebuilding in the 15th century. The fine carved font is probably original. The tower was rebuilt in 1902. It is short and squat, but this was not the architect's plan: the money ran out when the tower was this high.

On top of Withypool Hill to the west is one of Exmoor's very few stone circles. The circle, comprises about 40 very short stones, the tallest being barely 0.6m (2ft) high.

To the south of Withypool are **Tarr Steps**, one of Exmoor's prettiest sites. Close to Tarr Steps is the **Caratacus Stone**, another enigmatic megalith. The stone, standing in a shelter erected to protect its inscription, is carved with the words *Carataci Nepus* – kinsman of Caratacus. Caratacus led the Welsh Celts against the Romans in the first century AD, yet the inscription is 5th or 6th century work. The stone could be Neolithic, 2000 years earlier than the man or the carving, and the inscription faces away from the old track it stands beside – was it once erected elsewhere? As with Tarr Steps we will never know for sure.

Tarr Steps and Withypool are linked by a fine walk beside the River Barle, returning along a section of the Two Moors Way, an unofficial long distance footpath that crosses Exmoor and Dartmoor.

East of Exford the B3224 finds a way below the high moor to reach Wheddon Cross, passing a road which heads north, edging Dunkery Beacon before dropping down to Luccombe.

Wheddon Cross to Dulverton

The main road, the A396 which crosses Exmoor from north to south, passes **Wheddon Cross** before following the River Quorme to its confluence with the River Exe. On the Exe, just off the main road is **Winsford**, the prettiest of Exmoor villages – though not as favoured as Exford and Simonsbath. Ernest Bevin, Foreign Secretary in Atlee's post-war Labour government was born here. Beyond the turn to Winsford the A396 follows the River Exe past the secluded hamlet of Exton to the border with Devon. Just before the border, **Dulverton** lies on the B3222, west of the main road.

Dulverton was once a cloth making town, its mills driven by the River Barle, but has always been a centre for hunting and fishing. As a field sports centre it has a very long history, Sir Robert Corun, a local man, having been prosecuted for killing a royal stag in 1365. The now-controversial Devon and Somerset Staghounds was refounded by a town resident in 1855. At one time the hunting and fishing visitors came in such numbers that there were more than 20 hotels and inns in the town. Today there are fewer, and most visitors are using the town as a centre for exploring Exmoor, or just for admiring the town.

To the east of the centre, on the B3222, 'Woodliving' is a thatched, 13th century cottage, once a tannery. Walking back to the village centre, bear right after the Rock House Inn, then left to reach the church where Thomas Chilcott lies. Continue towards the centre, soon reaching Fore Street and the Town Hall, built in 1866. The double, outside steps were added in 1927 to a design by Sir Edwin Lutyens. Continuing along High Street, then Bridge Street, a right turn leads to **Exmoor House**, a National Park Information Centre housed in the Victorian Warehouse.

Nearby is the **Guildhall Heritage Centre and Art Gallery**. The centre explores Dulverton's history (including a reconstruction of Granny Baker's kitchen) and has a remarkable collection of photographs of old Exmoor. The art gallery has regular exhibitions.

Thomas Chilcott and other Dulverton Worthies

The tombstone of Thomas Chilcott who died in 1873 was once inscribed:

He was neglected by his doctor
Treated cruel by his nurse
His brother robbed his widow
Which makes it still worse

The doctor and nurse seem to have been sanguine about the libel, but the brother took Chilcott's widow to court. She was ordered to remove the words, refused and was sent to jail in Taunton. Her sentence required her to stay there until she agreed to the removal, and, eventually, she did. The space on the tombstone is now taken with the wife's details.

On happier notes, Dulverton was the birthplace of Sir George Williams, founder of the YMCA, who is commemorated in a window in the church, and of George Peppin who emigrated to Australia and bred the Merino sheep.

Dunster

Dunster is one of the highlights of Exmoor, a real gem of a village. It can be a little overcrowded in summer, and has rather too many tourist-based shops, but it is still worth every moment spent in it, still having quiet corners where it is possible to get away from the crowds and experience the old village. The best place to start an exploration is the car park at the main road end of the village, where there is an Information Centre for the National Park. The Somerset Guild of Craftsmen have a gallery here. The tower to the north-west is **Conygar Tower**, built in 1776 by a member of the Luttrell family, lords of the manor, for the mighty sum of £192. It is named from the hill on which it stands and is a folly in the grand style, having been built for no better reason than to create a landmark. A local tale maintains that a subterranean passage links the tower and the castle. If that is so it is a very long tunnel.

Walk down High Street to reach the **Yarn Market**, a wonderful building built in the first years of the 17th century by a member of the Luttrell family as a market for cloth when the village was a centre for the local wool trade. The market was damaged in the Civil War, some roofing timber still showing the impact marks of a cannonball. Opposite the market is the Luttrell Arms Hotel, built for the Abbot of Cleeve Abbey but taken over by the Luttrell family in 1499.

About half-way down High Street, on the right, is the **Dunster Doll Museum**, which has a good collection of antique and ethnic dolls. The collection was started by a local resident and presented to the village on her death. A burglary in 1990 resulted in the loss of some of the most interesting dolls, but the collection is still worth visiting. At the bottom of the High Street **Dunster Castle** is straight ahead.

There is a legend that a Celtic fort stood here and was used by the Celtic St Carantoc to exhibit a dragon that he had charmed from the sea on the orders of King Arthur. It is known that Aluric, a Saxon, built a castle here, and it is likely that a Norman castle was built on the same site. Of that first Norman building only a tower and part of a curtain wall remain, though there are other sections of the building that represent additions from the 13th century. One addition was the gatehouse, a formidable structure, one tower of which was known to have been used as a dungeon even before the discovery, in 1869, of the skeleton of a 2m (7ft) man. He had been manacled to a wall

***Above:* Dunster Castle from the coast road**
***Below:* The Yarn Market at Dunster**

Civil War Action

The castle saw service during the Civil War when it was twice besieged. At first it was held for Parliament and withstood a Royalist siege in 1642 before the Luttrells changed sides in 1643. In 1645 it was besieged again, this time by Parliament. The siege lasted for six months, until long after all other West Country castles had surrendered and the King's cause was hopeless. Then near starvation caused the castle garrison to surrender, though they found the strength to march out with honour. Acknowledging the castle's great strength as a fortress, Cromwell had the castle slighted, a semi-demolition that included the razing of the original Norman keep.

with iron bands on his feet, hands and neck, and then walled up to die.

In Victorian times the whole building was re-structured as a domestic building. Inside, the castle is a fine mix of Elizabethan and later work, with wood panelling and plaster ceilings and, in the Leather Gallery, some remarkable leather 'tapestries'. One room was used by the Prince of Wales, later Charles II, during a stay in 1645 when the Civil War was going badly for his father. Equally good are the castle gardens which include, among the more unusual plants, orange and lemon trees, camellias and magnolias.

The Capture of a Man-o'-War

The second siege of Dunster Castle gave English military history one of its most bizarre moments. At one stage a Royalist ship sailed towards Dunster from Wales loaded with supplies meant to help break the siege. The ship put in locally but the crew were surprised by a really low tide and were left beached on the mud. At that stage a force of Parliamentarian cavalry arrived and attacked the ship, boarding and taking it. This incident is the only known record of cavalry defeating a man-o'-war!

At the bottom of High Street bear right into Church Street, passing, to the right, the **Nunnery**, a superb, triple-storeyed, double-overhung building. Despite the name there was never a house of nuns in Dunster, the house dating from the mid-14th-century when it was built as a guest house for Cleeve Abbey. Next to the right are the village gardens – once part of the Priory – and the church. The church holds several monuments to members of the Luttrell family, but the most interesting memorial is the cover slab from the grave of Adam of Cheddar, Dunster's prior in the mid-14th-century.

To the right, beyond the church, St George's Street leads to the **Butter Cross** and the **Dovecote**. The Butter Cross is thought to have been the original village market cross, perhaps moved here when plague was rife so that local farmers did not need to enter the village. The dovecote is all that now remains – apart from some outbuildings – of Dunster Priory. The charming round building, with a conical slate roof topped by what, for all the world, is an up-market bird-table, held 500 pairs of doves.

Bear left along West Street. First left is Mill Lane at the end of which is **Dunster Water Mill**. There were mills in Domesday Dunster, but the present mill dates from the 17th century. It still grinds flour for local bakeries. Visitors can watch the process (and buy flour), see a collection of old agricultural machinery or enjoy the tea room.

The second left, Park Street, leads to **Gallox Bridge**, a fine medieval packhorse bridge. The name is believed to be a corruption of gallows and is called after the hill to the south on which a gallows once stood.

Beyond Dunster

From Dunster the A39 heads east to **Carhampton**, a large village reputedly founded by the Celtic St Carantoc who sailed across the Bristol Channel from South Wales on

Dispute between the Villagers & the Monks

A Benedictine priory was built in Dunster in the early 12th century, but very unusually the Priory Church was shared between the village folk and the monks. Eventually a dispute arose between the vicar and the prior over the times of service and use of bells. The dispute over the bells was brought to a head when the villagers removed the bell ropes so that the monks could not toll them. The incensed prior wrote that *'to fulfill and satisfie theire croked appetities, thei take up the bell roopis and said that the Priour and convent there should have no bellis there to ryng'*.

The dispute was taken to Glastonbury where an unsatisfactory decision was reached that the building should be divided into two. That decision resulted in one of the longest rood screens in Britain, over 16m (50ft) long and massively constructed. The screen was built locally and erected in 1499.

a large stone altar. He set this up in a church he built, after he had disposed of a fiery dragon which was plaguing the locals (see Dunster above). From the village a turn left heads to the coast, reaching it at **Blue Anchor**, a small holiday resort named for a 17th century inn. The local station of the West Somerset Railway has a **Museum of GWR memorabilia**.

To the east of the hamlet are crumbling cliffs on which stood a chapel, built in the 15th century, until a section of cliff collapsed, dumping the building into the sea.

The road follows the shore line at Blue Anchor, passing **Home Farm** where visitors can make friends with the animals and enjoy the home-made cakes or home-produced ham.

The coast road continues to Watchet, but before going that way, head inland to **Old Cleeve**. Here, in the churchyard, is the grave of George Jones, the village blacksmith, marked with the famous blacksmith's epitaph. There is also a sheepskin tannery which can be toured.

Close to Old Cleeve is **Washford**, a village bisected by the A39. Here, the station on the old **Somerset and Dorset Railway** – the West Somerset Railway runs on the adjacent line – is a museum of the old line. The museum has a huge collection of memorabilia and a reconstructed signal box. To the south of the village is **Cleeve Abbey**, the most complete monastic house in Somerset and with one of the finest cloisters in England. The abbey was founded in the 1880s for Cistercian monks. The 13th-century gatehouse remains, as do many of the abbey's domestic buildings, set around the cloisters. The chamber near the Chapter House retains a medieval wall painting, while the 15th-century refectory has a magnificent timber roof with carved angels.

To the east of Washford, on the A39 near Washford Cross (and the radio masts) **Tropiquaria** has a collection of small animals and birds, lizards and spiders, some of which can be handled. There is also an aquarium. The site has a café and a picnic room, and a puppet theatre. The site is housed in an old BBC transmission building and so it is appropriate that it is also home to **Wireless in the West**, a history of radio broadcasting with a collection of old transmission equipment and wirelesses.

Watchet

Watchet is a lovely little port and town, justifiably popular with visitors. It has been popular ever since seaside holidays became the vogue.

Medieval tiles exhibited at Cleeve Abbey

Poetic Inspiration

Samuel Taylor Coleridge is said to have been enchanted: the town claims that his visit inspired *The Rime of the Ancient Mariner*, though given the mournful nature of the great work that would seem to be a poor compliment.

The town is set at a natural break in the coastal cliffs and was obviously of importance as a port in Saxon times because a royal mint was set up here. Some of the minted coins can be seen in the town museum. Interestingly, others can be seen in museums in Scandinavia, having found their way there as booty from Viking raids or, perhaps, as *danegeld*, the 'protection money' paid to the Vikings to avoid raids. The town museum, housed in the old Market House in Market Street, close to the port, also has fossils excavated from the local cliffs and a collection on the Brendon Hills iron ore mines and the railway which brought the ore to the port. The railway followed the Washford River to the port, the shipment of ore to South Wales making Watchet a very prosperous place in the mid-19th century. The line was later incorporated into what is now the West Somerset Railway which has a station in the town.

Close to the station, is the church, dedicated to St Decuman, the 6th century Welshman whom we have met before at Oare: legend has it that Decuman was murdered at Watchet. The church has several good monuments to the Wyndham family.

Cleeve Abbey, where many of the buildings are intact

Soon after her marriage to John Wyndham, Florence Wadham died suddenly. Her body was taken to the Wyndham family vault in Watchet church. After it had been laid out the sexton, left alone with the corpse, decided to steal the expensive rings left on her wedding finger. These proved impossible to pull off, so he took a knife to the finger. At the first cut Florence promptly sat up, fully conscious and revived. Florence lived a full life, though whether the sexton survived the experience, or what happened to him is not recorded.

Just to the south of Watchet, on a road which passes ancient earthworks known as Battle Gore, reputedly the site of a battle between Saxons and Vikings in the 10th century, is the larger, but less attractive, town of **Williton**. Here Orchard Mill, powered by an over-shot water mill, is now home to the **Bakelite Museum** with a collection which explores the fascinating history of plastics from Victorian times (when substances as varied as egg-white, crushed beetles, pigs' blood and soot were used to create mouldable materials) to more modern materials. There is also a rural life collection and a tea room.

The Brendon Hills

The Brendon Hills are the eastern outliers of Exmoor. The name 'brendon' means 'brown hills' and, interestingly, is different in origin to the village of Brendon on Brendon Common, on the west side of Exmoor, near Doone Country, which derives from 'broom', the plant. The hills are nose-shaped, poking themselves at Taunton Deane and the Quantocks. To explore them, go

• R D Blackmore and Lorna Doone •

Richard Doddridge Blackmore was born in 1825, the son of John Blackmore, the curate of Longworth, Berkshire. Sadly, when young Richard was only three months old his mother died and much of the responsibility for his upbringing fell to his grandparents, his grandfather – also John – being the rector of Oare church.

Richard was boarded at Blundell's School, Tiverton and spent holidays here on Exmoor, learning at first hand the old stories of the Doones, a 17th-century family of local outlaws. Richard qualified as a barrister after graduating from Oxford but when ill-health forced him to give up his practice he turned to writing full time. Though he lived in Middlesex he retained an affection for Exmoor, visiting frequently before his death in 1900. *Lorna Doone* remains Blackmore's most popular book.

Considerable research has now been carried out on the story of Lorna Doone, and it is now established that the book is essentially factual, though elaborated to create a compelling drama. It is, therefore, 'faction' rather than fact or fiction.

The facts are that a very small, perhaps only three of four, group of Scots under the leadership of a knight of Clan Stewart were outlawed in the early years of the 17th century as a result of a family feud. The head of the group, Sir James Stewart, took the Gaelic, poetic version of his name when he settled in a remote Exmoor valley, calling himself Iain Ciar Duine – Ian, the chosen man, a name which suited his bitterness at the loss of family lands – but retaining his knightly 'Sir'. The locals, not understanding the Gaelic, called him Sir Ensor Doone and the name stuck.

The lands that Sir Ensor had lost were those of Lorne in North Argyll. This land – now called Lorn – was named for a Viking settler and had on occasion been called Lorna. In his Exmoor valley Sir Ensor's sons grew up to become real outlaws, holding the county to ransom, while Sir Ensor dreamed of recapturing his former wealth and title. In an attempt to do so he kidnapped the daughter of the new lord, with the intention of marrying her to his eldest son Charles (Carver) when she came of age. To hide her identity she was called Lorna (from her lands) Doone (from Sir Ensor's newly acquired local name). It was this girl that John Ridd, a real man who truly was a local wrestling champion, met when he climbed the water-slide one day.

In the story John marries Lorna, but only after Carver Doone has shot her at the altar. The Doones are defeated and their village burned. Then John and Lorna live happily ever after. In reality most of this is also true: the Doones leaving Exmoor to return to Scotland and Lorna staying locally even when her true identity was known. As records from Oare church do not go back far enough no marriage record exists, so it is not definite that John and Lorna really did marry.

Only in one respect did Blackmore positively alter the story, rather than just embellishing it. The real Lorna Doone was born in 1645 but in the book this is taken 20 years forward to 1665 so that the author could weave in some local intrigue about Monmouth's rebellion and Judge Jeffreys' Assize: these latter dates could not be altered.

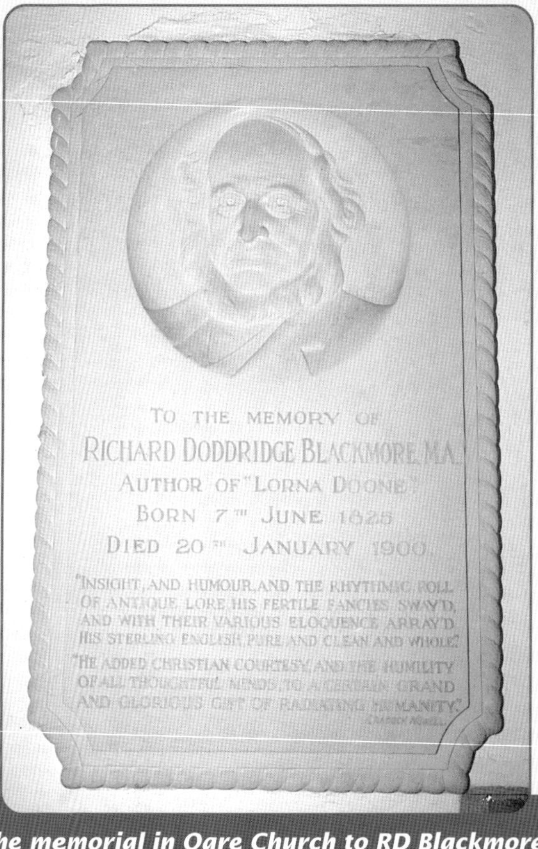
TO THE MEMORY OF
RICHARD DODDRIDGE BLACKMORE M.A.
AUTHOR OF "LORNA DOONE"
BORN 7TH JUNE 1825
DIED 20TH JANUARY 1900

***The memorial in Oare Church to RD Blackmore, who wrote* Lorna Doone**

Above: The Bakelite Museum, Orchard Mill, Williton

Below: The steam-hauled service at Crowcombe Heathfield Station

eastwards from Wheddon Cross on the B3224, a road which makes the most of this area of the National Park, and allows visits to interesting, secluded places such as Luxborough and **Brompton Regis**. The 'king' (*regis*) of Brompton Regis was William the Conqueror who took the estate himself as it had been held by King Harold's mother. Close to the village is **Wimbleball Lake**, a reservoir created in 1974 which is now also a water park with sailing, rowing and fishing, shoreline nature trails and a café.

After its junction with the B3190 the B3224 forms the boundary of the National Park. To the south here is **Clatworthy Reservoir**, created in 1960, which is also popular with sailors and anglers. To the south of the reservoir tiny **Huish Champflower** is another of Somerset's romantically named hamlets.

Finally, we leave the National Park to visit **Stogumber** a picturesque village whose name – after permission, which he sought in writing from the vicar – was used by George Bernard Shaw for the priest in *Saint Joan*. In the village church, a fine building in red sandstone, is an excellent monument to Sir George Sydenham, father of Elizabeth, the wife of Sir Francis Drake. Sir George had two wives, their effigies being crammed in on either side of his own. Downhill from the church are the village almshouses, founded by Sir George in the late-16th century. Originally for six poor widows, the almshouses are now a single house.

To the east of the village, close to the Stogumber station of the West Somerset Railway, lies **Bee World and Animal Centre.** Here there are working hives – safely displayed behind glass – and collections of farm animals (including rare breeds) and pets. There is a lake which attracts many species of birds, and a nature trail. The site shop sells honey and beeswax candles. There is also an adventure play area and a restaurant/tea room.

Combe Sydenham Country Park

The B3224 leaves the National Park just beyond the village of Elworthy. To the north of the village is the **Combe Sydenham Country Park**, centred on the fine Elizabethan manor house built by Sir George Sydenham.

The house can be toured: one of the items on display is the cannonball supposedly fired from the other side of the world by Sir Francis Drake to (successfully) cause the abandonment of Elizabeth Sydenham's wedding to a local man so that Drake could marry her on his return.

The site also includes a restored medieval mill and the **National Museum of Baking** with a collection on the trade. The mill is used to grind floor for making 'monksbread' to a recipe reputedly unchanged since its use by 14th-century Benedictine monks. The country park beside the house has 16km (10 miles) of waymarked trails. North of the country park is **Monksilver** where, in the church on 18 June 1583, Sir Francis Drake married Elizabeth Sydenham.

Allerford

Allerford Museum

(West Somerset Rural Life Museum)
The Old School
Allerford
Open: Good Friday – October, Monday – Friday 10.30am – 1pm, 2 – 4.30pm, Saturday 2 – 4.30pm. Also open Sundays from mid – July to early September 10.30 – 12.30pm.
☎ 01643 826529

Bossington Farm and Birds of Prey Centre

Allerford
Open: March – October, Sunday – Friday 10.30am – 4.30pm. Also open on Saturdays at Easter, Whitsun and in July and August, same times.
☎ 01643 862816

Blue Anchor

Blue Anchor Railway Museum

Blue Anchor Station
Open: Easter – September, Sunday and Bank Holidays 11am – 5pm.
☎ 01643 821092

Home Farm

Blue Anchor
Open: Easter – September, Sunday – Friday 10.30am – 5.30pm.
☎ 01984 640817

John Wood's Sheepskin Tannery

Old Cleeve
Open: Factory tours: Easter – October, Monday – Friday at 10.45am, 11.30am, 2.15pm and 3pm
Shop: All year, Monday – Friday 9am – 5pm, Saturday and Bank Holidays 10am – 4pm.
☎ 01984 40291

Dulverton

Guildhall Heritage Centre

Monmouth Terrace
Dulverton
Open: Easter – October, Daily 10am – 4.30pm.
☎ 01398 324081

Dunster

Dunster Castle (NT)

Open: Castle: April – October, Saturday – Wednesday 11am – 5pm (closes at 4pm in October)
Gardens and Park: April – September, daily 10am – 5pm; October – March, daily 11am – 4pm.
☎ 01643 821314

Dunster Dolls

Memorial Hall
High Street
Open: Easter to September, Daily 1030am – 4.30pm.
☎ 01643 821220

Dunster Water Mill

Mill Lane
Open: Easter – October, Daily except Saturday 10.30am – 5pm. (Also open on Saturdays in July and August, same times).
☎ 01643 821759

Somerset Guild of Craftsmen – Gallery

National Park Information Centre

Open: Easter – October.
Daily 9.30am – 5pm.
☎ 01643 821235

Porlock

Doverhay (Dovey House) Museum
High Street
Porlock
Open: One week from Maundy Thursday, then May – October, Monday – Friday 10am – 1pm and 2 – 5pm, Saturday 10am – 12noon, 2.30 – 4.30pm.
☎ 01643 863150

Stogumber

Bee World and Animal Centre
Stogumber
Open: Easter – October, Daily 10am – 6pm or dusk.
☎ 01984 656545

Combe Sydenham Country Park
(Elizabethan mansion/medieval mill/ National Museum of Baking)
nr Monksilver
Open: House/Museum: Spring Bank Holiday – September, Monday, Thursday and Friday – Tours at 2pm
County Park: March – September, Sunday – Friday 9am – 5pm.
☎ 01984 656364

Washford

Cleeve Abbey (English Heritage)
Washford
Open: April – October, Daily 10am – 6pm or dusk, November – March, daily 10am – 1pm, 2 – 4pm.
☎ 01984 640377

Somerset and Dorset Railway Museum
Washford Station
Washford
Open: March – October, Daily 10am – 5pm.
☎ 01984 640869

Tropiquaria/Wireless in the West
Washford Cross
Open: Easter – mid – September, Daily 10am – 6pm, mid – September – October, daily 11am – 5pm. November, February and March, Saturday, Sunday and School Holidays 11am – dusk. Also open from 28 December – 3 January, 11am – dusk.
☎ 01984 640688

Watchet

Watchet Museum
Market Street
Open: Easter, May – September, Daily 10.30am – 12.30pm, 2.30 – 4.30pm. Closes at 7pm in July and 9pm in August.
☎ 01984 631345

Williton

Bakelite Museum
Orchard Mill
Williton
Open: March – October, Tuesday, Thursday – Sunday and Bank Holiday Mondays 10.30am – 6pm. Monday and Wednesday 3.30 – 6pm.
☎ 01984 632133

2 The Quantocks

Stogursey Village

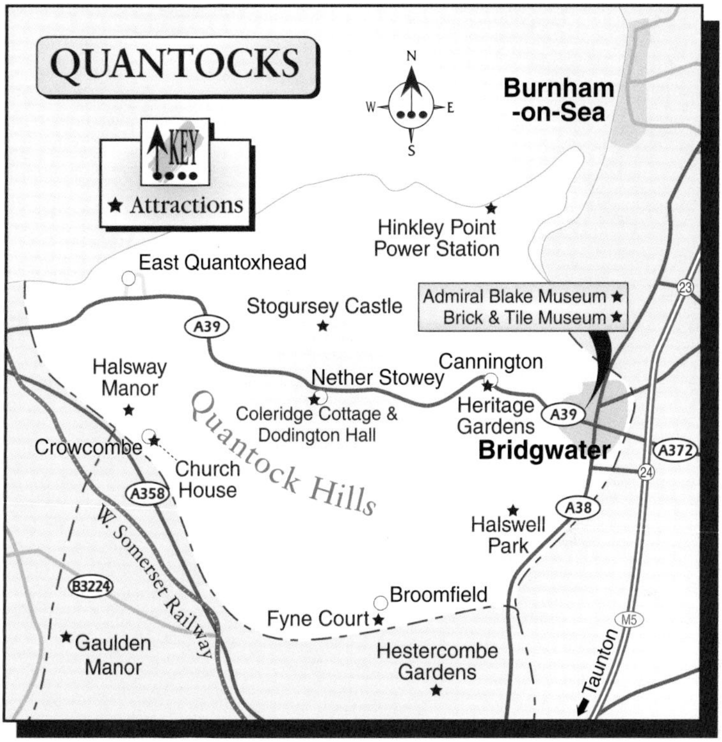

In this chapter we explore the Quantocks, and that area of the Somerset Levels which lies to the west of the River Parrett. The Quantocks are the smallest of the distinct areas of Somerset, but scenically one of the most spectacular.

The Quantocks

Following the establishment of ten National Parks in England and Wales in the 1950s it was recognised that there were other areas of the countries which, for a variety of reasons – size, population density, etc. – were not suitable for designation as National Parks but were, scenically, outstanding. It was decided, therefore, to designate these as Areas of Outstanding Natural Beauty (AONB) offering them a degree of protection for their natural habitats and scenic 'highspots' along the lines of those for the Parks. The first AONB to be designated, on 1 January 1957, was the Quantocks.

The Quantocks are occasionally called the Quantock Hills, though the use of 'hills' is something of a misnomer for a raised, dissected plateau that forms a single north-south ridge just 20km (12.5 miles) long and barely 5km (3 miles) wide. The Quantocks cover an area of about 100sq kms (38.5sq miles) which by National Park standards is very small indeed, yet within that area there is a quite remarkable range of scenery, the result of rapidly changing geology along the ridge's length.

The Quantocks rose from a sea of New Red Sandstone as a geological island of Devonian rocks some 450 million years old. But that island appearance does not mean a homogeneity of rock. In fact there is a rapid variation. To the north are grits and quartzitic sandstones hard enough to have merited quarrying for road stone. These have resisted erosion, giving a poor, acidic soil so that the northern end of the hills appears as a high (relatively) barren moor, but drained by narrow stream valleys (combes) in which the vegetation is slightly lusher.

In the middle section of the hills are a mixture of sandstones and limestones – rocks which weather more easily and give a more sustaining soil. The vegetation here is both more varied and more plentiful. South again are the shales, geologically the youngest, a softer rock weathered down to low, rounded hills with a deep, rich soil.

But though these changes sound dramatic they are, in fact, very gradual and visitors who walk the Quantock ridge walk could be forgiven for failing to realise that any change had taken place until they were asked to compare the view – both local and afar – at each end of the walk. Then they would recognise that at one end the local view was of short shrubs and windswept moor flowers, with South Wales and Exmoor visible, while at the other end it was of trees – trees thick enough to block out any far views.

As mentioned above, the Quantock ridge is a dissected plateau with streams draining from the ridge watershed on both sides of the hills. Indeed, the name derives from this geography, stemming from *cantocks* (stream headlands), a name mentioned as early as the seventh century when it appeared (as *cantucudio*) in a charter of the West Saxon King Centwine. These streams have formed combes that tend to be narrower at the northern end – though this generalisation fails when account is taken of stream volume flow, ie. bigger rivers cut bigger combes than do smaller ones. The combes are an impressive feature of the Quantocks, creating lush, wooded valleys that are a delight for both the plant-seeker and birdwatcher, and in which the patient visitor – particularly one who arrives at dawn or stays until twilight – can see deer.

The Western Edge

West Quantoxhead, a straggling village is interesting mostly for its fine church and for having two names. It might be assumed that the second name, St Audries, would be from the church, so it comes as a surprise to discover that it is dedicated to St Etheldreda. But St Etheldreda and St Audrey are the same person – the seventh-century Queen of Northumbria who became the first Abbess of Ely and died in 679. It seems odd that an East Saxon noblewoman should be associated with a Somerset church.

Odder still is that the Queen's early liking for cheap jewellery – before she renounced materialism for a spiritual life (changing a bad habit for a nun's habit as it were) – gave us the word 'tawdry'.

The church was built in 1856 though some items from an older building were incorporated. The font is Norman, while two of the church's five bells are dated 1440. The organ is a working Kilton barrel organ, built in London in 1782 and originally installed in Kilve church. It is the only one in Somerset that is still playable.

A minor road leads on to Bicknoller, passing a turn, on the left, for a car park on the high ridge beside Staple Plantation from where **Beacon Hill** (302m – 1,019ft) is easily reached. From it there is a fine view, northward to the Welsh hills, and westwards to Exmoor. Dominating the coast below are the reactors of the Hinkley Point nuclear power station.

Bicknoller is a very picturesque village of thatched cottages, some dating from the 16th century, and a church with some beautiful carvings, in both wood and stone. Beyond the village is **Halsway Manor** – pronounced Halsey – an imposing mansion which mostly dates from 1870, but includes medieval sections. It is now a 'college' for folk song and dance.

Next is **Crowcombe**. The most interesting building here is the Church House. This was certainly in existence by the early years of the 16th century and is probably even earlier. It is a simple construction of two floors. The upper floor is reached by an external stairway, the stone steps of which have centres hollowed out by the tramping of countless feet.

The church across from the house has a fine 14th-century tower that was once completed by a 24m (80ft) spire which was destroyed by lightning in 1725. The top section is preserved in the churchyard – near the east window. Pevsner maintained that the south aisle of the church was the finest Late Perpendicular building in Somerset. Beside the church is Crowcombe Court, built in the early 18th century. A few hundred metres or so to the west of the church is the 13th-century Crowcombe Market Cross. Its steps were once used as market stalls.

From Crowcombe a minor road follows the base of the Quantocks, passing through Triscombe and West Bagborough, a pretty village, to reach **Cothelstone**. Here, in the churchyard, Ianthe, the daughter of Percy Bysshe Shelley is buried. She was married to the owner of Cothelstone

Church houses

Sometimes called church-ale houses, these were built as village halls and were used for social gatherings at certain times of the year – saint's days, fair days, etc. – at which food and drink were available. All profits went to the upkeep of the church – hence church-ale. In the absence of shops the houses were also used by travelling salesmen who showed off their goods under a dry roof.

Though most villages had such houses very few now survive: the only other in Somerset is at Chew Magna.

Above: Halsworthy Manor
Below: The Church and Church House, Crowcombe

Manor. Earlier owners of the house, the Stowells, are remembered in memorials in the church. One, Lord Ralph Stowell, criticised the brutality of the Bloody Assizes, incurring Judge Jeffreys' wrath. The judge ordered two rebels to be hanged at Cothelstone in revenge, legend having it that the unfortunate pair were hanged from the gateway arch to the manor.

The Eastern Edge

East Quantoxhead is an ancient settlement, Bronze Age burials having been found in the area. There was a mill at the time of Domesday, the mill pond now being an attractive feature of the village. Beyond the pond is the Court House, once home of the lord of the manor. The village is unique in Somerset for the lordship having stayed in the same family from the Conquest.

From close to East Quantoxhead the A39 follows the base of the hills to **Kilve.** The village's church lies to the north, towards the sea, a simple building close to a farm that was originally, in the 14th century, a chantry chapel for the lord of the manor. The sea can be reached from here, passing a brick tower that is all that remains of a failed attempt to extract oil from oil shales.

Continue along the main road, going through **Holford**, a popular starting point for walks on the Quantocks. The walks head up on to the Quantocks through one of several fine combes. Hodder's Combe and Lady's Edge lead to Bicknoller Post, on the ridge top. The Combe is said to derive its name from Odda, a Saxon general of King Alfred who camped here while preparing to do battle with another raiding party. It is said that he lit a beacon fire on Longstone Hill, which is possible because it is actually a little higher than the neighbouring peak of Beacon Hill, despite the latter being more obviously named for such a fire.

An alternative walk follows Holford Combe to wooded Dowsborough. To the east of the village is the hamlet of **Dodington** where the Hall, former seat of the lords of the manor, is open to the public. It is a fine Tudor mansion, with an

The Holford Dog Pound

To the west of Holford, on a track which follows the southern edge of Alfoxton Park, is an animal pound marked with a seated wolf, the crest of St Albyn, the family who owned the park when the pound was built. It was, apparently, built to house any stray animal found on the park, but legend maintains it was solely for stray dogs after an unpleasant death at the park.

The legend has it that meat to feed the park's foxhounds was hung in a tree close to the kennels, where it attracted all the neighbourhood's stray dogs who would spend time slavering beneath the tree, vainly trying to reach the food.

One night there were so many strays and they made such a noise they set the hounds howling. Hurriedly the huntmaster dressed and went to quieten them, but failing to recognise him without his fine hunting dress the hounds tore him to pieces. The pound was built to stop a recurrence.

The Viking Sweetheart

Tree-clad Dowsborough is topped by a superbly sited Iron Age hill fort. An alternative local name for the hill fort, Danesborough, derives from a time when Viking raiders landed on the Somerset coast near Combwich. One story tells of the Danes coming inland to shelter in the fort. From here, it is said, they were lured by local women to the cottages at the hill's foot and murdered one at a time.

But one young girl fell in love with her Viking, a handsome young lad who played the harp, and hid him when the murderers arrived. A few days later he was discovered and killed: today his ghost haunts the hill fort where his harp can still be heard. Wordsworth knew of the story of the ghostly Dane, including a reference in one of his works to one who 'warbles songs of war, that seem like songs of love'.

excellent oak roof and plasterwork, set in good gardens.

To the west of Holford is Alfoxton Park (a Georgian mansion, now a hotel) where William and Dorothy Wordsworth stayed in the 1790s. Next along the main road is **Nether Stowey**, where Samuel Taylor Coleridge stayed. Coleridge stayed at a cottage then called Gilbards, but now known as **Coleridge Cottage**. The cottage is owned by the National Trust and part of it, with its memorabilia of the poet, is open to the public. Thomas Poole, Coleridge's patron, was a local tanner, a very successful one as his house, the seven-bay mansion at 21 Castle Street, shows. In the house Poole held meetings of his literary circle, not only bringing Coleridge to the village, but persuading Charles Lamb, Robert Southey and, of course, the Wordsworths to visit.

There is a delightful story that Poole once asked his charming young cousin Penelope to sing 'Come, ever smiling Liberty' from Handel's *Judas Maccabeus* to Wordsworth and Coleridge, but she declined. She claimed that this was because she had no singing voice, but later told a friend that it was because she suspected what liberties the poets had in mind.

Thomas Poole's tannery brought prosperity to the villagers of Nether Stowey, a prosperity reflected not only in his house but in many others. The dominant feature of the village is, however, the castle mound to the west of the centre. This is the remains of a Norman motte and bailey castle.

Another ghost is supposed to haunt the Quantocks above Nether Stowey, that of John Walford. His body hung at Walford's Gibbet (to the south-west of the village) after his execution for the murder of his simpleton wife whom he had been forced to marry despite his love for another village girl. His true love knelt beside the scaffold at his hanging. Dead Woman's Ditch, to the south-west of the Gibbet is said to derive its name from this murder.

Nether Stowey lies just outside the AONB, on a minor road heading south to return to the Quantocks base. This minor road then heads uphill to reach the heart of the hills – Crowcombe Park Gate (from where Crowcombe can be reached) and the **Triscombe Stone.** From the car park near theTriscombe Stone it is a short walk along Alfred's Road to Will's Neck. The 'road' is an old drove trail – used to deliver animals on the hoof to market in the days before refrigeration. A drove must have been a grand sight, for not only cattle and sheep, but pigs and even turkeys (their feet dipped in pitch to harden them for the journey) were driven.

From **Will's Neck**, the highest point of the Quantocks at 384m (1,260ft), on a good day the Mendips, Brecon Beacons, Exmoor and Dartmoor can all be seen, as can Pilsdon Pen, Dorset's highest peak. The name is Saxon. To the Saxons all non-Saxons were the same: they called them *wallas*, which just means foreigners, a term they derived from their first meeting with a Celtic tribe, the Velcae. This word has given us Wales – the land of the foreigners according to the Saxons – and also the Vlachs in Romania, Valais in Switzerland and the Walloons in Belgium. It also gives us Will here.

To the south of Nether Stowey is **Broomfield**. The church here has the best position of any on the Quantocks, being surrounded by trees. Inside there is some excellent wood carving. To the west of the church stood **Fyne Court,** once the seat of the Crosse family, but destroyed by fire in 1894. The **Crosse**

The Lake Poets in the Quantocks

In December 1796 Samuel Taylor Coleridge, his wife Sara and their new baby, Hartley, moved to Nether Stowey, close to the poet's benefactor Thomas Poole. In March 1797 William and Dorothy Wordsworth arrived at Alfoxton Park. The two poets already knew each other, but over the next 12 months their friendship grew and kindled what many regard as the most creative period of Coleridge's life. Wordsworth sought inspiration from nature and wrote with a simplicity that reflected this. Coleridge was a great reader and his florid style at that time reflected his scholarship. Each poet gained from the relationship, but Coleridge much more so, producing the first part of *Christabel, Frost at Midnight, This Lime-Tree Bower My Prison, Kubla Khan* and *The Rime of the Ancient Mariner.*

But the poets' lives were not always straightforward ones. The Wordsworth's (and Coleridge when he joined them) habit of walking the cliffs – a strange one for the time – led to them being followed by the locals who became convinced they were spies looking for a good landing spot for a French invasion. London was alerted and a government spy-catcher was despatched. Legend has it that the spy-catcher, hearing the poets discussing Spinoza assumed they had realised he was watching them – he being the spy nosey!

Andrew Crosse, the Thunder and Lightning Man

Andrew Crosse was born in 1784. He was educated in Bristol and Brasenose College, Oxford, before returning to Somerset to manage the Fyne Court estate after the death of his mother in 1805. At the Court he pursued his joint interests in electricity – the new science – and natural history. He rigged several kilometres of copper wires through trees close to the Court, using it to conduct electricity from lightning into his laboratory where he experimented with Leyden jars, electroscopes and copper balls.

As early as 1816 he was claiming that the new energy source would eventually allow communication around the world and revolutionise manufacturing, remarkably prescient notions. His work brought great scientists of the day, including Sir Humphrey Davy, to Fyne Court, but terrified the locals who referred to him as the 'thunder and lightning man'.

During experiments in which Crosse attempted to grow crystals on volcanic stone soaked in hydrochloric acid and stained with potassium carbonate, the whole exposed to a low electrical current, he was astonished to discover a previously unknown species of mite crawling from the stone. The newspapers immediately seized on Crosse having created life and it is claimed (though without much justification) that this gave Mary Shelley the idea for *Frankenstein*. Crosse categorically denied creating life, though quite where the mites came from – and they were found in similar experiments later – has never been satisfactorily explained.

estate, amounting to 26 acres, is owned by the National Trust which rents it to the Somerset Wildlife Trust. The Trust's headquarters is housed in the surviving outbuildings of the Court, one of which is named the Andrew Crosse Hall.

Around Bridgwater

Bridgwater, Stogursey and surrounding low-lying land as far as the River Parrett are more correctly placed with the Somerset Levels than the Quantocks. But the river forms a natural barrier – one that once separated the Saxons from the Celts – and so here we include the area within the Quantocks chapter.

Before exploring **Bridgwater** it is worth noting that there is no spelling mistake in the name, the 'e' having been omitted when the spelling of the town's name was 'regularised' in the 19th century.

Only those born and raised in the town could possibly think it beautiful – and not too many of them either perhaps – yet Bridgwater does have interest and also has a certain unpolished charm. It grew up at the tidal reach of the River Parrett,

The little shop set in the garden of the former Fyne Court

becoming a port of some importance before bigger ships, unable to negotiate the river, carried the trade away. The town's most prosperous era was in medieval times, but only St Mary's Church survives from this. It is a fine building with a tall spire. Close to the church there are several good 16th/17th century houses, among the oldest in the town. There are others of similar age near the west quay. There, too, are all that remains of Bridgwater castle. The Duke of Monmouth slept at the castle at the start of his rebellion, and was proclaimed king by the town council.

The Triscombe Stone

The stone lies above the village for which it is named, but is easy to miss as it is only about 0.6m (just over 2ft) high. There are several stories told about it, all revolving around its use by the Devil as a mustering-point for the Yeth Hounds, hounds of death who hunted the Quantocks. The hounds are accompanied by ghostly riders who ride at breakneck speed. To see, or even to hear, the hounds could mean death and, as they were thought to ride on moonless and stormy nights, the locals would walk miles in order to avoid the stone on such nights. Surprisingly, the locals also believed that it was a wishing-stone and would visit in daytime to sit on it and make a wish.

In 1841, after Bridgwater had been linked to Taunton by canal, a dock was created on the north side of the town linking the river to the canal. Now disused, the development of this dock area has created one of the town's most attractive areas. The canal towpath is now enjoyed by walkers and cyclists, while the waterway is popular with canoeists and anglers.

The town has two museums. One is named for Admiral Robert Blake and housed where he was born in 1598. Blake was a staunch Parliamentarian – as were most of the town, though it was held for the Royalists until it was captured by Col Fairfax in an attack which destroyed many of the buildings by fire – and rose to be Cromwell's General-at-Sea. The museum explores Bridgwater's history. The **Somerset Brick and Tile Museum** is a new venture illustrating the town's brick and tile industry at the (now-restored) site of the last surviving kiln.

To the south of Bridgwater is **North Petherton** close to which the famous Alfred Jewel was discovered in 1693. The jewel is an enamel figure, protected by rock crystal, set in gold filigree and bearing an inscription which translates as 'Alfred had me made'. The jewel is believed originally to have been mounted on a reading pointer. It is now in Oxford's Ashmolean Museum, but a replica is kept at North Petherton Church.

West of North Petherton, at **Goathurst** stands **Halswell House**, built in 1689 and claimed by Pevsner to be the most important of its date in Somerset. It is an imposing, though hardly beautiful, building. Presently empty, it is hoped that it will eventually be restored and opened to the public. The builder, Sir Charles Kemys Tynte, built several follies in the grounds and one of these, the Temple of Harmony – based on Rome's Fortuna Virilis – has already been restored and can be visited.

Close to Goathurst is **Enmore** where a vast mock-medieval castle complete with moat and drawbridge was built in the 1750s, though only a small part – seen from the churchyard – now exists.

A local resident of Enmore, Dr Jasper Porter, who died in 1795, had been disinherited by his father in favour of his sister, a slight from which he clearly never recovered. In his will he left money to be used to make effigies of the pair. On 5 November each year, these effigies, suitably labelled, were to be carried around the village before being

Carnival Processions

In Somerset, Bridgwater is also famous as the main centre for the series of carnivals held in the county during November each year. The town carnival grew out of Bonfire Night celebrations, and has involved decorated floats from the mid-19th century.

Now the floats create a procession that is several kilometres long and takes hours to pass. Prizes are given for the best floats. After Bridgwater, many of the floats tour the other carnivals of the Somerset series.

burned on a bonfire. Historians doubt the effigy making and processing ever took place.

From Bridgwater the A39 heads west, soon reaching **Cannington**. There was a priory of Benedictine nuns here, founded in the 12th century. The priory was dissolved in 1536 – having survived a 14th century scandal involving illicit sex between nuns and the vicar of the local church (said to have taken place in the nave and leaving one nun pregnant) – and incorporated into Cannington Court. The Court now forms the heart of Somerset's Agricultural and Horticultural College. The college grounds can be visited – they include numerous walled gardens and greenhouses which delight gardeners.

A minor road heading north at Cannington bypasses pretty **Combwich**, an old port on the River Parrett, and continues to the Hinkley Point Power Station. Here there are four nuclear power reactors, two of the first generation Magnox type (the blue cubes) and two of the later AGR (Advanced Gas-cooled Reactor) type (enclosed within the single pale building). Since privatisation of the electricity supply industry the two types are run by different companies, but these share a Visitor Centre which explains nuclear power. Guided tours of the stations are possible. There is an interesting nature trail from the Visitor Centre.

Of equal interest is the local shore. Off-shore, and revealed only on very low tides) are the petrified remains of an ancient forest, while the lias cliffs – which can be followed westwards to Kilve – are a re-emergence of the well-known Lyme Bay strata in which Mary Anning found her famous dinosaur fossils.

Also on the coast, to the east of the power station, is Stert Point. The shore here is well known for its ducks and wading birds.

Stogursey, as with Stogumber to the south-west, derives its name from 'stoke', Saxon for a dairy farm. Here the addition to the name is from the Cowey Family that owned the manor and also built the castle whose ruins lie to the south of the village centre. The village also had a Benedictine Priory, founded in about 1100 by the first Norman lord. The village church is the priory church and is a marvellous building with many interesting architectural features. It houses some excellent monuments, including one to William Varney (died 1333), who is shown holding his heart.

Fossils

The local beach is littered with ammonites, and other fossils are found in the cliffs – but please be careful, the rock is fragile and, as a result, the cliff is unstable and dangerous.

Bridgwater

Admiral Blake Museum
Blake Street
Bridgwater
Open: All year, Tuesday – Saturday 10am – 4pm.
☎ 01278 456127

Somerset Brick and Tile Museum
East Quay
Bridgwater
Open: July and September, Sundays 2.30 – 4.30pm.
☎ 01278 320200

Broomfield

Fyne Court (NT)
Broomfield
Open: All year, Daily 9am – 6pm or dusk.
☎ 01823 451587

Cannington

Cannington College Heritage Gardens and Plant Centre
Cannington
Open: All year, Daily 2 – 5pm.
☎ 01278 652226

Crowcombe

Church House
Crowcombe
Open: Only during regular art exhibitions between May and September.

Goathurst

Temple of Harmony
Halswell Park
Goathurst
Open: Easter, May Bank Holiday and Late May – September, Saturday, Sunday and Bank Holidays 2 – 5pm.
☎ 01823 443955

Nether Stowey

Coleridge Cottage (NT)
Nether Stowey
Open: April – September, Tuesday – Thursday 2 – 5pm.
☎ 01278 732662

Dodington Hall
Nether Stowey
Open: June, Saturday and Sunday 2 – 5pm.
☎ 01278 741400

Stogursey

Hinkley Point Power Stations and Visitor Centre
nr Stogursey
Open: April – September, Daily 10am – 4pm, October – March Sunday – Friday 10am – 4pm.
☎ 01278 654334

Coleridge Cottage, Nether Stowey

3 Taunton Deane & the Blackdown Hills

Wiveliscombe

The fertile valley of the River Tone, which rises on Exmoor (though is now more readily seen as the overflow of Clatworthy Reservoir) has always been an important feature of the Somerset landscape: it is no surprise that the county town of Taunton stands on its banks and is named for it. Taunton Deane is the name given to the equally fertile land around the Tone Valley, a land extending to the foot of the Exmoor, Quantock and Blackdown hills. In this chapter we explore the Deane, and also that section of the Blackdowns AONB which lies in Somerset.

Taunton

Somerset's county town is an attractive and interesting town, and an ideal centre for touring the local area. The site was first settled in Saxon times, King Ine of Wessex building a fort beside the river in around 700AD. The exact date is uncertain, but it is known that his queen, Ethelburga, had the fort destroyed in 722 to stop it falling into the hands of rebels. The site was soon re-established, legend having it that a church was built during the reign of Ine's successor. In 904 the church and its estates were bought by Denewulf, Bishop of Winchester and under his and his successors' lordship the town prospered, mainly due to the market they established.

The bishops maintained the lordship after the Norman Conquest, and even built a castle in the 1130s. The bishops also began the town's wool industry, supplying fleeces which were processed at mills driven by the Tone's waters. Wool made Taunton wealthy, silk weaving and lace making maintaining its prosperity when the wool industry declined.

Today Taunton is still prosperous – a lively place, typical of England's small provincial towns. But the town has also played its part on the national scene. There was a minor battle here during the Wars of the Roses and the rebellion of Perkin Warbeck ended here in 1497. During the Civil War the siege of the town and castle (1644-45) included a prolonged cannon bombardment which destroyed most of the medieval buildings.

"A Fair and Pleasant Town"

Before the Civil War Thomas Gerard, an early 17th-century traveller, noted that Taunton was a 'faire and pleasant towne' noting 'the bewtie of the streetes and markett place... the sweet situation.' Gerard would not recognise today's town, but he might well make the same comments.

To explore, start at the Tourist Information Centre in Paul Street, conveniently located below a multi-storey car park. Walk down Paul Street and turn right along East Street. Along here, on the right, are the **Gray's Almshouses**, founded by Robert Gray in 1635. Close by stood the town's East Gate. During the Civil War siege, when Taunton was held by Admiral Robert Blake for Parliament, this area was heavily bombarded, the almshouses being lucky to escape intact.

The walk to the almshouses is a detour, our route crossing East Street and taking Magdalene Lane to reach **St Mary Magdalene Church**.

The tower of St Mary Magdalene Church is 50m (163ft) tall and quite magnificent, one of the great sights of Somerset. It was built over a 25-year period from 1488, but by the 1850s it had become precarious and it was decided to dismantle and re-build it. This was done with meticulous care, with no change to the medieval concept.

The work began at ground level, but as it progressed a pulley and hauling system was constructed to raise stone to the working level. The hauling was carried out by a donkey who patiently plodded down Hammet Street for 4 years. When the tower was complete, the masons felt that the donkey should share their satisfaction, so it was strung from the pulley and man-hauled to the top of the tower to enjoy the view. The donkey's reaction is not recorded, but can be easily imagined.

The tower is the church's jewel, but the inside is worth a look. The full-size painted effigy of Robert Gray, builder of the almshouses, is particularly good. Gray was a London merchant tailor and despite the effigy is actually buried in London.

Continue along Whirligig Lane and bear right along Middle Street to reach Cannon Street. Turn left to reach Priory Avenue. Turn right here to reach, to the left, Priory Barn. The barn was originally the gatehouse of a medieval Augustinian Priory.

Perkin Warbeck

Perkin Warbeck, a Flemish youth whom the Yorkists claimed was Richard, Duke of York (one of the princes in the tower reputedly murdered by Richard III) was captured in Taunton after launching a rebellion in Devon. Henry VII travelled to Taunton to meet Warbeck, whom he ordered to be executed, and to extract fines from those who had supported him. Legend has it that the king made rather more money beating the prior at cards.

The Barn is now home to the museum of the **Somerset Cricket Club** whose ground lies beside it. The museum has an interesting collection of photographs and memorabilia and an excellent reference library.

The Cricket Museum is a detour: turn left along Priory Avenue, soon passing St James' Church on the right. St James' also has a fine tower, though less grand than that of St Mary Magdalene. Inside there is one of the most elaborate 15th-century fonts in the county, and a pulpit and rood screen from the early 17th century.

Beyond the church, also to the right, is Coal Orchard which leads to the Brewhouse Theatre. The theatre is named after the brewery which once stood here. The 'coal' of the street's name remembers the delivery of Welsh coal to wharves here. Continue along St James' Street to

Continued on page 56...

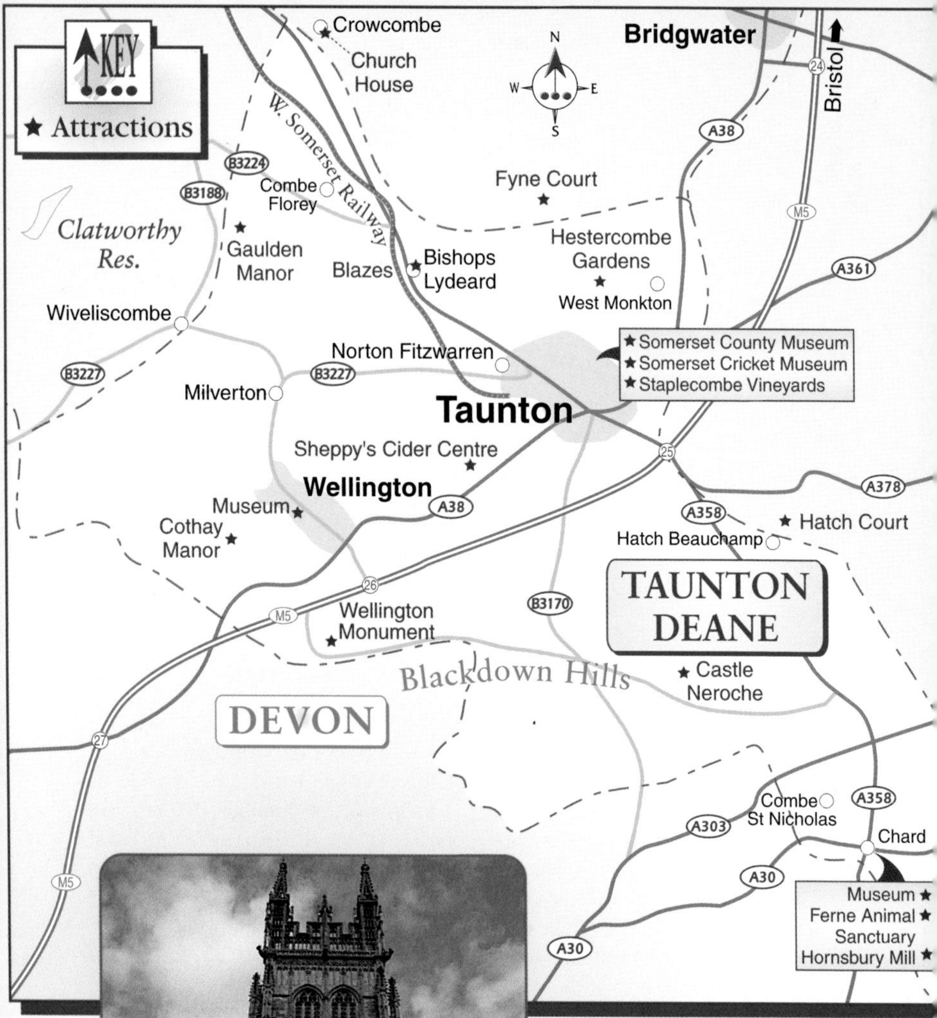

Left: St Mary Magdalene Church, Taunton

Opposite page: Wellington Monument

• The Wellington Monument •

After Napoleon's retreat from Moscow, with his exile to Elba looming, a grateful British nation decided to honour the man who had helped foil the Emperor's European ambitions with his victories in the Peninsula War. Arthur Wellesley was to be ennobled, and legend has it that an estate was purchased for him close to a town whose name was sufficiently close to his own. Wellington was chosen and Wellesley become the 1st Duke of Wellington.

The celebration of Napoleon's defeat was premature, but after Waterloo in 1815, a committee of local gentry decided that this final defeat of the 'little Emperor' should also be commemorated. A public subscription was therefore opened. The committee envisaged a fitting memorial on the Duke's estate – a huge column surmounted by a statue of Wellington (in iron, of course – what else for the 'Iron Duke'). The columns would be set on a plinth of concentric circles on which two dozen cannons from Waterloo would be mounted. Three cottages would be built around the base, housing veterans from England, Ireland and Scotland.

But the funds raised were insufficient to realise the dream and the early building work was dogged with problems – one story suggests that the builders employed turned out to be rogues and that their mortar was washed away by the first rain storm, leaving a pile of tottering stone. Eventually it was decided to redesign the monument. A triangular shaft was agreed: it is occasionally said that the shape was a reference to the bayonet used by the British at Waterloo – in fact it was, as the architect pointed out, because a triangle used only half the stone of a square.

Troubles continued. When the '24' cannons eventually reached Exeter it was found there were only 15, and as the money had run out they could not be transported to site: Exeter Corporation used them as bollards. The Duke made his only visit to his estate in 1819, but work was nowhere near completed. Eventually it was abandoned.

Then, after Wellington's death in 1852, a further appeal raised enough money to complete the spire and to top it off with a pyramid. An attempt was made to rescue the cannons from Exeter, but during the course of this it was discovered that they were Russian not French, had been made in Scotland, and never been anywhere near Waterloo. The rescue was abandoned. In 1892 the monument was in such a poor state of repair that a major refurbishment was carried out, raising its height a little to the present 53m (175ft). In 1911 one more effort was made to rescue the Exeter cannons. Four were brought to the site, but these were taken away during the 1939-45 War when metal was scarce. A single cannon was placed at the base of the monument in 1985.

Despite the tribulations, the resulting monument is an impressive work. It can be climbed – there are over 200 steps – for a marvellous panorama of Taunton Deane.

Children's Wood

Although it is too far to walk, one site should be visited before you leave Taunton.

To the east of the centre, sandwiched between the railway line and the River Tone (and most easily reached from the car park of the Creech Castle Hotel) is Children's Wood. Begun by the Borough Council in 1992 the aim is to plant a tree for every child born in Taunton Deane: over 3,000 trees have been planted to date. Wildflowers have also have planted making the wood a fine place throughout the year.

reach North Street. Turn left and follow the street towards the triangle of **The Parade.** This was the site of Taunton's market until 1929: the old Market House was built in 1772. After the Battle of Sedgemoor, Col. Percy Kirke marched rebel prisoners to Taunton and hanged 19 without trial on The Parade.

Just before reaching The Parade, turn right along **Castle Bow**. The gateway is the only remnant of the outer castle and town walls.

Guests of the nearby Castle Hotel have included Tsar Nicholas I and the Duke of Wellington.

Beyond the arch is Castle Green, once the outer bailey of the castle. Go past the 'sword in the stone' sculpture (remnant of a 1987 exhibition/show on King Arthur in Somerset) to reach what remains of the 12th-century castle. The medieval work was considerably refurbished from the 1780s onwards when the castle was the venue for the Assizes Courts, and was also the judges' lodgings. The Great Hall was also the scene of one of Judge Jeffreys' Bloody Assizes. Now the castle houses the **Somerset County Museum** which explores the history and natural history of the county, and the **Military Museum** of the Somerset Light Infantry.

From the castle, go along Castle Walk, following the line of the old walls from Castle Bow, to reach Corporation Street. The **Old Municipal Buildings** to your right include the old grammar school (to the right of the main entrance) built in 1522 by Richard Fox, Bishop of Winchester. The grammar school was badly damaged during the Civil War siege, but carefully restored.

Turn left along Corporation Street to regain The Parade. To the right here is the now-pedestrianised High Street. Along it, on the right, a plaque marks the spot where the Duke of Monmouth was declared King in June 1685.

Monmouth stayed at a house in East Street for three days and was presented with a banner made by local schoolgirls, the Maids of Taunton.

First right in High Street is Bath Place with some lovely medieval buildings while at the top of the street are the elaborate gates to **Vivary Park**, named for the Winchester bishops' fishpool (*vivarium*). There is a fine Victorian bandstand and a memorial fountain to Queen Victoria in the park.

The plaque, close to where the town's old High Cross stood, is a detour: continue along Fore Street, with The Parade to your left, soon reaching the gabled, half-timbered **Tudor House**. This is the oldest house in the town, dating, in part, from the 14th century (though the façade is 200 years later) and was the home of Sir William Portman who escorted the Duke of Monmouth to London after his capture on Holt Heath, Dorset. Beside the house is Pig Market Lane which leads to the Old Market Shopping Centre with its wooden pigs and sculpted toads. Walk past the Tudor House and turn first right to return to Paul Street.

Around Taunton

To the north-east of Taunton, beyond **Cheddon Fitzpaine**, a little village trying hard not to be swallowed by its large neighbour – be sure to look for the gargoyles on the church – is **West Monkton**, a larger village. The church has a tall, but very plain, tower and, inside, a memorial slate to a local 17th-century doctor noting that 'Thou hast conquerd death, Now death hath conquerd thee'.

To the west of the village (towards Kingston St Mary) are **Hestercombe Gardens**, one of the highlights of this area of Somerset and, indeed, one of the most important gardens in Britain.

The estate dates back to medieval times, though the house is largely the work of the first Viscount Portman who acquired it in the early 1870s. The gardens were begun much earlier by an amateur artist/architect/landscape gardener with the unlikely name of Copplestone Warre Bampfylde. In the late 1750s he laid out the first (Georgian) garden and also built several follies of which two still survive. Viscount Portman added a Victorian garden and a third was added in 1903 when the second Viscount's eldest son asked Sir Edwin Lutyens and Gertrude Jekyll to work at Hestercombe.

The combination of Georgian, Victorian and Edwardian gardens make Hestercombe a remarkable place for following the evolution of the English garden. The last Portman died in 1951 and the property was leased (and then bought) by Somerset County Council who have replanted and restored the gardens – in the case of the Edwardian section to the original specification of Gertrude Jekyll. This painstaking work was only completed in 1997 when the gardens were opened for the first time.

To the west of Taunton is **Staplegrove** whose church contains a memorial to Joseph Poole who sailed with Captain Cook. Near the village **Staplecombe Vineyards** has about 3 acres of vines producing good quality wines. The vineyards and winery are open to visitors, and tasting and purchasing are available at the shop.

To the north of Norton Fitzwarren is an Iron Age hillfort where, legend has it, after a fierce battle which left many dead, a dragon was born from the heap of rotting corpses. The dragon devastated local crops with its fiery breath and devoured farm animals and children alike until a brave local man killed it by stabbing it with a lance and beheading it with his sword.

The story is told in a carved frieze on the rood screen of All Saint's Church. The screen, inscribed with the name of Ralph Harris the churchwarden who died in 1509, is itself a wonder. It was dismantled in Victorian times, a later vicar finding it in a Taunton junk shop. The frieze is wonderfully vibrant, showing the

Continued on page 60...

• Cider Making •

Cider is the fermented juice of apples. Cider making in Somerset is almost as old as recorded history, the county's farmers maintaining small orchards and pulping the apples to create their own brews. The apples were pressed either in a stone trough in which a millstone was rolled by a horse (which walked around the trough), or in a hand press in which a top plate was screwed down on to layers of apples separated by straw or sacking. Farmers made 'scrumpy', the apple juice being left to its own devices, fermenting on the mix of juice, bits of apple skin and pulp that had floated in with the juice, and any other odds and ends that somehow managed to get into the barrel the juice was stored in. There are legends of the brew being 'started' by the addition of things that range from the disgusting (a dead rat) to the bizarre (bird's nests) but in truth it usually fermented on natural yeasts found in the apple skins.

So important was cider making to the locals that there was an annual worry over the likelihood of a good apple crop. What concerned the farmers most was frost killing the apple blossom. Early blooming or late frosts were feared: if the apples blossomed in March there was likely to be little cider, but if blossoming was as late as May then there could be more juice than barrels. The deadline, according to a local saying, was May 21, the date of Culmstock Fair. 'Til Culmstock Fair be come and gone, there might be apples and might be none', folklore claiming that there were no frosts after 21 May.

Commercial cider making is more particular about the fermentation, and also pays great attention to the blend of apple varieties. It comes as a surprise to many just how many cider apple varieties there are, and what exotic names they have – Royal Somerset, Somerset Redstreak, Tremlett's Bitter, Brown Snout, Porter's Perfection and many more.

Visiting a cider farm is one of the joys of a trip to Somerset. Visitors can watch the cider making process (and sample and buy the end product). Many of these are mentioned in the main text as they include factory visits and museums. These, and a couple of others, are collected together.

Coombes Somerset Cider
Japonica Farm, Mark.
☎ 01278 641265

WE Hecks
9-11 Middle Leigh, Street.
☎ 01458 442367

Perry's Cider Mills & Museums
Dowlish Wake, nr Ilminster.
☎ 01460 52681

Sheppy's Cider Farm Centre
Three Bridges,
Bradford-on-Tone.
☎ 01823 461233

Somerset Cider Brandy/ Burrow Hill Cider
Pass Vale Farm, Kingsbury Episcopi.
☎ 01460 240782

Tanpits Cider Farm
Dyers Lane
Bathpool, nr Taunton.
☎ 01823 270663

Torre Cider Farm
Washford.
☎ 01984 640004

The Cider distillery at Kingsbury Episcopi

Continued from page 57

crocodile-like dragon devouring a man in one panel and, above, its last moments. The lower panel has three naked figures portrayed in a pose that is extremely unchurch-like.

Bishops Lydeard and Northern Deane

Nestling below the Quantock edge, **Bishops Lydeard** is a large, attractive village grouped around a red sandstone church. The 'bishop' of the name was Bishop Asser of Sherborne who was granted the manor by King Edward the Elder in the early tenth century: the Sherborne bishops held the village until the 16th century. The village church has a fine tower and one of the county's best sets of carved benches. These date from the early 16th century and include some non-religious motifs – a windmill, a stag and a ship. In the churchyard there is a medieval cross. A short distance from the church are the village almshouses founded in 1616.

Bishops Lydeard is the present terminus of the **West Somerset Railway**, the station lying across the A358 from the main village. At 32kms (20 miles), the line is the longest preserved railway in Britain. It was constructed by a private company, its chief engineer being Isambard Kingdom Brunel, and linked Taunton to Watchet by 1862 and was extended to Minehead in 1874. The company was taken over by Great Western Railways in 1897. The line closed in 1971 but was re-opened – a triumph of enthusiasm – in 1976. It was originally hoped that it would again connect Taunton and Minehead, but the final link between Bishops Lydeard and Taunton has remained elusive: passengers on this section travel by bus.

Close to the station is **Blazes**, a new museum devoted to fire and fire fighting. The museum is housed in Sandhill Park, a fine early 18th-century mansion and explores the mythology of fire, fire prevention and safety, and the history of fire fighting. The latest audio-visual techniques are used to excellent effects and the collection of fire engines (real and model) and fire-fighting memorabilia is fascinating.

Also close to the railway station, just a short distance to the west, is **Ash Priors Common**, a local nature reserve set up to preserve an area of heath and grassland. The common's plant life is excellent and supports a wide variety of butterflies including the rare pearl-bordered fritillary.

From Bishops Lydeard the A358 heads north-west, defining the base of the Quantock edge. From it, turn left along B3224 to explore the quiet country that lies between high Exmoor and the Quantocks.

Lydeard St Lawrence, to the right of the B3224 has a neat red sandstone church with an airy interior. Legend has it that the font was inverted after the Restoration as John Venn of Pyleigh, a hamlet on the other side of the B3224, had been baptised in it. Venn had been a colonel of the Parliamentarian army and a signatory of the death warrant of Charles I.

Beyond the turn to Lydeard St Lawrence, to the left of the B3224, is **Tolland**, close to which stands **Gaulden Manor**. The manor house dates, in part, from the 13th century when it was owned by Taunton Priory. After the Dissolution the manor had several owners before being bought by John Turberville, a

Combe Florey

Set midway between the B3224 and the A358 is **Combe Florey**, a pretty red sandstone village with an elegant 17th-century manor house which was the home of the novelist Evelyn Waugh from 1956 until his death in 1966 and is presently the home of his son Auberon.

Evelyn Waugh is most celebrated for his book *Brideshead Revisited* which explored the complex lives of a Roman Catholic family, a book written after Waugh's conversion to Catholicism. The book was recently the subject of a highly successful TV adaptation.

The village church, which has some fine medieval effigies, has a window which commemorates Rev Sydney Smith the renowned essayist and wit who was vicar here from 1818-1845. Smith had claimed to be fearful of a country parish, seeing the country as 'a kind of healthy grave' but seems to have become very attached to Combe Florey. Smith had a lovely line in self-deprecating humour, claiming that there were three sexes – men, women and clergyman, but was equally unimpressed by the foibles of others. My favourite line is his suggestion to a colleague that 'I am just going to pray for you at St Paul's, but with no very lively hope of success'.

Devonian and distant relative of the Dorset family made famous by Thomas Hardy.

During the Civil War the house was occupied by Parliamentarian soldiers who, John's son (also John) maintained, were such enthusiastic drinkers and smokers that 'a barrell of good beere trembles at the sight of them, and the whole house is nothing but a rendezvous of tobacco and spittinge'.

The house survived the onslaught, its famous plasterwork remaining intact. There are also good collections of furniture and china, and excellent gardens. The gardens are small and themed – scent garden, butterfly garden – and very attractive. The rear of the manor is also planted with old-fashioned roses.

Milverton and Wiveliscombe

From Taunton the B3227 heads west through Norton Fitzwarren. To the right is Heathfield where the church has a curious Elizabethan monument. A man and woman kneel, facing each other across a prayer desk, not an unusual form for the time – but who are the two smaller figures in leg irons? On the minor road beyond Heathfield is **Halse**, a pretty village of thatched cottages. A left turn reaches **Oake**, another very attractive little village: the church has some 15th century stained glass said to have come from Taunton Priory.

Milverton lies off the B3227 on the road to Wellington (the B3187).

There was a Saxon settlement here, but the Saxons were only re-occupying the site, the building of the town's bypass revealing Neolithic and Bronze Age artefacts. Medieval Milverton was a market town, successful in a small way, but achieving real prosperity when the cloth trade was at its height: the row of Georgian houses in North Street is testament to the wealth the trade brought the town's merchants.

The church built, like many Deane churches, in red sandstone, is late 14th century, too early to have benefited from the town's later prosperity. Just to the east of it is The Parsonage, a fine late 15th century house that was originally the local residence of the Archdeacons of Taunton. Stephen Gardiner, Bishop of Winchester, and Thomas Cranmer both held that position, though there is no evidence that either of them lived in the house. There is a fine collection of carved bench ends in the church, one of which bears the Arms of Henry VIII. Thomas Cranmer was responsible for negotiating the king's divorce from Catherine of Aragon and was the first Protestant Archbishop of Canterbury. He was burned at the stake after the accession of the Catholic Queen Mary.

To the south of Milverton there are several attractive villages, **Bathealton** with its late-18th century Court and **Langford Budville** where the church stands above picturesque cottages. From the church there are fine views towards the Tone.

Anciently the church was circled by the villagers who held hands to form a continuous chain. The ceremony was known as 'clipping', but had nothing to do with the trimming of hedges. The name derives from *ycleping*, Saxon for circling and is likely to have been of pagan origin, perhaps a ritual show of communal unity to drive away evil spirits. Similar ceremonies are held in other

Thomas Young, Milverton's Scientist

Thomas Young was born in North Street, Milverton in 1773, the son of a cloth merchant and banker. He was a precocious child, fluent in several languages by the age of 14 and with a keen interest in the natural world. He studied medicine at London, Edinburgh, Göttingen and Cambridge, and became a physician in London, but being of independent means was soon able to study science full time. In 1801 he was appointed Professor of Natural Philosophy (as physics was then – and is occasionally now – called) at the Royal Institution.

As a physicist he is best known for his pioneering work on the wave theory of light, but he is equally famous for work in a quite unrelated field. He was a keen Egyptologist and did important early work on the Rosetta stone. This work led to the translation of Egyptian hieroglyphs by the French scholar Champollion. Thomas Young died in 1829.

Above: Detail on the bay above a main street shop, Wiveliscombe
Below: In the garden at Hestercombe, near Taunton

places in Britain, most notably at Painswick in Gloucestershire. The Langford ceremony was followed by a 'revel', with music, dancing and feasting. Unfortunately the drinking of the revellers got out of hand and the clipping was ended.

North of Milverton, **Fitzhead** is another pretty village: look for the gargoyles in the church, a collection saved from the early church on the site, and the 14th-century cross and tithe barn, now the village hall, in the churchyard.

To the west of Milverton is **Wiveliscombe**, beautifully positioned in a fold of the Brendon Hills. The Romans built a fort to the south-east of the present town in the third century AD, and the Saxons had a settlement here, but as elsewhere in Somerset, Wiveliscombe was a cloth town.

Clothing Made to Shrink

The speciality of Wiveliscombe's clothiers was 'penistones', a cloth stretched well past normal limits, a fact which led it to shrink dramatically when wetted. This sounds a severe drawback, but was popular with West Indian slave owners, the shirts and trousers made for their slaves shrinking in the rain to a fit which restricted movement, allowing work (uncomfortably), but limiting the likelihood of escape. The pictures of slaves in too small, too tight clothes are the result of using penistones.

In medieval times the Bishops of Bath and Wells had a palace here, though of this only an arched entrance gateway, visible from the eastern end of the churchyard, remains. The church fell into disrepair in much the same way as the palace and was in such a state that it was completely rebuilt in the 1820s by Richard Carver whose name can be seen on the west gallery. Inside there is a fine monument to Humphrey and Margery Wyndham, the pair lying in alabaster effigy. The inscription extols Margery's abilities as an amateur doctor.

Taunton to Wellington

The A38, once the holiday route which served Devon and Cornwall, but quieter now that the M5 has been built, heads south-west from Taunton, soon reaching a turn, to the right, for **Bradford-on-Tone**, a large, but attractive village. The bridge over the Tone here is 15th-century, though it needed major repair work in 1698 and minor repairs several times since. Beyond the turn, at Three Bridges, **Sheppy's Cider Farm** centre can be visited. There are orchard and cellar tours, a shop where cider can be tasted and bought, and a museum of cider-making. The farm also has a nature trail, a children's play area and a licensed restaurant.

Wellington is a pleasant town, though some may be disappointed that the place which named the most famous of British soldiers is not more dazzling. As with so many other south Somerset towns a Saxon settlement grew into a prosperous clothmaking town, Wellington's particular claim being the 'invention' of the official khaki colour. The town can also claim the invention of the aerosol spray at a local chemical works: the first spray was fly killer.

At the centre of the town is the Town Hall, built in 1833 to replace a medieval market house. Close by is the town museum, housed in the old Squirrel Inn, which explores the town's history and its association with the Duke. From the Town Hall the High Street, lined with elegant Georgian buildings, leads to the town church, a fine church with a slim sandstone tower. Inside there is a very grand monument to Sir John Popham and his wife. Popham had a mansion near the town (destroyed during the Civil War) to which he retreated from his duties as Speaker of the House of Commons and Lord Chief Justice under Elizabeth I and James I.

He is said to have sent the official message of the sighting of the Spanish Armada off the Devon coast to London from the town. As Chief Justice, Popham presided over the trials of Mary, Queen of Scots, Sir Walter Raleigh and Guy Fawkes and his co-conspirators.

Popham was not a man lacking in self-confidence (as his monument shows) and was quite willing to converse with Elizabeth I in a manner which would have daunted many noblemen. When he was Speaker of the House of Commons the Queen is said to have asked him what had passed there in the time since her last query. 'If it please your Majesty, seven weeks' Popham is said to have replied.

Finally, before leaving Wellington, head along North Street from the Town Hall, then turn left along Coram's Lane to reach the sports centre. Close by are the Wellington Basins, two large ponds formed in 1803 to provide water to a cloth mill. The basins now form the centre of a small nature reserve which is explored by a trail with several information boards. Kingfishers live on the streams that feed the basin's.

Around Wellington

To the south-west of Wellington, Somerset drifts quietly into Devon, the famous red soil of the latter county being formed from the red sandstone that colours this part of Somerset. **Sampford Arundel** lies below Sampford Point, the western extreme of the Blackdown Hills, and is worth passing through for a glimpse of the delicate 13th-century tower on the church. From **Thorne St Margaret** there are superb views of the Quantocks.

To the west of the village, beside the River Tone, is **Cothay Manor**, which Pevsner maintained was one of the most perfect smaller English manor houses of the late-15th century. The house has remained virtually untouched since completion, making it a rare, as well as beautiful, building. The house is reached through a gatehouse and across a courtyard, and there are period outbuildings to the side: when viewed across the lake which fronts it, the collection of buildings is delightful. The manor's gardens are open to the public and are equally serene, laid out as small, themed plots on each side of a long yew walk.

Further west there is a scattering of pretty villages close to the Devon border. Of these **Stawley** is worth visiting for its church, which largely escaped the Victorian restorers, a rare find.

The Blackdown Hills

The Blackdown Hills are formed from Cretaceous Greensand a darker rock than the red sandstone which underlies the plain at their foot. This darker rock creates a darker soil, this being the origin of the name which means no more than it seems to imply – these are the black downs. The hills are still deeply wooded in places, and no less beautiful where the trees have been cleared, a fact that has led the range to be included in the Area of Outstanding Natural Beauty (AONB) that comprises part of south Somerset and a section of Devon to the south.

To the east of the Wellington Monument only a thin sliver of the Blackdowns lies in Somerset. Not

Cothay Manor

Castle Neroche

Between Staple Fitzpaine and Buckland St Mary lies **Castle Neroche**, a Norman fortification which might sit on an earlier hill fort. The castle lay at the western end of the Neroche Forest, a royal hunting ground, 'neroche' being thought to derive from a Norman word for hunting dogs. The castle, a motte-and-bailey, but with outer rings of banks and ditches, was raised by Robert, Count of Mortain, and half-brother of William the Conqueror, in 1086 as a base for operations to thwart a western rebellion against the Normans. It was abandoned within a few decades.

With its massive undulations and tangled trees, it is a marvellously atmospheric site. If the wind is blowing and the sky overcast it can be an eerie place, and it is no surprise that a local legend maintains the Devil took up residence here, the better to harass the local villages. It was from here that he threw the stone that stands beside Staple Fitzpaine church.

until Luxham Reservoir is reached does the county acquire a sizeable piece of the Hills. Scattered within that section of the AONB are a number of pretty villages. **Churchstanton** was Devonian until a shift of the county boundary in 1896. There is actually no true village, just a series of hamlets, the church of the name sitting in isolation beside a minor road that traverses the parish. **Corfe** and **Pitminster** lie at the base of the Blackdowns' northern slope. In the church at Corfe there is a fine Norman font, while close to Pitminster is Poundisford Park. The house here is architecturally interesting as it was one of the last to have been built in Henry VIII's reign and, therefore, before the change to the Elizabethan style.

At the eastern edge of the AONB are **Staple Fitzpaine** and **Buckland St Mary**. The 'staple' of Staple Fitzpaine's name is said to derive from the standing stone near the church. Legend has it that the stone was thrown there by the Devil and that it bleeds if pricked with a pin. The church at Buckland St Mary was built in the 1850s by the vicar, the Rev. John Lance, as a memorial to his beloved wife who had died in childbirth. Inside there is a touching, though a little macabre, monument to his wife showing her rising from her grave with her baby son, having broken the lid of the tomb.

Hatch Court from the deer park

Hatch Beauchamp to Chard

The A358 has been moved to the west of **Hatch Beauchamp** making it a quieter place but, on the definition of the Somerset Levels used in this book, shifting the village into that area. It is a somewhat arbitrary definition, though, and Hatch is a Blackdown edge, rather than a Levels, village.

Hatch Court, lying a little way to the north-east of the village, was built in 1750 – in Bath stone and Palladian style – by a local clothier on the site of an earlier manor house. It is an elegant building, angular in design but very simply decorated to soften the lines. Inside there are cantilevered staircases and a fine use of columns. The furnishings are in period and there are numerous family portraits, some by Sir Alfred Munnings, and a superb collection of porcelain. It also houses a small museum of the Princess Patricia's Canadian Light Infantry, the British Empire's last privately raised regiment which was founded by Brig Hamilton Gault, an uncle of the present owner.

Outside, there are good formal gardens and lovely parkland, part of it occupied by a herd of fallow deer. An arboretum has recently been planted.

To the west of Hatch Beauchamp are a couple of attractive villages – **Stoke St Mary** with an interesting modern village hall and **West Hatch** where the church was lovingly restored after a disastrous fire in 1989. Southwards, minor roads reach the A303 at **Broadway**, a large village named for the 'broad way' which ran to the Neroche Forest. South of the A303 is **Combe St Nicholas**, the last – and very attractive – village before Chard is reached.

A Zulu War Reminder

Behind Hatch Court stands St John the Baptist's Church, built in the 16th century but extensively remodelled. In the chancel there is a memorial window to Col John Rouse Merriot Chard VC who died in the village in 1897. John Chard was born in Devon in 1847 and was commissioned as a lieutenant in the Royal Engineers in April 1868.

On 22 January 1879 Chard found himself in charge of the mission station at Rorke's Drift in Natal just hours after the Zulu warriors of King Cetshwayo had annihilated a British army column at Isandhlwana. The ensuing battle between the hundred or so British soldiers, some of them sick as the mission had been taken over as a hospital, has been immortalised in the film *Zulu*, Stanley Baker playing Chard with Michael Caine as Lt Bromhead, the

Chard

Chard is another clothmaking town, one which grew from a medieval

other senior officer at the station. Though somewhat fanciful, the film does present an essentially true story, the British repelling repeated Zulu attacks for the loss of only 17 men. Several hundred Zulus were killed before they retreated (due to tiredness and hunger rather than as a salute to brave opponents as the film maintains). After the battle eleven VCs were awarded, including one to Chard, the highest number ever awarded for a single engagement.

Chard continued his army career, being promoted twice. He developed cancer of the tongue in 1897 and retired from the army in August, coming to Hatch Beauchamp where his brother Charles was rector. Within three months he was dead. Queen Victoria sent a personal wreath to his funeral and this was kept in the church for many years. Both Chard and his brother are buried in the churchyard.

market town, a market having been held here since the 13th century. To explore, it is really only necessary to stroll gently down High and Fore Streets. Start at the top of High Street, where the museum, housed in 16th-century Gadworthy House, explores the history of the town with a series of excellent exhibits. Stringfellow and his model aircraft take pride of place, but there is also a remarkable collection on the work of John Gillingham.

He was a Victorian shoemaker who became a pioneer in the production of artificial limbs after an accident in 1863, during the firing of a celebratory cannon, left a local man with only one arm. Gillingham's work was of such a high standard that he was in demand throughout Britain.

There are a lace making machine from a local lace mill, a 1940s garage, a blacksmith's forge and much more. Other local people honoured by the museum include Margaret Grace Bondfield who became Britain's first woman cabinet minister in the Labour Government of 1943.

Also in High Street are Choughs Inn, dating from about 1600 and Harvey's Hospital, a group of almshouses found in the 17th century though rebuilt in the 1840s. As the plaque notes, John Stringfellow lived at No. 121. Go past the intriguing sculptures and the fine model of Stringfellow's aircraft to reach the Guildhall, on the right, an impressive porticoed building raised in 1834. Opposite the Guildhall, and a little way back up towards High Street, the Court House is Elizabethan, while the George Hotel is an old coaching inn. Further along Fore Street, and also to the left, is the old Grammar School, built as a private house in 1583 but which became a school in 1671.

Turn right into Silver Street and continue along Old Town to reach St Mary's, the town church, a low,

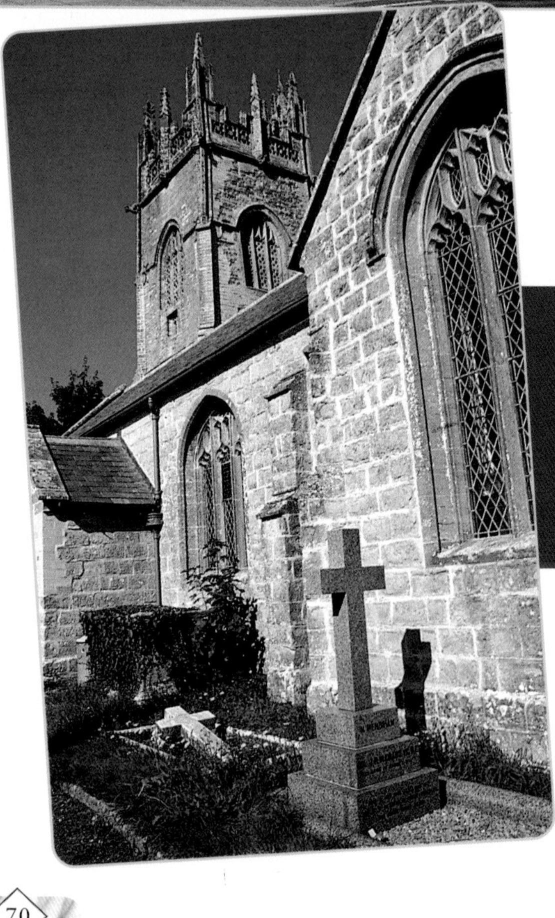

Above: The High Street, Chard

Below: The grave of John Chard VC, St John the Baptist Church, Hatch Court

embattled building in Perpendicular style. Inside there is an interesting monument to William Brewer, a physician who died in 1618 having fathered 'only' eleven children.

There are several interesting places within easy reach of Chard. To the north west of the town the land surrounding **Chard Reservoir** is a nature reserve explored by a waymarked trail: roe deer and kingfishers are often seen here. North of the town **Hornsbury Mill** is a 19th-century mill building now a hotel and restaurant, but with much of the mill machinery intact. There is also a rural life museum and a picnic area beside the mill pond. Finally, to the east of Chard at Wambrook, the **Ferne Animal Sanctuary** has farm and pet animals on a 51-acre site. There are farm and gift shops, a tearoom and a picnic area.

Chard: Birthplace of Powered Flight

The signs that welcome visitors to Chard refer to it as the 'birthplace of powered flight', an intriguing notion. John Stringfellow, born in 1799, was a Chard lace bobbin and carriage maker with an amateur interest in flight. In June 1848 he flew a model – but a large model, it had a 3m (10ft) wingspan – at a disused lace factory in the town. In 1868 he flew a similar model at the Crystal Palace in London. Stringfellow's plane was steam powered, steam being generated by a methylated spirit burner. One of the problems with the model was that as it accelerated, the wind it generated blew the flame out.

In progressing from a model to man-powered flight Stringfellow's major difficulty was the sheer weight of steam engines and the fuel to power them. Consequently interest in his achievement faded. Not until the discovery of the internal combustion engine was it revived. The Wright Brothers have the fame, but Chard's pioneer should not be forgotten.

Bishops Lydeard

Blazes
Sandhill Park
Bishops Lydeard
Open: April – October, Tuesday – Sunday and Bank Holiday Mondays 10am – 5pm.
☎ 01823 433964

Gaulden Manor
Tolland
Open: Last week of May – August, Sunday, Thursday and Bank Holidays 2 – 5pm.
☎ 01984 667213

West Somerset Railway
Bishops Lydeard
Trains run all year except November and February, but are limited in December, January and March. From April to October there are regular services (daily June – September) with several trains each day.
☎ 01643 707650
(24 hour talking timetable)
01643 704996 (other enquiries)

Chard

Chard Museum
Godworthy House
High Street
Chard
Open: May-October, Monday – Saturday 10.30am – 4.30pm.
Also open Sundays in July and August, same times.
☎ 01460 65091

Ferne Animal Sanctuary
Wambrook
Chard
Open: All year, Daily 10am – 5pm.
Closed Christmas Day and Boxing Day.
☎ 01460 65214

Hornsbury Mill
Eleighwater
Chard
Open: mid – February-December, Daily 10am – 4.30pm.
☎ 01460 63317

Hatch Beauchamp

Hatch Court
Open: House: mid – June – mid-September, Thursday 2.30 – 5.30pm
Gardens and Park: mid-April – June, Daily 10am – 5.30pm,
July – September Monday – Friday 10am – 5.30pm.
☎ 01823 480120

Taunton

Hestercombe Gardens
nr Cheddon Fitzpaine
Open: All year, Daily 10am – 6pm (last admission 5pm).
☎ 01823 413923

Somerset County Museum and Military Museum
Taunton Castle
Open: Easter – October, Tuesday – Saturday 10am – 5pm, November – Easter, Tuesday – Saturday 10am – 3pm. Also open on Bank Holiday Mondays, times as above.
☎ 01823 320201

Somerset Cricket Museum
7 Priory Avenue
Open: April – November,
Monday – Friday 10am – 4pm.
☎ 01823 275893

Staplecombe Vineyards
Burlands Farm
Staplegrove
Open: April – October, Monday – Saturday 2 – 5pm. Also occasionally open at other times: ring beforehand.
☎ 01823 451217

Wellington

Cothay Manor
nr Thorne St Margaret
Gardens open: May – September,
Wednesday, Thursday,
Sunday or Bank Holidays 2 – 6pm
House open by appointment to groups of 15 or over, throughout the year.
☎ 01823 672283

Sheppy's Cider Farm Centre
Three Bridges
Bradford-on-Tone
Open: All year, Monday – Saturday 8.30am – 6pm. Also open Sundays from Easter – Christmas,
12noon – 2pm.
☎ 01823 461233

Wellington Monument (NT)
Wellington
Open: Any reasonable time.
The key is available from nearby Monument Farm.

Wellington Museum
28 Fore Street
Wellington
Open: April – September, Monday – Saturday 10am-6pm, October – mid-December, Saturday 10am – 1pm.
Closed on Bank Holidays.
☎ 01823 664747

4 South-East Somerset

Alfred's Tower near Stourhead

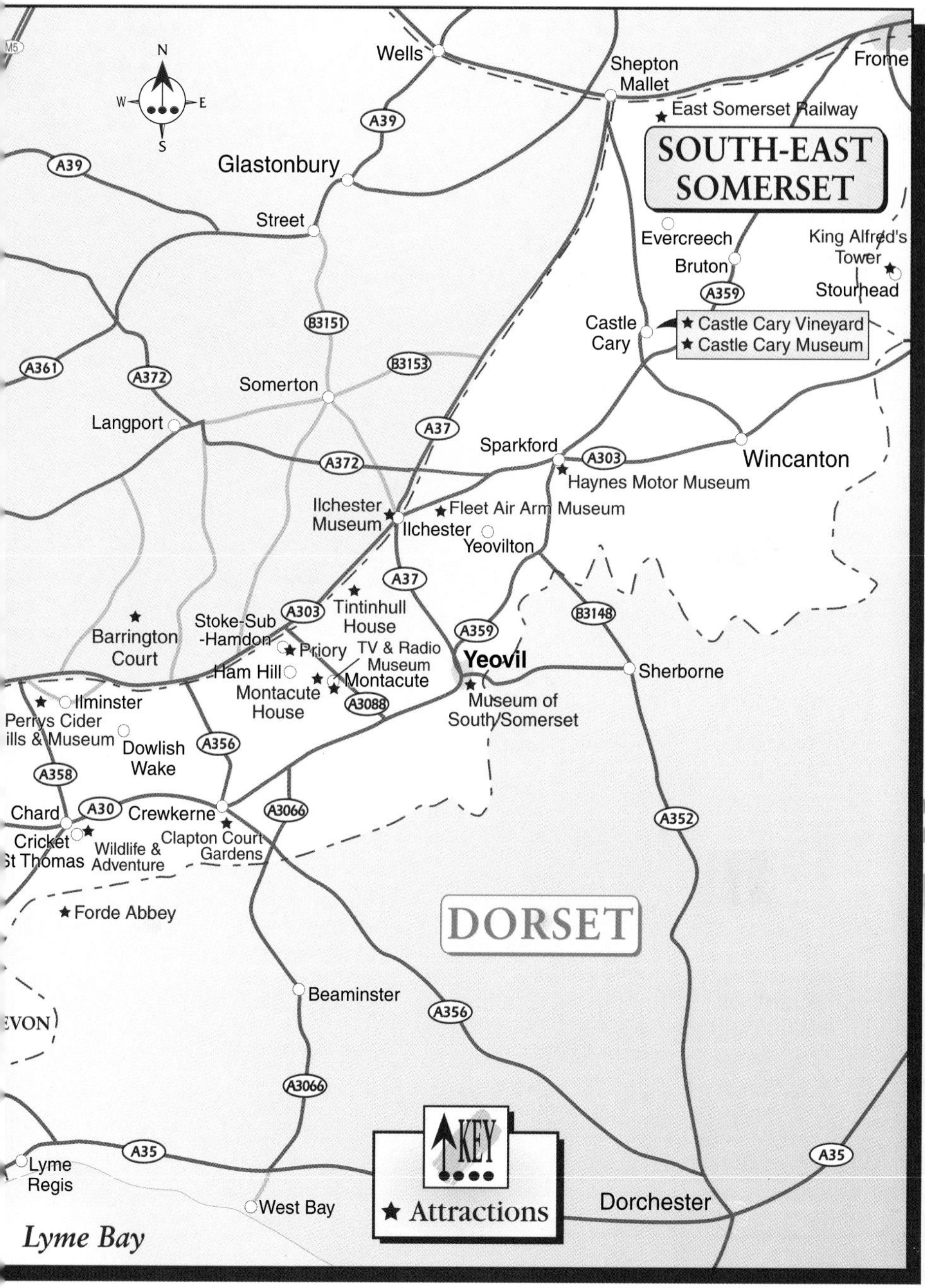

SOUTH-EAST SOMERSET
DORSET
N
S
E
W
M5
Wells
Shepton Mallet
Frome
East Somerset Railway
A39
Glastonbury
Street
Evercreech
Bruton
King Alfred's Tower
Stourhead
A359
B3151
Castle Cary
Castle Cary Vineyard
Castle Cary Museum
A361
A372
B3153
Somerton
Langport
A37
Sparkford
A303
Wincanton
Haynes Motor Museum
Ilchester Museum
Ilchester
Fleet Air Arm Museum
Yeovilton
Tintinhull House
Barrington Court
Stoke-Sub -Hamdon
Priory
TV & Radio Museum
B3148
Yeovil
Sherborne
Ham Hill
Montacute
Montacute House
A3088
Museum of South Somerset
Ilminster
Perrys Cider Mills & Museum
Dowlish Wake
A356
A358
Chard
A30
Crewkerne
A3066
A352
Cricket St Thomas
Wildlife & Adventure
Clapton Court Gardens
Forde Abbey
Beaminster
DEVON
A35
Lyme Regis
West Bay
KEY
Attractions
Dorchester
Lyme Bay

Exmoor, the Quantocks, the Mendips and the Somerset Levels are the famous areas of Somerset, but there is another, often overlooked piece of the country. Sandwiched between the Levels and the Dorset border is a strip of Somerset with interesting towns and places to visit, delightful countryside and, some believe, the real home of King Arthur.

YEOVIL

The largest town in south Somerset has many claims to fame – Paddy Ashdown as the local MP, a football team which holds the record for the number of appearances in the FA Cup 'first round proper' for a non-league side (and an enviable record as cup giant killers) and a helicopter company, Westland, whose fortunes were the cause of the resignation of two of Mrs Thatcher's cabinet ministers – but would not claim to be one of the county's major tourist centres. Nevertheless it has a number of interesting features and deserves more than a passing glance.

The town has the largest outdoor sports centre in the southern county and a good indoor sports centre too: there is also a dry ski slope. The pedestrianised town centre is excellent for shopping, particularly at the modern Quedam centre, and the car parks servicing it are well-positioned and spacious. The town centre also has historical interest, and this is complemented by the Museum of South Somerset which stands beside the Octagon Theatre, a venue for programmes which range from children's shows to ballet, variety to opera.

The town's site, close to the River Yeo's western bank, has been popular with man since earliest times. Neolithic and Bronze Age axe heads have been found locally, as has a Bronze Age torc (a form of twisted necklace), and Roman remains unearthed during excavations near the Westland site were found to be built on Iron Age foundations. There was certainly a Saxon settlement, with an estate held by Ethelweard, a son of King Alfred, and a church by 950AD at the latest.

Ivel

The Saxons named the river *gife* – crooked stream – and that name (as Ivel), together with the alternative river name of Yeo, named the town.

Ivel was resurrected as a name by Unigate when they had a major dairy products factory in the town, in the form of the St Ivel brand name.

Ivel is also spelt out by the initial letters of the town's motto – *Industria Virtute et Labore*.

After the Norman conquest the town was given to Hugh Maltravers whose name is remembered in Maltravers House, the new (1969) home of local government. Medieval Yeovil was prone to fire (as were all towns of the time, the combination of wooden, thatched houses and open fires being disastrous) and suffered a series of bad blazes. One, in

1640, left many townsfolk homeless, fuelling the resentment they already felt about Charles I's imposition of the 'ship money' tax.

When, in 1642, with Civil War looming, the king sent the Marquis of Hertford west to raise troops for the royal army, the Marquis was forced to retreat with those he had raised to the shelter of Sherborne Castle where he was surrounded by an angry mob, and then by a more organised force under the Earl of Bedford. The Earl eventually retired to Yeovil but advanced westwards quickly when Hertford took up a position on Babylon Hill, to the east of the town (and over the Yeo in Dorset).

The battle fought on the hill was short, but fierce, Hertford being forced to return to Sherborne. The battle ended Yeovil's direct involvement in the war, though any joy the townsfolk might have felt was short-lived, plague devastating them in 1646, its spread aided by the miserable, insanitary conditions most were still forced to endure as the war had hampered the rebuilding following the 1640 fire.

Prosperity returned to the town in the 18th century when a thriving leather industry, particularly glovemaking, developed. When Somerset's wool industry went into decline, the leather working allowed Yeovil to stay prosperous, resulting in the building of a fine array of houses. Later a dairy industry replaced the declining leather works and then, in about 1895, James Petter, a local ironmonger, built his first diesel engine. Within 20 years the company he founded had become Britain's major producer. After the 1914-18 War Petter began producing aircraft at a new site at Westland, to the west of the town centre. This works was the forerunner of the world famous Westland Helicopter works.

A Short Town Walk

To explore the town, use the car park near the South Somerset Museum, Octagon Theatre and Magistrates Courts. From here walk to the Tourist Information Office and continue down to South Street, with the Arts Centre (advertised by an eye-catching mural) to the left. Cross and walk ahead along pedestrianised King George Street to reach High Street. Bear right to reach **Silver Street**, on the left side of which, across the lawns and flower beds, is the town church.

St John the Baptist's Church is an impressive building, the more so for standing in isolated splendour beyond the lawns and flowers, its size and position giving it the air of a cathedral rather than a parish church. Perhaps this is no great surprise as it was begun, in 1362, by Robert de Sambourne, Canon of Wells Cathedral, who became Yeovil's vicar.

Inside there is a very rare mid-15th-century brass lectern inscribed *Frater Martinus Forester* (Brother Martin Forester) presumably the donor and the monk whose half-figure is engraved on it.

There are also some good memorial brasses and excellent stained glass in the east window. The glass is 19th century: note that Judas is depicted with a black halo.

Across the lawns from the church is Church Street in which an excellent coffee house offers outside tables for summer visitors wishing to relax beneath the shading trees and absorb the fine view.

Continue down Silver Street and turn right, opposite the church,

The parish church, Yeovil

into the **Quedam**, Yeovil's newest shopping precinct, elegantly pedestrianised. The name is curious, *quedam* is Latin for 'certain', some having suggested that Quedamstrate (the original name of the street replaced by the precinct) was 'a certain street' in the town at some early stage. Walk through the Quedam – the square set back on the left about half way along is Ivel Square, another reminder of the old name – and turn right along **Middle Street**.

Here stood some of the best of Yeovil's old buildings (including a fine half-timbered inn). These were demolished to widen the street for traffic twenty-five or so years ago – and then the street was pedestrianised during the next phase of development. It is still worth a look though: look up, above the shop fronts, to see snatches of prosperous old Yeovil.

Follow Middle Street back to the High Street/Silver Street junction and reverse the route back to the car park. Across the car park is the **Museum of South Somerset**, housed in the old coach house of Hendford Manor. The museum explores the history of the area from prehistoric times using tableaux with life-size wax models to recreate various periods – a Roman dining room, the Georgian era and the cottage leather industry for example. The exhibits on local industries are particularly good. There is also a good collection on local geology and another of fire-arms. The museum also has an interesting collection of paintings, Hendford Manor, just beyond the museum, is a fine building dating from the mid-18th century.

Eastwards from Yeovil

To the east of Yeovil the River Yeo forms the border between Somerset and Dorset, though even the most devoted Somerset fan will follow the A30 across the river and over Babylon Hill to reach **Sherborne** with its superb abbey and brace of castles.

South-east from Yeovil the A37 follows the line of a Roman road, bypassing the village of **Barwick** which has a neat little church and some attractive cottages. On the northern edge of the village is Barwick House, famous for its follies.

Jack the Treacle Eater: the Barwick Follies.

There are four follies set on the cardinal points and said to define the four extremities of the Barwick House estate which was owned by the Newman family when the follies were erected in the late 18th/early 19th centuries. The four are of rough stone and can all be seen from the roads around the village. To the north is Fish Tower, a 15m (50ft) cylinder once topped by a fish weathervane. To the south is a tall Egyptian obelisk oddly bent at the top. To the west is a 22m (75ft) spire topped by a ball. Finally, to the east is an arch supporting a thin tower, itself topped by a figure. The figure is said to be of Hermes, but locally it is known as Jack the Treacle Eater.

The Messiters, a banking family from Wincanton, who took over Barwick House from the Newmans, are said to have employed a lad called Jack to carry messages from their bank to London. Jack is said to have had two claims to fame, the first his phenomenal speed (he is said to have run from Wincanton to London), the second that his efforts were entirely fuelled by treacle. The locals named the statue in his honour.

Montacute and Around

From Yeovil the A3088 heads west, passing two fine National Trust properties before reaching the A303, the border of the Somerset Levels.

Firstly though, the road passes close to **Brympton D'evercy**, reached by a short detour to the left. This tiny hamlet is claimed by Pevsner to be the 'most perfect the county has to offer'. Built of the golden stone from the quarries on nearby Ham Hill, the manor house, church and Chantry House glow in bright sunshine and are beautifully set in lush country. The Chantry House (sometimes called the Dower House), beside the church, is the original 15th-century manor house of the Sydenham family who acquired the estate from the D'evercys of the name. The church is earlier and houses fine monuments to both families, as well as a stone rood screen. The new manor house was begun in the 16th century but was

The Odcombe Jester

Close to Brympton D'evercy is the village of **Odcombe**, set on a hill. The church is largely 19th century, but on an ancient site, there having been a church here since at least the 11th century.

In the late 16th century Thomas Coryate, the son of the vicar, became the unofficial jester to Prince Henry at the Court of James I. Calling himself the 'Odcombian leg-stretcher' Coryate kept the Prince amused for several years, but in 1608 left the Court to walk around Europe. In a 5-month expedition he visited Paris, Turin and Venice, returning home by way of Zurich and Strasbourg. He is said to have introduced the fork to England from Italy, the Italians being appalled by the English habit of eating with fingers.

Coryate also wrote a book entitled *Coryate's Crudities*, (and subtitled *Hastily gobled up in Five Moneth's Travells in France, Savoy, Italy, Helvetia, some parts of High Germany and the Netherlands, newly digested in the hungry aire of Odcumbe in ye country of Somerset and now dispersed to the travelling members of this kingdom*).

The book was published in 1611 and Coryate hung up his shoes – literally, hanging them in the church where they stayed until 1702. But the urge to travel was too strong and in 1612 he set out again, walking through Greece, Turkey and the Middle East and across Persia and Afghanistan to India. He died in India in 1617 at the age of 40.

extended in later years. The house is said to have the longest straight staircase in Britain, but is sadly not open to the public at present.

Beyond the turnings to Brympton D'evercy and Odcombe the visitor on the A3088 soon reaches **Montacute** and arguably the finest stately home in Somerset. The village is named for Mons Acutus, the pointed hill which overlooks the village. Immediately after the Norman Conquest Robert de Mortain, William's half-brother, built a castle on the hill. This may have been a deliberate slight to the Saxons who believed the hill was holy and provoked a furious reaction, the locals besieging the castle in 1068. The uprising failed, but within 35 years the castle had gone, demolished after the Mortains were implicated in a plot against the crown. As well as losing the castle the Mortains were required to found an abbey, a Cluniac Priory being founded in about 1102. Following the Dissolution the Priory was demolished, only a gatehouse (to the south-west of the church) and a small dovecote surviving.

Mons Acutus was originally Logworesbearh (Logor's Hill), a fortified Saxon settlement – there is also evidence of Roman occupation – and became famous in the early 11th century when a crucifix of black flint was discovered on the hill. The crucifix was given to Tofig, standard bearer to King Cnut who took it to Essex and placed it in a church he founded there. The church became Waltham Abbey and the Holy Cross became its most prized relic. When the Normans invaded in 1066, Harold's battle cry is said to have been 'Waltham's Holy Cross' and it was to Waltham that the Saxon King's body was taken.

Montacute House & Gardens

At the Dissolution the estate was owned by the Phelips family and it was one of that family, Sir Edward, the Master of the Rolls and Speaker of the House of Commons, who built **Montacute House**. The House was begun in 1588 and completed in 1601. Its eastern façade is in the E-form popular in Elizabethan times, though the overall form is a symmetrical H. The west façade was added, in an unusually sympathetic form, in the 1780s. With its warm Hamstone and elegant lines Montacute is one of the finest Elizabethan houses in Britain, the view of the eastern façade, with its niche statues of the Nine Worthies, across the well-manicured lawn, or along the gently rising avenue of lime trees, being quite superb.

It is astonishing to discover that after the last member of the Phelips family left in 1911, and after a tenantship by Lord Curzon, the house was put up for sale as 'scrap' in 1931 at an asking price of £5,882. Ernest Cook (the grandson of Thomas Cook, founder of the travel company) bought it and presented it to the National Trust which still owns it.

Inside there are some beautiful and interesting rooms and decorations. The Dining Room has superb 16th-century furniture, while the Great Hall – relatively small, a last echo of the medieval great halls – has portraits of the Phelips family and an extraordinary plasterwork panel. The panel, on the north wall, shows a man being hit with a shoe by his wife for drinking while minding the baby and then being made to endure a 'Skimmington ride'. This, also known as 'riding the Stang', was a medieval punishment for cuckolded or hen-picked husbands and involved being paraded around the village on a pole. The panel is a remarkable work of both levity and local culture which is most unusual in such a grand house.

On the first floor – reached by a grand stone staircase – are more excellent rooms, including that named for Lord Curzon who installed the cupboard bath during his tenancy.

Awaiting the Call

It was at Monacute that Curzon waited in 1923 for the call to become the new Prime Minister following the resignation of Bonar Law on health grounds. When the long awaited telegram arrived it was to tell him that the King had invited Baldwin to form a government.

On the second floor is the Long Gallery, at almost 53m (172ft) the longest now surviving in Britain. The gallery, and the small rooms at its ends, house a collection of 16th- and 17th-century paintings on loan from the National Portrait Gallery.

Outside, the house gardens are formal, the lawn in front of the east front enclosed by a stone balustrade, with small pavilions, below which there are excellent shrubberies. Close by are an ornamental pond and fountain, and an orangery. Beyond the formal gardens the lovely parkland can be explored. Look out for the ice house, to the north of the house: here food was stored, kept cold by ice cut from local ponds and packed in straw. Parkland walks can also return through the village or be extended to include St Michael's Hill.

St Michael's Hill

Mons Acutus is now known as St Michael's Hill, named for a chapel built on the summit after the destruction of Mortain's Castle. The chapel fell into disrepair and had disappeared by the 17th century. The hill was revered as a holy place for many centuries for not only was Waltham's Holy Cross found here, but a local legend claimed that a nail from the Crucifixion was also unearthed on the summit. This legend was related to another which claimed that Joseph of Arimathea (who is usually associated with Glastonbury) was buried on the hill. Joseph is said to have brought the nail to Somerset.

The south-eastern side of the hill was terraced in early medieval times, probably for a vineyard planted by the Cluniac monks. The terraces are now difficult to detect as the hill was planted with trees in the 18th century and is now deeply wooded. At the summit there is a folly, built as an observation tower by the Phelips family in 1760. The profound-looking Greek inscription above the door translates merely as 'Look Out'.

Montacute Village

Montacute village should not be ignored by visitors to the House. The church was the chapel in the monks' graveyard. It dates from about 1300, but has been remodelled. Inside there is a series of monuments to the Phelips family, though some of them

Above: Montacute House
Below: Stoke-sub-Hamdon Priory

have been defaced. C F Powys was vicar here from 1885 until 1914, the three famous literary sons of the vicar – John Cowper, Theodore and Llewellyn – being raised in Park House which was then the vicarage.

Park House is just one of many attractive Hamstone houses. In one, in South Street, the new **TV and Radio Memorabilia Museum** explores the radio/TV age with a collection of over 400 radios and radiograms, together with some early televisions and toys, games, books and magazines associated with radio and TV programmes. The museum also has an Alice in Wonderland collection and a Mad Hatters Tea Room.

Stoke-Sub-Hamdon

A short distance to the West of Montacute is **Stoke-sub-Hamdon**, a village with two distinct parts, East and West. East Stoke is reached first. It has the village church, a Norman building with some interesting details. The tympanum above the north door has a tree of life and a representation of the zodiac figures Sagittarius and Leo, a most unusual feature, while inside there are several fine monuments.

The village's better buildings are in West Stoke, particularly the National Trust property now called **The Priory**. Technically the name is incorrect as the buildings were never a priory. In the late 12th century the village was held by the Beauchamp family who built a fortified manor house about 400m (quarter of a mile) north-east of The Priory. The Beauchamps built a chapel beside their house and then built a chantry for a provost and four chaplains. The Beauchamps required this community to say five masses daily for the souls of their parents, family and friends. The first provost, Reginald de Monketon is believed to lie beneath the tomb in the south transept of East Stoke Church.

The last Beauchamp died childless in 1361 only 60 years after the founding of the chantry, though three masses were still being said daily when Leland, the Elizabethan traveller, visited the village. By then Beauchamp's manor house was in ruins, though the 'large house' (the chantry) noted by Leland was still intact. The chantry was, however, in a state of decay. It was suppressed at the Dissolution and converted into a farmhouse.

It was bought by the National Trust in 1946. Much of the property is occupied and cannot be visited, but enough is open to enable some idea of the original layout to be gained. When occupied by the provost and chaplains it had a number of private rooms for them, as well as a Great Hall and a range of outbuildings, including a fine barn, stables and a circular dovecote. Much of this remains intact, though the dovecote, which had 500 nest holes, has lost its conical roof.

Ham Hill

Stoke-sub-Hamdon acquired the addition to its name from Hamdon Hill which stands above it to the south. Now more usually called Ham Hill, the peak is distinctively crowned by a war memorial and forms a country park with superb views over south Somerset and the southern Levels. On clear days the view extends as far as the Mendips and the Quantocks.

FortNeolithic and Bronze Age artefacts have been found on the hill and in Iron Age times it was topped by one of the largest hill forts in Europe, the ditches and ramparts enclosing an L-shaped area of over 200 acres.

The hill fort was occupied by the Romans and it is speculated that they may have had to fight for its control, the local tribe of Durotriges having resisted strongly at the Maiden Castle fort to the south in Dorset.

Considerable evidence of the Roman occupation has been unearthed, but proof of a battle might have been lost when the hill was extensively quarried. Ironically the first to have quarried the hill were the Romans themselves, eager to exploit the golden limestone that has made Ham famous. After the Roman departure the Saxons certainly occupied the hill fort, though they probably did not continue the quarries. The Normans certainly did, and quarrying has been carried on almost continuously from that time. As well as quarrying, Ham Hill was also used for the annual fair of Cluniac Priory at Montacute and, several centuries later, for political meetings.

Walks at Ham Hill

The hill has several waymarked walks exploring its more interesting historical and natural sites, and is the start (or end) of the Leland Trail, a 45km (28mile) waymarked path which follows the route of John Leland's tour of south Somerset in the 1530s or early 1540s. The trail goes through Montacute and Castle Cary to reach Bruton.

Yeovil to Crewkerne

The A30 heads south-west from Yeovil, soon passing turnings to **East Coker**, to the left (south) of the main road. East Coker is a delightful Hamstone village, once owned by the Helyar family who modified an original 15th-century building to create the fine Coker Court beside the church. The Helyars also built the quaint row of almshouses with their gabled dormers and tall chimneys.

To the south of the village is **Sutton Bingham Reservoir**, created in 1956 and popular with trout fishermen and sailors. The tiny church in **Sutton Bingham** is Norman and has superb medieval wall paintings.

A minor road runs across the reservoir dam to reach **Closworth**. This last Somerset village sits on a hill top looking out across northern Dorset.

The great poet T S Eliot, born an American, but who became a naturalised British subject, traced his British ancestry to a man born in East Coker. Andrew Eliot was born here in 1627 (that is his baptismal date, but his birthday could not have been much earlier, 1626 at the earliest) and emigrated to the US in 1660. T S Eliot only visited the village once, but used its name as the title of one of the *Four Quartets*, which celebrated British life. Eliot was awarded the Nobel Prize for Literature in 1948. Following his request, after his death in 1965 his ashes were buried in East Coker churchyard.

The A30 goes through **West Coker**, cutting it in half, which is sad as it is another pretty Hamstone village.

William Dampier, Surveyor and Pirate.

To the north of East Coker lies **North Coker**, little more than a hamlet, in which stands Hymerford House, a fine Tudor manor with a two-storey porch.

William Dampier was born here in 1651. He had an adventurous life which involved several (probably three) voyages around the world. In addition to being a surveyor with the Royal Navy (where, reputedly, he was court-martialled for his brutal treatment of the men in his charge) he was several times a crewman on privateers. He was the first Englishman to set foot in Australia and has an archipelago off Western Australia named for him.

Dampier's adventures included being shipwrecked and marooned on an island in the Indian Ocean. This might have give him some sympathy for Alexander Selkirk, the marooned man who was the model for Daniel Defoe's *Robinson Crusoe*: Dampier was on the ship which rescued Selkirk. Towards the end of his life Dampier joined the crew of another privateer, living the hazardous life of a pirate until his death in 1715 at the age of 64.

Here, too, there is a row of almshouses, though they are more severe than those at East Coker.

To compensate there is an exquisite manor house, built after a fire in 1457 destroyed the original. The house seems to have been a place to avoid in the early 16th century. After the execution for treason of the Marquess of Exeter the house passed to Edward Seymour, Duke of Somerset. Somerset was a Protector of Edward VI, but was overthrown and beheaded by John Dudley, Earl of Warwick. Warwick took the title Duke of Northumberland, and took West Coker manor too, but was himself beheaded after Edward's death and the accession of Queen Mary.

To the south of West Coker, **Hardington Mandeville** has the distinction of having been the estate of Gunhilda, the sister of King Harold, a fact that caused it to be taken by the Conqueror himself after the Battle of Hastings. Gunhilda was sent to a nunnery in Bruges, far enough away to ensure she would not be a figurehead for Saxon discontent.

East Chinnock, the next village along the A30 is unique for its church having stained glass windows crafted by a German ex-prisoner of war. Gunther Anton was 18 years old and serving in the Luftwaffe when his aircraft was shot down in 1944. From his POW camp near Yeovil he was sent to work on a farm at East Chinnock. On his return to Germany Anton set himself up as a stained glass artist. His business became a success and he crafted a series of windows for East Chinnock Church in gratitude for the treatment he had received from the villagers.

The windows were dedicated by Bishop George Carey (later Archbishop of Canterbury) in early 1989. Sadly Anton had died just a few months before.

To the north of the A30 is a series of delightful villages, all worth more than a passing glance. **Norton-sub-Hamdon** is tucked beneath the western flank of Ham Hill. Not surprisingly its cottages are of Hamstone, the older ones – some as early as the 17th century – being thatched. **Chiselborough** has a 16th-century inn and a fine Early English church. It was the site of the October Fair, held from the 16th century until the 1890s, which is said to be behind Hilton St George's Punky Night (see below).

To the south of the A30, on the A3066, is **Haselbury Plucknett**, another of Somerset's romantically named villages. Haselbury was famous as the site of the cell of St Wulfric, an early-12th-century hermit. Wulfric is said to have worn chainmail constantly (much more troublesome than a simple hair shirt) and to have regularly plunged into cold water. He rapidly developed a reputation as a healer, and also for prophecy. He is said to have been visited by Henry I and to have correctly foretold the king's death.

Wulfric died in 1154 and his body was immediately the subject of an unholy clamour by those seeking to profit from it: any shrine over Wulfric's remains was bound to attract pilgrims. The monks of Montacute Priory attempted to take the body, but the vicar of Haselbury Church, close to which Wulfric had his cell, hid it. When the clamour died down a shrine was built in the church's north aisle and, as predicted, pilgrims came from all over England to touch it, many claiming miraculous cures for long-standing afflictions. Records of the shrine cease in the 16th century and its whereabouts, and those of Wulfric's remains, are not known.

Enjoying the sun in Yeovil. There are always lots of flowers near to the church in summer

The King's Evil

It is not clear exactly what the King's Evil was, but most experts now believe it to have been scrofula, an unpleasant skin disease. The name came from a belief that it could be cured by a touch from the king.

In 1680 the Duke of Monmouth was travelling through Somerset and stopped at Hinton House. There he touched Elizabeth Parcet who had walked from Crewkerne to be cured. It is said that her condition was so bad that her arms and hands were covered in open sores. The disease also affected her eyes. She had been afflicted for ten years and often could not work, this being a real problem as she had five children. After being touched by the Duke her sores dried and her eyes returned to normal.

The fact that the Duke's touch cured her led many locals to support his claim to the throne when, five years later, he led his rebellion against his uncle, James II.

Hinton St George is home to one of Somerset's strangest customs when, in October, on Punky Night, the locals walk through the village carrying hollowed out mangel-wurzels in which are lighted candles. (Mangel-wurzels are large beets grown as cattle food. The name is old English – from mangel or mangold, a beet, and wurzel, a root – but has become so associated with Somerset that it is now commonly assumed to be county dialect. Indeed, one of the county's most famous folk groups is called The Wurzels, the group's popularity having survived the unfortunate death of their lead singer Adge Cutler.)

The origin of Punky Night seems to be the habit of Hinton womenfolk using lanterns to find their husbands as they returned home, late and the worse for wear, having enjoyed themselves rather too well at Chiselborough Fair. Punky is an old local adjective meaning worthless.

Winsham to Ilminster

The south of England is crossed diagonally by a band of chalk, stretching from the Dorset coast to East Anglia. This band creates some of Dorset's most distinctive landscapes, as well as the Wiltshire and Berkshire Downs and the Chilterns. To the west of Crewkerne the northern edge of that band crosses the county boundary – which follows the River Axe – from Dorset to Somerset. The band creates Windwhistle Hill, such a distinctive feature of the South Somerset landscape, and the delightful folded country that lies south of the hill.

Tucked into the folds are **Wayford**, a pretty, unspoilt village with a fine medieval manor house, and **Winsham**, a larger village with an impressive church of unusual design, having the nave and chancel separated by a central tower. Near Wayford, is the hamlet of **Clapton**, Clapton Court has impressive gardens, both formal and informal, covering about ten acres. The gardens have well-labelled plants and shrubs and are very peaceful.

Winsham once had a cloth factory which employed many of the villagers. The manufacturing process required ammonia as part of the dye-fixing process, and the cheapest (and easiest to come by) source was human urine. As a consequence a cart trundled through the village each day, the villagers pouring their accumulated stock into the tank it carried. Those who maintained their supply (so to speak) throughout the year received a Christmas present from the factory. Presumably the queue for a vacancy in the cart-driver's job did not stretch around the corner.

To the south-west of Winsham, across the Axe (and, therefore, over the border into Dorset) lies **Forde Abbey**.

The abbey was founded in 1141 for Cistercian monks. It grew in wealth and influence, but had declined to just 12 monks at the Dissolution though building work continued almost to the day Henry VIII's men arrived. Forde was partially demolished, what was left being eventually sold, in 1649, to Edmund Prideaux, Attorney General to Oliver Cromwell. Edmund's son entertained the Duke of Monmouth at Forde in 1680. Though this visit was legal, Prideaux was seen (probably rightly) as a Monmouth sympathiser and was imprisoned after Sedgemoor. He was released, but fined a sum that ruined him. Later, the house was rented by the philosopher Jeremy Bentham.

Cricket St Thomas Wildlife park

The house incorporates the Great Hall (unfinished at the Dissolution), the monks' refectory and dormitory. The result is splendid – many experts claim Forde to be among the best mid-17th century houses in Britain – but slightly formal.

Inside, the house is wonderfully elegant, its high ceilings and classic windows making it light and airy. Of the furnishings, the greatest treasures are the Mortlake Tapestries, based on Raphael works for Pope Leo X, the present of Queen Anne to Sir Francis Gwyn, the owner in 1702.

The abbey's gardens are as attractive as the building, with trees and shrubs surrounding a large lake and excellent flower beds. There are specimen gardens – Bog Garden, Kitchen Garden etc – and in spring the crocuses and daffodils are beautiful.

The quick way to Ilminster from Cricket is to follow the A30 into Chard and the A358 north. The best way is to cross the A30 and meander through the pretty villages that tumble down the northern slope of Windwhistle Hill. **Chaffcombe** has a neat church with 19th-century stained glass and some delightful thatched cottages. **Cricket Malherbie**, named for 13th-century Norman lords, is a tiny place with a fine court built in about 1820 for Admiral Pitt. The historian Nikolai Tolstoy whose work was the subject of a recent infamous libel case once lived here.

World of Wildlife & Adventure

North of Winsham lies **Cricket St Thomas**, nestling below Windwhistle Hill. Cricket – the village name derives from the Celtic for hill, the same route that produces craig in Welsh: it has nothing to do with the game – was never a large village, little more than a church and Cricket House. It is now given over almost entirely to the **World of Wildlife and Adventure**, one of Somerset's major tourist attractions.

The house was built (or, rather, rebuilt) in 1801 for Admiral Hood, later ennobled as Lord Bridport. The second Lord Bridport demolished some houses in the village to create a series of lakes that are now a feature of the wildlife park. He also rebuilt the village church which is worth visiting for its memorials to the Hoods and their friends. One memorial is to Earl Nelson, brother of Admiral Nelson and father-in-law of the second Lord Bridport.

The house was the centrepiece of the television series *To the Manor Born* which starred Penelope Keith and Peter Bowles.

The wildlife park began in 1967 and has expanded to include an elephant reserve as well as other animals (including sea lions, whose shows are very popular). There is a safari ride through some of the animal enclosures. There are water and land based adventure rides, an adventure fort and undercover play area for younger children, and a miniature train. There is also a licensed restaurant.

Dowlish Wake is another pretty village with a packhorse bridge over its stream.

Dowlish Wake was held for several centuries by the Speke family of Dillington House, Ilminster. One member of the family was John Hanning Speke, the Victorian explorer. Speke, who was born in 1827, accompanied Sir Richard Burton in an expedition to discover the source of the Nile. The pair were the first Europeans to see Lake Tanganyika in 1858, after which Speke continued alone to discover the lake which is the Nile's source. He named it for his Queen – Lake Victoria.

Back home in England Speke was feted as a national hero, but having survived his treks across Africa, in 1864 he was killed while shooting partridge, having accidentally shot himself. David Livingstone attended the funeral when Speke was buried in Dowlish Wake's churchyard.

Ilminster

Now bypassed by the main road and so a great deal quieter, **Ilminster** is worth an hour or two, particularly for its church and old Market House. The town was founded by the Saxon king Ine in the late-seventh century – or so it was claimed by the monks of Muchelney Abbey when they were trying to regain possession of land here during the time of Ethelred the Unready. The monks had a charter to prove both the founding and their claim to the land: the charter may well have been a forgery – the monks did, after all, have a considerable vested interest, but that does not mean the tradition of King Ine's founding is untrue.

After the Norman Conquest Ilminster became an important cloth town, a legacy of this prosperity being a number of elegant houses close to the town centre. The church is large and very grand, the soaring Perpendicular lines of its tower being said to have inspired the design of Wells Cathedral. Inside there are several monuments to the Wadham family, including that of Nicholas and Dorothy Wadham, the founders of Wadham College, Oxford. Another famous Ilminster son was John Taylor, founder and first editor of the *Guardian* (or *Manchester Guardian* as it then was).

At the heart of the town is the delightful Market House, its roof held aloft by open columnwork. Elsewhere, be sure to visit Court Barton, beside the churchyard, which has an array of fine houses, mostly 15th and 16th century, but remodelled in Georgian times. Further away, along North Street, the George Hotel is 18th century and accommodated Princess Victoria in 1819 as she was travelling to meet her parents at Sidmouth.

To the north-east of the town centre, near Whitelackington, is **Dillington House**, now an adult education college but built by the Speke family in the last years of the 16th century. The house is open to visitors. There is a small theatre in the 19th-century mews and the grounds have good gardens, both formal and informal, and a small arboretum. Herne Hill, a well-known landmark to the south-west of the town, is explored by a nature trail set up as part of a protection scheme for the hill's wildlife, which includes the dormouse.

To the west of the centre is **Perry's Cider Mills** where cider is made in a

Muchelney Abbey, near Langport

The Unfortunate Charles Speke

When the Duke of Monmouth was rallying an army to support his claim to the throne, dozens of Ilminster men joined him. One was John Speke. The Spekes knew the Duke, who had stayed at their house during his visit to Somerset in 1680. When he returned, the Duke's army camped near Ilminster and he met John and his younger brother Charles in the market place. Charles Speke shook the Duke's hand.

After Sedgemoor John Speke fled the country, but Charles was arrested and brought before one of Judge Jeffreys' Bloody Assizes. Charles had not joined the Duke, but Jeffreys was heard to say that 'his family owes a life, he shall die for his brother'. And so, for the crime of shaking Monmouth's hand Charles Speke was one of the twelve men hanged, drawn and quartered in Ilminster's market square.

sixteenth century thatched barn, using traditional apples, including the Somerset Redstreak. The barn has a collection of old cider making equipment and farm tools, while a new thatched barn houses a collection of farm wagons (and the barrels where the best cider is matured). Visitors can watch cider making and buy the product, and other things, at the farm shop.

Tintinhull and Ilchester

From Yeovil the A37 heads north-west, taking a winding course until the line of an old Roman road is reached near the turn to **Chilthorne Domer**, where the church has a 13th-century effigy said to be of Sir William De Domer who gave his name to the village. The Roman road was proverbially straight, as is the main road which follows it to Ilchester, but a detour beyond Chilthorne Domer is worthwhile, reaching **Tintinhull**, a lovely village of Hamstone cottages. There are several very attractive houses, including Tintinhull Court, a Jacobean manor.

Tintinhull House is early 17th century and has walled and hedged gardens laid out by the Rev S M Price at the turn of the 19th century. The gardens, which include several small ponds, manicured lawns and good borders are now in the hands of the National Trust.

Ilchester lies on Roman Fosse Way and was the largest Roman settlement in what is now Somerset. *Lendiniae*, Roman Ilchester, was a stop-over on the route that took Mendip lead to the south coast for shipping to mainland Europe. Lendiniae had been a Durotriges settlement before the tribe was defeated by the

Haynes Motor Museum

Romans. It had grown up at a ford of the River Yeo – called the *Yle* by the Celts, explaining the 'Il' of the town's name – but the better organised Romans built a bridge across the river. The history of the Roman settlement, which has been well excavated, is explored in the town museum in High Street.

It seems that after the Romans departed Lendiniae was abandoned for several centuries, then occupied by the Saxons. There was a royal mint in the town in the tenth century, and this was re-established in the 13th. By then Ilchester was Somerset's county town, a prosperous place with six churches. It remained the county town until the middle of the 19th century.

The only church now surviving is St Mary Major, close to the town centre. It is largely 13th century with a massive tower which changes shape (from square to octagonal). Inside there is a plaque recording the birth of Roger Bacon, philosopher and scientist, in the town in about 1214. North of the church is the town centre where the Town Hall houses a 13th-century brass civic mace, one of the oldest in Britain.

North again the Yeo is crossed by a bridge that is, in part, late-12th-century. The town jail once stood at the bridge centre, an extraordinary place to have erected it. Beyond the bridge is Northover, once a village, but now a part of the town. It is named for its position relative to Ilchester, being 'north over' the Yeo.

From Northover a road follows the Yeo, then the edge of Yeovilton Airfield, soon reaching the **Fleet Air Arm Museum**, one of the most impressive in the county. Here over 40 aircraft trace the history of the 'Flying Navy', pride of place going to the Harrier jump jet, still one of the world's most versatile fighter aircraft. The museum also has Concorde 002, the first British-built version of the supersonic airliner. The museum has a mock-up aircraft carrier control centre and a vast collection of photographs, models and uniforms relating to the development of the Fleet Air Arm.

There is also an adventure playground for younger children while older children (and adults) can try the Super X Flight simulator for a real taste of flying. The site has a picnic area and a licensed restaurant.

Yeovil to Sparkford

The A359 heads north-east from Yeovil, soon reaching **Mudford** where the church has some finely carved Jacobean pews. North again, across the Yeo, is **Marston Magna** with a lovely church and some very attractive cottages.

Beyond Marston Magna is **Queen Camel** where the church contains many memorials to the Mildmays, manorial lords for several centuries, including one to Humphrey Mildmay who was killed at the first battle of Newby while fighting for the Royalists. Ahead now the A359 joins the A303 dual carriageway. The road can be followed eastwards to Wincanton, but must be left quickly to reach two interesting local sites.

The first is **Sparkford** where the **Haynes Motor Museum** is a must for all car enthusiasts. The museum was set up by John Haynes OBE, famous as the publisher of the Haynes Workshop Manuals, and has over 200 cars ranging from early forms to

The Screaming Skull of Chilton Cantelo

To the west of Marston Magna lies the village of **Chilton Cantelo**, little more than a huddle of houses around a church which was rebuilt in Victorian times. The village was the birthplace of a headmaster of Eton, but is rather better known for the macabre story of Theophilius Brome's skull.

Brome was a Warwickshire man who came to Somerset to stay with relatives at Higher Farm, opposite the church, to escape the Civil War. Brome must have been a very curious man as he requested that after his death his head should be kept at the farm while his body was interred in the churchyard. His relatives (equally oddly it must be said) complied with this bizarre request, Brome's body alone lying below the headstone beside the church. His head was placed in a cupboard. Whether the head decomposed to a skull or was rendered down is too unpleasant a question to dwell on.

Later occupants of Higher Farm wanted to remove the skull – not surprisingly you might feel – but at every attempt 'horrid noises, portentive of sad displeasure' were heard. The skull continued to scream each time an attempt was made to move it and reputedly it still lies in the cupboard.

Lamborghinis. There is a test track where the exhibits are regularly run, and visitors can also see the workshops where they are maintained. In addition to the cars there is a collection of motoring memorabilia and a shop where the full range of Haynes Manuals (and much more besides) is available.

On the other side of the dual carriageway lies **South Cadbury** where a scattering of houses and the very pretty church lie beneath the imposing remains of Cadbury Castle.

South of South Cadbury, and visible from Cadbury Castle, is the folded country around Corton Ridge, Corton Hill and Pen Hill. Here there are some pretty, largely unspoilt villages: **Compton Pauncefoot** – another of Somerset's romantic two-word names – with its fine Georgian rectory and the early 19th-century, but Gothic-inspired, Compton Castle built in parkland which includes a delightful lake; **Charlton Horethorne** and the **Cheritons**, North and South. In North Cheriton Church the handcuffs used by the village constable are preserved – and the stocks still stand by the churchyard gate.

Charlton Horethorne was where the first recorded cheese-making in Somerset took place in 1086 when a hundred cheeses were used to pay the manorial rent

Wincanton & Around

Joining the A303 at Sparkford allows a quick journey to **Wincanton**,

Continued on page 100...

• Cadbury Castle – Camelot? •

'At the very south ende of the chirch of South-Cadbyri standith Camallate, sumtyme a famose town or castelle.... the people can telle nothing thar but that they have hard say that Arture much resortid to Camalat'

This passage, written by Leland in 1542 is the first to link Cadbury Camp with King Arthur. But before considering whether the link is reasonable two questions must be asked – who was Arthur and what is the history of Cadbury Castle?

There is little hard evidence for the existence of a real Arthur, what there is suggests he was a sixth-century Celtic warlord who won a series of battles against the Saxons. The Saxon settlement of Britain began soon after the Romans departed, but was at first limited to the south-east of the country – the coastal areas of Kent. But the Saxons were not content to stay in Kent and began a westward push in the late years of the fifth century.

Their westward drive was halted in the early sixth century when, according to Nennius, writing in the eighth century, Arthur won a series of twelve battles, culminating in a decisive battle at Mons Badonicus – Mount Badon. The site of some of the battles has been identified, but Badon remains elusive, with claimants from Dorset (Badbury Rings) all the way to Scotland. Many experts believe that the battle took place on the Ridgeway, the ancient trail that follows the scarp edge of the chalk downlands of Wiltshire and Berkshire, pointing out that this was the obvious route from the south-east to the Severn, one of the Saxons' objectives.

Victory at Badon, which probably took place around 500AD, halted the Saxons advance for 50 years or more. Then the Saxons pushed west again. In 565 they won a battle at Barbury Castle (on the Ridgeway, lending confidence to the suggestion that Badon lay in the same area) and in 577 split the Celts in half by winning at Dyrham, just outside Bristol. The Celts were then pushed into Wales and across Somerset and Devon into Cornwall. So, if Arthur was a real man, he was a fifth/sixth-century Celtic warrior, quite unlike the romantic hero of the famous stories. The chivalrous Knights of the Round Table, the magnificent castle of Camelot, Lancelot and Guinevere are all later inventions, marvellous tales, but wholly founded in myth.

Cadbury Castle is an obvious place for a defensive fort, excavations showing that Neolithic man occupied the hill as long ago as 2,000 BC. The first major workings were in the early Iron Age, perhaps 500 BC, when four huge banks and ditches were constructed around the hill's perimeter. The sheer engineering work involved is staggering: in

Cadbury Camp – was this Camelot?

places the distance from bank top to ditch bottom was over 12m (40ft). The defences, which were penetrated by three gateways, enclosed an area of 7.3 hectares (18 acres) occupied by a small settlement, probably of the Durotriges tribe.

The Romans destroyed the settlement in about 70AD, but do not seem to have occupied it themselves. Then, after the Romans had gone, the site was re-occupied by the Celts. A wall of dry stone and wood was built on top of the inner bank, the gateways being fortified, probably with wooden towers. Inside these walls a large timber hall was erected.

This new work at Cadbury Castle took place in about 500AD, just the time when Arthur was stopping the Saxon advance, leading Leslie Alcock, who was in charge of extensive excavations of the site in 1966-70, to conjecture that the castle was Arthur's headquarters. Alcock wrote a brilliant book on the excavations and his beliefs – *By South Cadbury is that Camelot.*

Cadbury Castle can be reached by a short, but steep, track from the village road (there is a car park beyond the church). The walk around its rim offers magnificent views over the local country and the wonderful thought that you might just possibly be following in the footsteps of the real King Arthur.

Continued from page 97...

well-known to anyone with an interest in horse-racing.

The site was first settled by the Saxons and, as with most local towns became prosperous on cloth-making. The decline in the industry coincided with the town's rise in importance as a local stop on the coach route from London to Exeter. A devastating fire around the same time meant that many of the buildings in the steep High Street are elegantly Georgian. Several of the old coaching inns still exist and have their original inn signs – look out for the Bear, the White Horse, and the Greyhound. The latter entertained Princess Victoria as she travelled south to join her parents at Sidmouth (presumably the night before her stop at the George in Ilminster).

One of the most interesting buildings in the town is Ireson House, in Grant's lane, just off High Street. Nathaniel Ireson, the Warwickshire architect/mason moved to Wincanton after completing Stourhead in 1726, running a successful business from the town until he died in 1769. His monument can be seen in the churchyard – he is said to have created the tomb's terracotta statue himself.

In 1688 Wincanton saw the first battle of the forces of Prince William of Orange and James II. The Prince had sent a small band of soldiers to the town to buy horses, the men being surprised by a much larger group of troops from the royal army. The royalists moved away from the town after the skirmish and Prince William spent the night here, staying at a house in South Street known variously as Wincanton Manor and The Dogs. The latter name derives from stone dogs that sat on the house's gateposts. The Dogs is said to have been the birthplace of Jack White, the murderer hanged at Batton Seymour (see below).

In the area around Wincanton there are several fine villages. These include **Stoke Tryster** and **Cucklington**, to the west. At the former a document of 1547 noted that one John Chycke held land for which the rent was one penny, but that he would be excused payment if he was able, at the tenant's Christmas meal, to 'leape over the borde (table) and lette farte'. Sadly history does not record whether he was successful. By contrast, Cucklington seems staid, its only claim to fame being a 1703 storm which damaged the church tower. The restoration work included the pretty cupola to house the clock bell.

The Knights Templar and the Head of Christ

Templecombe's name derives from a preceptory of the Knights Templar, and the Templars are believed to have been the original owners of a medieval panel on which is painted the head of Christ.

The face bears an astonishing resemblance to that on the Turin Shroud which many claim to have been the cloth in which Christ was wrapped for burial. The panel hangs on the south wall of the village church.

Southwards from Wincanton the A357 passes through **Templecombe**, a stop on the S and D (Somerset and Dorset) Railway. The S and D was known as the Slow and Dirty or Serene and Delightful depending upon the passenger's point of view, but everyone agreed that Templecombe Station was one of its most scenic.

Beyond Templecombe is **Henstridge** where, it is claimed, stood the inn in which Sir Walter Raleigh was smoking his pipe of tobacco when a servant threw water over him believing him to be on fire. The incident may be apocryphal, and the Virginia Ash Inn's claim seems to date only from the 19th century. But Raleigh did live in Sherborne, just a short distance to the west, beyond **Millborne Port**, a small town set close to the Dorset border. The 'port' of the name is an old word for a market. At the town centre is the 18th-century Town Hall and the Guild Hall which incorporates a Norman arch. To the south-east of the centre is Ven House, an elegant Georgian mansion built by a local MP.

Sparkford to Castle Cary

From the Haynes Motor Museum the A359 heads north-east towards Castle Cary. To the left of the road is a surprisingly open country stretching across to Fosse Way (the A37), with a few scattered villages – Babcary, Lovington, Alford, East Lydford and North and South Barrow. **Alford** was a minor spa in the 17th century, Celia Fiennes noting its efficiency for 'gauty cases and bilious colic', though the village folk were a 'clounish, rude people'.

To the right of the main road is **North Cadbury**, less famous than its southern cousin, but with a superb Elizabethan mansion that is clearly seen from Cadbury Castle. The house, North Cadbury Court, was built for Sir Francis Hastings, a Puritan writer. Sadly the house is not open to the public. It is believed that Sir Francis lies below one of the two Jacobean tomb chests in the village church: the other tomb chest probably holds his wife.

Castle Cary

Castle Cary is one of the most picturesque small towns in Somerset, and well worth a visit.

The town is named for the stream, the Cary, beside which it sits, the name probably being Saxon for nothing more than 'pleasant stream'. The castle of the name was built in the early 12th century and had an eventful few years, being besieged by King Stephen and then the focal point of a feud between local lords before disappearing from the records barely a hundred years after its building. Castle Cary was a market town in medieval times, and was then prosperous as a cloth centre and for the manufacture of horsehair stuffed seating. Unlikely as it might seem, horsehair sustained the town until the early 20th century.

The town's history is explored in the museum in the **Market Hall**: the museum also has a collection of memorabilia of Rev James Woodforde, curate to his father, the town vicar, and famous as a diarist. His writings reflect local life on the late 18th century, noting the introduction

Jack White's Gibbet

To the north-east of North Cadbury, beyond the tiny village of Yarlington at the junction of the A371 and the road to Bratton Seymour is the site of Jack White's gibbet. There are two versions of Jack White's story, one – the most likely – has it that he was a layabout, inclined to drink too much, and one night spotted a stranger in a local inn buying drinks from a well-filled pouch. When the stranger asked for a guide to Castle Cary, White offered his services, killed the stranger at this crossroads, stole the purse and pushed the body into a ditch. White was quickly caught, confessed and was sentenced to hang.

The less likely version of the tale has White born at The Dogs in Wincanton and having a brother who went to sea after the death of their father. Years later, after the death of his mother, White became a lazy drunk (the stories agreeing on this point). One night White killed a sailor who showed up at the inn where he was drinking. The sailor's body was found at this cross-roads and was taken to Wincanton church where the authorities set up a trial-by-ordeal, asking local men to touch the body, assuming that a man's guilt would somehow reveal itself. When White touched the corpse blood trickled from its mouth. White let out a strangled cry and immediately confessed. Worse was to follow when an examination of the sailor's effects showed he was Jack White's long-lost brother.

Jack White was hanged at the crossroads, his body then being hung in an iron cage so that his rotting form would 'encourage the others'. Not until 1840 did the gibbet post collapse. Today there is no sign of the terrible crime or its aftermath, but it is said that on dark, stormy nights the creaking of the iron gibbet cage can be heard and a ghostly voice moans 'Jack's cold, terrible cold'.

of Edward Jenner's inoculation for smallpox, but also leave no doubt that the curate was fond of his food.

On 28 January 1780 the Rev James Woodforde dined on calf's head, boiled fowl, tongue, saddle of mutton and swan in currant jelly – and that was only the first course: he followed it with wildfowl, larks (!), blamange (sic), tarts etc, and finished with fruit and cheese.

The Market Hall is a good place to start an exploration of Castle Cary. The present building is mid-19th century, replacing one erected in 1616. It is possible that some of the columns are from the earlier building: with its mix of styles it is a lovely building. Opposite stands the George Hotel where Parson Woodforde ate many of his finest meals. Behind the Market Hall is the **Post Office**, a superb creeper-encrusted 18th century building. Close by is the **old town lock-up**, a surprising circular building erected in 1779. It is said that in addition to town miscreants and drunks, truant children, from school and Sunday school, were locked up here.

From the lock-up head back into High Street and turn right along Fore Street with its array of delightful houses. The horse pond with its 'island' war memorial is very picturesque. The castle stood behind it. Fore Street leads to Park Street and Church Street, and All Saints' Church (12th century but largely rebuilt in 1855) with its elegant spire, a landmark of the town.

In the opposite direction from the church, and rather too far to walk, is the **Castle Cary Vineyard.** The vineyard can be toured and wines tested and bought.

Bruton

Just a short distance north-east of Castle Cary is Bruton, a town that is equally picturesque and, historically, even more interesting. Bruton is a fascinating place, the death of its wool industry sparing it from development over the last two centuries so that it is a time capsule of late medieval architecture. It is also a place of surprising sights making an exploratory walk both a necessity and a joy.

An exploration should start with **St Mary's Church** which stands on the southern side of the River Brue, close to the site of the priory/abbey. It is a magnificent building, one of the best in the county, and is built on the site of St Aldhelm's church. The present building is mostly 14th century, work from this period including the unusual north porch tower. The west tower is late 15th century: it is 31m (102ft) high and a masterpiece. In about 1740, Nathaniel Ireson of Wincanton added a chancel to the church. Inside there are some fine monuments, including 16th century effigies of Sir Maurice Berkeley (who acquired the abbey at the Dissolution) and his wife, and some fine Jacobean woodwork.

Cross the Brue into the town. To the right here is Patwell Pump the communal parish pump, until the early 1900s. Turn left and follow the river to view the exquisite 15th-century **packhorse bridge** which once linked the priory to the town. Just a little further on stepping stones cross the river to reach a delightful narrow street which leads to **Plox,** reaching it close to Old House, built as King's School in 1519. The school was supported by the abbey and closed at the Dissolution. The school was

The old lock-up at Castle Cary

reformed in 1550 and now has buildings on both sides of Plox.

Our walk only detours to Plox, following one of several little alleyways away from the river to reach High Street. Turn left to reach **Priory House** (on the left), a part-timbered, 15th-century building which was the Abbey Court House.

Further on, also on the left, is **Sexey's Hospital**, founded in 1638 with money left by Hugh Sexey, a Bruton man who was auditor to Elizabeth I. Sexey built almshouses, a hall and chapel, but interest on his legacy allowed the establishment of schools for girls (in 1877) and boys (in 1892). Sexey's School still flourishes and, doubtless, the pupils have heard all the obvious jokes relating to the unfortunate name.

Return along High Street, admiring its many gracious buildings. At the crossroads the church can be regained by bearing right down Portwall Street, but there are fine buildings in the curiously-named Quaperlake Street ahead. Bruton's final worthwhile site involves a rather longer walk – go along Plox and turn first left – or a short drive to the car park beside the Jubilee Park playing fields. On the hill above the park, and the town, is the huge dovecote which once served the abbey. The gabled tower was one of the first buildings acquired by the National Trust.

Bruton to Evercreech

To the west of Bruton lies **Wyke Champflower**, a strong contender for the title of having the loveliest Somerset place name, and an equally lovely little hamlet with a Georgian manor with its own chapel. The hamlet can be visited on a route which rounds the western flank of Creech Hill. In the third century AD the hill was topped by a Roman

Bruton's Monks

St Aldhelm, the great eighth century Christian and scholar (Abbot of Malmesbury Abbey and first bishop of Sherborne) founded the first church at Bruton, a fact which may have persuaded the Norman lord William de Mohun to found an Augustinian Priory in about 1125.

Though started with great piety with monks brought from France, the priory gradually declined as a centre for strict orthodoxy. Eventually in the early 15th century the prior was sacked after it was found that the monks had taken to gambling and were not only sharing each other's beds (!), but entertaining women from the town, 'especially Margaret Stawel' a report of the time notes with obvious disgust. Clearly Ms Stawel had something of a reputation in Bruton.

A later prior, William Gilbert, restored the priory's reputation, and also rebuilt it, to such an extent that the house was 'upgraded' to an abbey in 1511. This triumph was short-lived: within 25 years Henry VIII had dissolved all of England's monastic houses. Today only a buttressed wall in the delightfully-named Plox, remains of the abbey.

The Royal Bath and West Show

North-west of Evercreech, close to where the B3081 joins the A371, is the showground for the Royal Bath and West show. The show is organised by the Bath and West Society, founded in 1777 by Edmund Rack, a Norfolk Quaker who had moved to Bath some years earlier. Rack had seen the effect of 'Turnip' Townshend on the agricultural practices of East Anglia and was keen to bring the same improvements to the West Country. Rack was the founder of the Society, and its first secretary, and used it to promote not only improved agriculture but also the use of steam engines to pump out the collieries of the Somerset coal field.

At first the Society's show moved from site to site, but since 1965 it has had this permanent site between Shepton Mallet and Evercreech. It is now one of Britain's foremost agricultural shows.

temple, statuettes of several gods having been unearthed. Later, probably in the sixth century a Christian cemetery was laid out beside the temple.

The western route around Creech Hill joins the B3081, which leads up the eastern flank of the hill, near the village of Milton Clevedon. Further along the road is Evercreech.

The west tower of St Peter's Church, **Evercreech**, is claimed to be the most perfect of any in the county, better even than that at neighbouring Bruton. It is 34m (110ft) high and is in purest Perpendicular style. On the outside of the south aisle is a collection of gargoyles sculpted in 1843 when the aisle was being built. Legend has it that they represent the vicar, a local innkeeper and two village woman with whom the master mason fell out while he was staying in Evercreech and working on the aisle.

Close to the church, in Church View, Phoenix Cottage is the well-restored and converted village almshouse, originally built in the 1820s. To the north-west of the town is the showground of the Royal Bath and West Show and, close to the site, **Bagborough Vineyard**, where the vineyard can be visited and wines sampled and bought.

North-east from Evercreech – take the minor road towards Stoney Stratton, then north through Chesterblade, passing Small Down Knoll which is topped by an Iron Age hill fort – is **Cranmore**. The village is actually an amalgamation of two hamlets, East and West Cranmore. East Cranmore was once the home of the Paget family who built Cranmore Tower on the hill across the A361 from the hamlet. The Pagets lived at Cranmore Hall, a neo-Jacobean reconstruction of an early 17th century manor house. The Hall now houses Hallows School.

West Cranmore has a fine church with an elaborate tower. To the south of the church is a preserved section of the **East Somerset Railway**. The line closed in 1963, but is now a museum and art gallery of the steam age, with several engines, coaches and wagons and a replica Victorian engine shed.

Bruton to Frome

Take the A359 north-eastwards from Bruton, a road that passes through beautiful pastoral country with few, all well scattered, villages. **Batcombe**, to the left of the main road, is an extremely attractive village in a secret valley. It was 'owned' by Glastonbury Abbey which might, perhaps, explain the distinctive appearance of the church with its ornate, truncated tower. The view eastwards from the churchyard alone is worth the detour to the village.

Further north the A359 goes through **Wanstrow**, somewhat spoiling a pretty little village.

In the 1860s Wanstrow was involved in a scandal. The vicar, a man with the unlikely name of Rev Cicero Rabbitts, was reported to the bishop for living with a woman to whom he was not married and carrying out his parish duties only when his shooting did not claim his time.

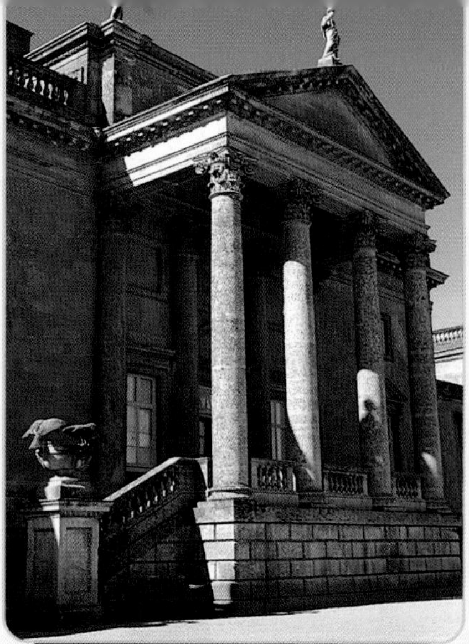

Above: Stourhead
Below: The River Brue at Bruton

Beyond Wanstrow the A359 joins the A361 close to Marston Bigot where there is a fine early 18th-century house and a church with interesting stained glass in the east window. The glass is early-16th century and was painted in Flanders and the Rhineland. One panel – depicting a scene in the life of St Bernard, the saint ordering an innkeeper's wife from his bed – has been traced to the monastery at Altenberg.

To the east of Bruton the skyline is dominated by the triangular **King Alfred's Tower** erected in 1772 by Henry Hoare, owner of Stourhead. According to local tradition the tower marks the spot where Alfred the Great raised his standard in 878 when gathering his army to fight the Danes. Unfortunately history does not support this claim, the now accepted gathering point being Egbert's Stone further south in Wiltshire. The tower is 49m (160ft) tall and for those willing to climb its tight spiral staircase offers a marvellous view westwards across Somerset.

• Stourhead and Longleat •

Stourhead, Henry Hoare's house and park lie over the border in Wiltshire, but are definitely worth a visit. The house was one of the first of the great Georgian houses, designed by Colin Campbell and completed in 1722, Henry Hoare, a banker, having bought the estate from the Stourton family who had owned it since the Norman Conquest. The house was badly damaged by fire in 1902, but rebuilt in fine style. One of the parts most seriously damaged was the library where, legend has it, Edward Gibbon, then aged 14, was inspired to write the *Decline and Fall of the Roman Empire*. The house is superbly furnished, with carved woodwork by Grinling Gibbons, statues by Michael Rysbrack and a fine collection of paintings.

About 20 years after completion of the house Henry Hoare's son laid out the gardens, adding lakes and temples – a copy of the Roman Pantheon and the Baalbeck Temple of the Sun among others – statues and bridges. The whole is one of the finest 18th-century gardens in Britain, especially pleasing in spring when the azaleas and rhododendrons are in bloom, and in autumn when the beech trees turn to gold. One entrance to the estate – which is now owned by the National Trust – is marked by a late-14th-century High Cross brought here from Bristol. The lower niches of the Cross hold original statues of Kings John, Henry II, Edward III and Edward IV. The upper statues, of Henry VI, Elizabeth I, James I and Charles I were added in 1663.

Nearby **Longleat** is also in Wiltshire. It stands on the site of an Augustinian (later Carthusian) Priory. At the Dissolution the estate was bought by Sir John Thynne for £53. He lived in the monastery buildings, but gradually rebuilt and extended: what the visitor now sees is mostly from the mid-16th century, though the work was completed after Thynne's death in 1580. The huge house is in fine Elizabethan style, with a uniform design on all four façades, an unusual feature for the time. The interior is as grand as the exterior with beautiful furnishings and priceless artwork. Longleat is the home of the Needlecraft Centre, and there are excellent collections of costume and Flemish tapestries. The house, now the home of the Marquis of Bath, was one of the first of the great stately homes to be opened to the public.

Longleat's gardens are in formal, Italian style, but the parkland was the work of Capability Brown who spent five years here, from 1757 to 1762. Later the park was remodelled by Sir Humphrey Repton. Today the grounds are more famous for the Safari Park, one of Britain's first. Vehicles are required to enter the big cat, wolf, rhinoceros and elephant enclosures, but visitors can walk among giraffes, zebras, camels and llamas. The park also has sea lions and gorillas, and a tropical house with stunning butterflies. At the pets' corner children can get much closer to the animals. To complete the attractions there is the world's longest hedge maze, a railway and a collection of dolls' houses.

Castle Cary

Castle Cary Museum
The Market Hall
Open: Easter and May – September, Monday – Friday 10.30am – 12.30pm, 2.30 – 4.30pm and Saturday 10.30am – 12.30pm.
☎ 01963 350680

Castle Cary Vineyard
Honeywick House
Hadspen
Open: Vineyard: May – September, Monday – Saturday 10.30am – 5.30pm, Sunday 10.30am – 4pm
Shop: All year, same times.
☎ 01963 351773

Crewkerne

Clapton Court Gardens
Clapton
Open: April – September, Tuesday – Thursday 2 – 5pm.
☎ 01460 73220

Forde Abbey
nr Winsham
Open: House: April – September, Wednesday, Sunday and Bank Holidays 1 – 4.30pm (last admission)
Garden: All year, Daily 10am – 4.30pm (last admission).
☎ 01460 221290

Lower Severalls Garden and Nursery
Nr Hazelbury Plucknett
Open: March – October, Monday – Wednesday, Friday and Saturday 10am – 5pm, Sunday 2 – 5pm.
☎ 01460 73234

The World of Wildlife and Adventure
Cricket St Thomas
Open: All year, daily 10am – 6pm or dusk. Not all attractions are open all year, but there is the full range from Easter – October.
☎ 01460 30755
At the time of writing the park is in the process of being sold. It is believed that the new owners will continue with the present attractions and opening times for 1999.

Evercreech

Bagborough Vineyard
Pylle
Open: April – September, Monday – Saturday 10am – 5pm.
☎ 01749 831146

East Somerset Railway and Museum
West Cranmore
Open: May – September, Wednesday – Sunday 10am – 5.30pm, October – April (but closed throughout February) Saturday and Sunday 10am – 4pm.
☎ 01749 880417

Ilchester

Fleet Air Arm Museum
Yeovilton
Open: All year (except 24 – 26 December) Daily 10am – 5.30pm (4.30pm from November to March). Last admission is 30 minutes before closing.
☎ 01935 840565

Haynes Motor Museum
Sparkford
Open: March – October, Daily 9.30am – 5.30pm (6.30 during school summer holidays), November–February, Daily 10am – 4.30pm, Closed Christmas Day and New Year's Day.
☎ 01963 440804

Ilchester Museum
Town Hall
High Street
Open: Easter – September, Thursday and Saturday 10am – 4pm.
☎ 01935 841247

Tintinhull House Gardens (NT)
Farm Street
Tintinhull
Open: April – October, Wednesday – Sunday and Bank Holiday Mondays 12noon – 6pm.
☎ 01935 822545

ILMINSTER

Perry's Cider Mills and Museums
Dillington House
Ilminster
Open: All year, Monday – Friday 9am – 5pm, Saturday 9am – 1pm.
☎ 01460 53427

Dowlish Wake
nr Ilminster
Open: All year, Monday – Friday 9am – 1pm and 1.30 – 5.30pm, Saturday 9.30am – 1pm and 1.30 – 4.30pm, Sundays 10am – 1pm Open Bank Holidays (9.30am – 4.30pm) except Christmas and New Year.
☎ 01460 52681

Longleat
Warminster
Wiltshire
Open: House: Easter – September, Daily 10am – 6pm, October – Easter, Daily guided tours only 10am – 4pm. Closed Christmas Day
Safari Park: mid – March – October, Daily 10am – 6pm
Other Attractions: mid – March – October, Daily 11am – 6pm
☎ 01985 844400 or 0891 884581 (24 hr information line).

MONTACUTE

Montacute House (NT)
Open: House: April – October, daily except Tuesday 12noon – 5.30pm, Gardens and Park: All year, daily except Tuesday 11am – 5.30pm.
☎ 01935 823289

TV and Radio Memorabilia Museum
1 South Street
Montacute
Open: Easter – October, Monday – Saturday 10am – 5pm, Sunday 11am – 5.30pm (but occasionally close on Tuesdays early and late in the season).
☎ 01935 823024

Stoke–sub–Hamdon Priory (NT)
North Street
Stoke–sub–Hamdon
Open: April – October, Daily 10am – 6pm.
☎ 01985 843600 for information

STOURHEAD

King Alfred's Tower (NT)
South Brewham
Open: Easter – October, Tuesday – Friday 2 – 5.30pm, Saturday, Sunday and Bank Holiday Mondays 11.30am – 5.30pm.

Stourhead (NT)
Stourton
Wiltshire
Open: House: Easter – October, Saturday–Wednesday 12noon – 5.30pm
Garden: All year, Daily 9am – 7pm or sunset
☎ 01747 841152 or 0891 335205 (24 hr information line).

YEOVIL

Museum of South Somerset
Hendford
Yeovil
Open: April – September, Tuesday – Saturday 10am – 4pm, October – March, Tuesday – Friday 10am – 4pm.
☎ 01935 424774

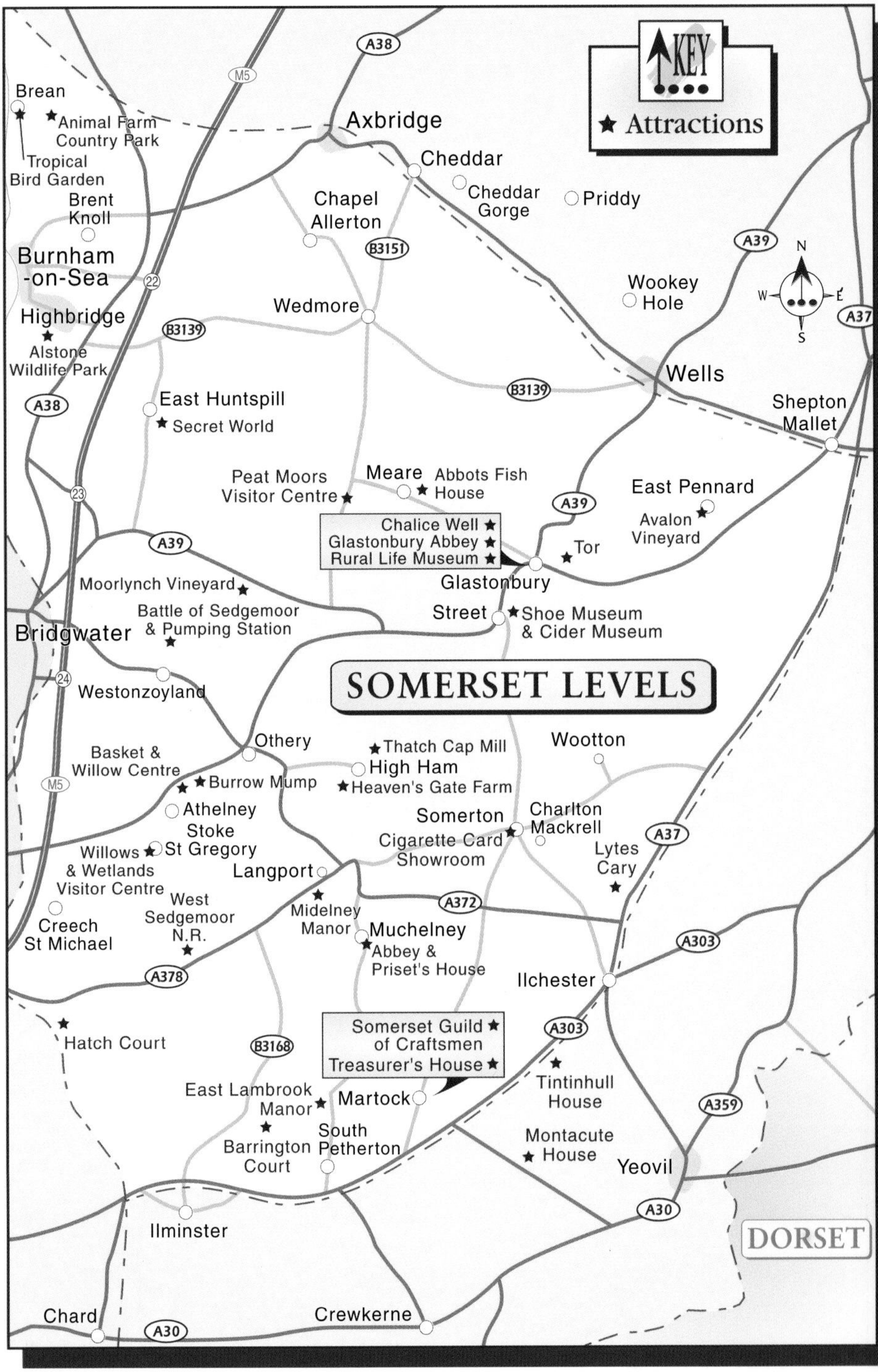
KEY
★ Attractions
SOMERSET LEVELS
Brean
Animal Farm Country Park
Tropical Bird Garden
Brent Knoll
Burnham -on-Sea
Highbridge
Alstone Wildlife Park
Axbridge
Cheddar
Cheddar Gorge
Priddy
Chapel Allerton
Wedmore
Wookey Hole
Wells
Shepton Mallet
East Huntspill
Secret World
Peat Moors Visitor Centre
Meare
Abbots Fish House
East Pennard
Avalon Vineyard
Chalice Well
Glastonbury Abbey
Rural Life Museum
Tor
Glastonbury
Moorlynch Vineyard
Battle of Sedgemoor & Pumping Station
Bridgwater
Street
Shoe Museum & Cider Museum
Westonzoyland
Othery
Thatch Cap Mill
High Ham
Heaven's Gate Farm
Wootton
Basket & Willow Centre
Burrow Mump
Athelney
Stoke St Gregory
Willows & Wetlands Visitor Centre
Somerton
Cigarette Card Showroom
Charlton Mackrell
Lytes Cary
Langport
Midelney Manor
Muchelney
Abbey & Priset's House
Creech St Michael
West Sedgemoor N.R.
Ilchester
Hatch Court
Somerset Guild of Craftsmen
Treasurer's House
Tintinhull House
East Lambrook Manor
Martock
South Petherton
Barrington Court
Montacute House
Yeovil
Ilminster
DORSET
Chard
Crewkerne
A38
M5
A39
A37
B3151
B3139
A372
A303
A378
B3168
A359
A30
22
23
24
N
S
W
E

5 The Somerset Levels

Thatch Cap Windmill

At the heart of Somerset lies another example of the county's extraordinary range of landscapes. Bordered by the Quantocks, the Blackdown Hills, the Mendips, the south-western chalk downs, and the sea lies the second largest area of fenland in Britain: the Somerset Levels.

The Levels

The Levels are a low-lying area of bog, water meadow, drained farmland and the surprising uplands of the Polden Hills, the hills emphasising the flatness of the surrounding land.

The basin of land now occupied by the Levels was flooded by a rise in sea level about 6,000 years ago, a layer of clay and silt being deposited beneath the shallow sea as rivers drained the surrounding hills. Over thousands of years the sea receded, the gradual lowering of the water level allowing a range of habitats to develop. Reeds and sedges grew beside pools and rivers, trees took root on drier sections. It is thought that an increase in rainfall at some stage caused local changes, some areas of soil becoming more acidic. Such acidic, poorly drained land prevents the total decay of dead plants, producing a layer of semi-rotted material – peat. This adds another plant habitat, peat bog. The drying of areas of bog creates heathland, yet another habitat.

When man arrived in the area he wanted access to the Levels where the fishing was good and wildfowl could be hunted. Using timbers and hurdles of hazel, birch, ash and oak he laid trackways across the quaking bogs. One of these, called the Sweet Track after its discoverer, is now thought to be almost 6,000 years old, making it the oldest man-made track in the world.

Settlements grew up on the Levels, the so-called Lake Villages. Despite the name these were not built on stilts in the lakes, but at their edges, the hurdle tracks connecting the settlements and reaching out into the Levels for hunting and fishing. Boats were also used to reach better fishing grounds or more remote wildfowl areas. At first these were just dug-out canoes made from tree trunks, but became more sophisticated as the earliest settlers were replaced by iron users.

Eventually man built sea walls to keep the sea at bay and began to drain the Levels so as to farm the land rather than hunt across it. Drainage ditches were dug: the local word is rhine, sometimes spelt rhyne, but always pronounced *reen*. The land the drainage created was very fertile, excellent for crops and farm animals. The hazel and willow that grew beside the rhines could be pollarded for cane to make baskets and, later, furniture. The exposed peat layers were dug for fuel. The Levels became an important area.

Today mechanical diggers can excavate deep, wide drainage ditches and sluice gates can regulate the flow of water. More land can be reclaimed, more peat dug, and the loss of wildlife habitat is accelerated. Concerns are now being expressed that the character of the Levels might be lost in the rush to 'civilise' the area. It is to be hoped that a compromise can be reached, leaving parts of the area as a reminder of a unique landscape.

GLASTONBURY

Glastonbury is the undoubted capital of mystical England, a wonderfully atmospheric town, its pavements alive with believers in Earth magic, their clothes as brightly coloured as the candles in the shops that line the streets; shops that also sell joss sticks, books on ancient wisdom and clothes that would frighten the horses. In summer the New Age travellers arrive for the Glastonbury Festival (actually held at Pilton), Britain's biggest pop concert, while smaller, less colourful, but quieter, groups arrive at the abbey ruins for one of the Anglican Church's most important pilgrimages.

Two thousand years ago Glastonbury Tor, an isolated hummock of Triassic rock rising 158m (518ft) above sea level, rose above an area of marshland that was occasionally flooded by the sea. As lately as 1607, when the Somerset Levels sea walls were breached, the sea lapped the foot of the tor. Excavations have shown that the tor was settled by Neolithic peoples and that a lake village was established at its foot.

Wildlife of the Levels

The plant life of the Levels can be, very roughly, divided into two, that of the rhines and that of the reclaimed meadows. The former is chiefly rushes and sedges, including marsh horsetail, and such delights as arrowhead, water violet and iris. In the wetter meadows there are marsh orchids and beautiful yellow marsh marigolds (kings cups), while the drier areas support meadowsweet, birdsfoot trefoil and pepper saxifrage.

The Levels are famous for birdlife, waders especially, though they are the threatened by any change in the drainage pattern. They are one of the very few places in Britain where the black-tailed godwit nests (though it has yet to settle permanently), and there are nesting colonies of heron, curlew, lapwing, redshank, snipe, yellow wagtail and winchat. Visitors interested in birds of prey will be keen to see the rare marsh harrier. In winter flocks of migratory birds, use the Levels for 'refuelling', with many species of plover and duck, dunlin and jack snipe. Flocks of Bewick's swans also arrive from the Arctic. The merlin, hen harrier and short-eared owl are also frequent winter visitors.

Animal species are limited. The once common otter is now very rare, though mink are quite common, taking water voles and water shrews. Of the insects, dragon and damsel flies are, not surprisingly, common, one of Britain's rarest damselflies being relatively abundant in certain small areas. Butterflies include the rare marsh fritillary and the increasingly rare marbled white.

Joseph of Arimathea, the Thorn and the Grail

The fact that the tor was reachable by ship allowed the legends of Joseph of Arimathea to take hold at Glastonbury, that and some curious facts which believers suggest are not coincidences. The legend has it that Joseph founded the first abbey at Glastonbury, but that tale has been further embellished to suggest that Joseph, a merchant, once brought his nephew Jesus to the Tor.

On one journey Joseph is said to have docked his ship beside Wearyall Hill, to the south-west of the town. He went ashore and placed his staff on the ground: it instantly took root. This was the Holy Thorn which blossoms at Christmas. During the Civil War soldiers took cuttings from the tree, so many that it died, but luckily several locals had also taken cuttings and these had taken. A Holy Thorn still grows on Wearyall Hill – partially protected by a cage, and another grows in the Abbey Grounds. Each Christmas a sprig of blossom is cut and sent to the monarch.

Joseph is also said to have brought the Holy Grail, the chalice or cup from which Christ drank at the Last Supper. The cup, a sacred relic, was hidden near a spring of healing waters at the foot of the Tor.

These legends have taken such a hold at Glastonbury that it seems sacrilegious to question them, but it is worth dating their appearance. The legend of Joseph founding Glastonbury Abbey dates from the 13th century, the Holy Grail appearing as late as the 19th century. But, the thorn (*Crataegus praecox*) is certainly of Middle Eastern origin, being a native of Syria, and the well where the Grail is said to have been hidden was known as Chalcwelle in the 13th century. Of course this is likely to mean 'chalk well' as the water is highly mineralised, but the low mound to the north of the well was called *chalewe* at the same time, which some see as being too close to 'chalice' for coincidence.

Glastonbury Abbey pre-dates the first recorded settlement here, having been founded in the seventh century by the Saxon kings of Wessex and Mercia. King Ine built a stone church in 720, replacing the earlier timber church. Over the next 200 years the abbey was repeatedly attacked by Vikings and might have passed from history, but in 940 St Dunstan was appointed Abbot.

Under Dunstan's stewardship the abbey grew in importance and wealth, both of which outlasted his appointment as Archbishop of Canterbury in 960. Dunstan crowned Edgar King of England at Bath in 973, the first acknowledged king of the entire Saxon realm. Edgar was buried at Glastonbury as were other Saxon kings and five of Dunstan's successors to the Canterbury archbishopric came from

Above left: The Tribunal at Glastonbury

Above right: The main shopping centre from the entrance to the Abbey, Glastonbury

Right: Glastonbury Tor

Glastonbury Abbey: by the time of the Norman Conquest the abbey's place in English religious life was unrivalled.

Extensive building work took place in the 11th century, but then, in 1184, a disastrous fire destroyed the abbey, consuming most of its treasures and almost all the buildings. To rebuild, particularly on the scale of the earlier building, a huge amount of money was required. More pilgrims were therefore needed, and fortuitously, in 1191, the monks claimed to have found the bodies of King Arthur and Queen Guinevere buried in the abbey graveyard. The bodies were identified by an inscription on a lead cross found with them.

It is now widely believed that the 'grave' and cross were faked, but the effect was immediate, Glastonbury was identified as the Isle of Avalon and the abbey's fortunes rose. Rebuilding on a grand scale began and the 'bodies' of Arthur and Guinevere were re-interred (about 80 years later, the delay due to rivalry between the abbey and local bishops) with great ceremony in the presence of Edward I and Queen Eleanor.

The lavish scale of the building and the abbey's importance did not save it at the Dissolution: in 1539. Richard Whiting, the last Abbot, an old, frail man, was found guilty on trumped-up charges and hauled to the top of the Tor where he was hanged, together with two colleagues. Abbot Whiting's head was placed on a spike by the abbey's gatehouse. The abbey buildings were plundered for their stone and for 350 years what was left decayed away. In 1907 the site was bought by the Church of England and what remained was stabilised.

The abbey ruins are an impressive site, covering 14.5 hectares (36 acres) and including evocative remains of the church and the rather more complete remains of the Abbot's kitchen. The latter gives some idea of the abbey's wealth. The parkland includes a fish pond and a picnic site. The Holy Thorn grows close to the entrance to the site.

From the abbey entrance walk towards the Market Cross, erected in 1846, but in medieval style. Close by is the George and Pilgrims Hotel, built in 1455 to accommodate wealthier pilgrims to the abbey. Walk up High Street with its array of New Age shops, soon reaching the **Tribunal**, on the left, built in the 13th century but with a façade from about 1500. The building now houses the town's Tourist Information Office and a museum of local pre-history.

The Glastonbury Zodiac

In 1925 Katherine Maltwood claimed to have discovered the figures of the zodiac laid out in natural features centred on Glastonbury, while working on a translation of an ancient text on the Holy Grail. Since then the study of the zodiacal figures, or Glastonbury Giants as they are sometimes known, has continued, with other investigators also finding outlines of King Arthur and the Knights of the Round Table in the landscape.

Further along High Street, also to the left, is St John's Church, an early 15th century building with an impressive tower which, at 41m (134ft), is second only to St Mary's in Taunton as Somerset's highest. Inside are some good monuments and a window of the 1930s which retells the Glastonbury legends.

Continue up High Street and turn right at the T-junction. This is Lambrook Street and leads into Chilkwell Street. Neither is impressive, but have the advantage of visiting the best of Glastonbury's sites without the need to re-park a car, parking in the town being notoriously difficult. Where Chilkwell street reaches Bere Lane, to the right, on the diagonally opposite corner is the Abbey Barn, a superb 14th century tithe barn. The barn now houses a **Rural Life Museum** with exhibits on country life in Victorian times.

Bear left with Chilkwell Street – passing the wonderful scrap iron ostriches – to reach the **Chalice Well** on the left. The mineral spring has been known since at least the thirteenth century, but achieved nation-wide fame in about 1750 when an asthmatic claimed to have been told in a dream to drink the waters, and had been cured when he did so. Thousands of pilgrims with a variety of illnesses and afflictions arrived and a pump house was soon built. The attempt to set up a spa to rival Bath failed very quickly when smallpox broke out among the pilgrims. Today the well is the centrepiece of gardens laid out by a Trust which administers the site as a religious retreat.

Around the corner from the garden is Wellhouse Lane, opposite the Chalice Well water tap is the town's old reservoir. The stone tank, once filled by the 'white' and 'red' springs is now another mystical place to Glastonbury Earth Magic believers, the springs denoting man and woman.

From Wellhouse Lane a path leads to the Tor, following a direct line to the tower of St Michael's Chapel.

Healing Water

The water can be tasted – there is an outlet in Wellhouse Lane when the gardens are closed. It has a high iron (chalybeate) content and emerges at 52°F (11°C). Over 110,000 litres (25,000 gallons) per day emerge. The source has not yet been found, but is believed to be on the Mendips

Most investigators claim the figures are very ancient, but not all the suggested features are natural, some following roads which clearly post-date medieval times – because before that the area was flooded and such roads did not exist – or hedgerows, which were planted only after the Enclosures Act. Nevertheless, the proponents of the figures are adamant that sufficient features are ancient, and that the outlines are real. In most plans, the Tor is incorporated into the figures of Aquarius and Sir Perceval.

The chapel was built in the 14th century, replacing one destroyed by an earthquake in 1275.

Finally, to reach **Wearyall Hill** and the site of the original Holy Thorn, go along Bere Lane, with the Abbey Barn on your left, and continue ahead along Hill Road when the main road bears right down Fishers Hill. There is a footpath ahead as Hill Road bears left.

Glastonbury Tor is ringed by terracing (obvious to all visitors) which has been the source of speculation for many years. Suggestions that the terraces were for agriculture seem unrealistic as the terraces are too narrow. They are also too regular to have been made by sheep or cattle. It is now thought – especially by Earth Magic believers – that the terraces form a maze known as a Cretan Spiral (as it appears on coins from Crete, though it is also known from other places, including North America). Crete was, of course, home of the famous Labyrinth of Greek mythology. Quite who would have constructed such a maze at the Tor, and why, is not clear. Was the Tor, in profile a little like a prone, pregnant woman, the centre of a fertility rite or Earth Mother worship in Celtic, or even earlier, times?

Following the spiral maze is not easy because of erosion and tree growth. It also requires a journey of several kilometres as it climbs up the tor to summit. It is said that if it is followed accurately on the night of a full moon a door to the underworld will be found at the top. The author's attempt, by the light of a very bright moon and starting around midnight was not successful.

Glastonbury to Shepton Mallet

Heading east from Glastonbury the A361 skirts the Tor and Pennard Hill before climbing up the southern slope of the Mendips to reach Shepton Mallet. To the north of the road is **North Wootton**, a picturesque village set on a stream draining down from the Mendip foothills. On the road itself lies **Pilton**, now famous as the site of the Glastonbury

West Pennard's Record Cheese

West Pennard is famous for an octagonal cheese weighing 11cwt (about 550kg) which was made here in June 1839 and presented to Queen Victoria in 1840. The Queen declined the cheese, claiming it was unripe, so the cheesemakers exhibited it instead, making a tidy sum from visitors. The makers had a good time with the cash, much to the annoyance of the farmers whose milk had been used to create the cheese and who had been paid nothing.

The farmers had a plaster model made which they, too, exhibited in London. They also took the cheesemakers to court, forcing them to withdraw their cheese from show. When the Queen showed no enthusiasm for changing her mind, the makers took the real cheese back to West Pennard where, in a final irony, it was fed to local pigs.

pop festival – at Michael Eavis' Worthy Farm, to the south of the village – but worth visiting, too, for a lovely little church nestling in trees and a superb tithe barn over 30m (100ft) long. The barn stands above the Manor House, which occupies the site of a summer house for the Abbot of Glastonbury.

To the south of the road are the villages of West and East Pennard.

The church at **West Pennard** has some good Victorian stained glass. At **East Pennard** the **Avalon Vineyard** can be visited for a self-guided tour of the vineyard and a look at the grape and cider presses. Wines and ciders can be tasted and bought. To the south of West Pennard are two interesting villages. **Baltonsborough** is an attractive place – though somewhat spoiled by unsympathetic development – famous as the probable birthplace of St Dunstan, the greatest of Glastonbury's Abbots. The church is dedicated to the saint and has a delightful weathervane made by a local blacksmith.

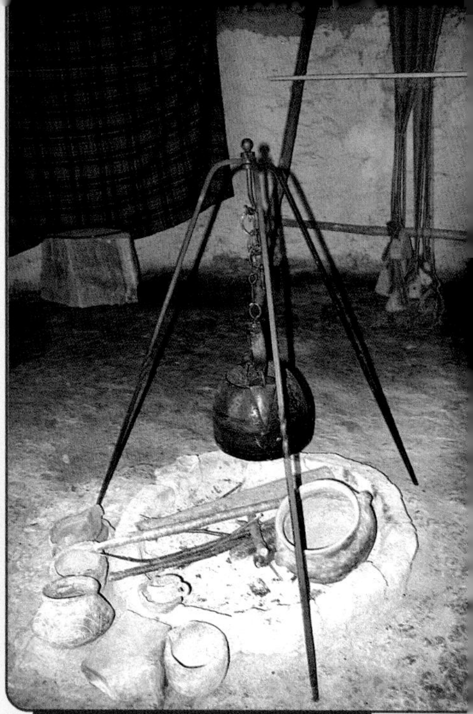

Above & below: The Peat Moors Visitor Centre

Butleigh is a larger, but more harmonious village, with a fine Court, built in 1845 but in Tudor style and a neat church which houses memorials to several members of the Hood Family of nearby Butleigh Wootton. The Hoods were seafarers: Samuel and Alexander, sons of the Rev. Samuel Hood both became Admirals and were ennobled. Viscount Samuel Hood is remembered in a Tuscan column monument on the hill to the west of Butleigh. Another Hood, Capt Alexander, was killed while sailing with Cook: a table tomb in the churchyard is inscribed with an epitaph by Robert

Southey, Poet Laureate and friend of Wordsworth, which details his death.

Glastonbury to Wedmore

To the north-west of Glastonbury are a succession of moors drained by North Drain into the River Brue. The B3151 follows the river, then cuts across the Levels to reach the 'island' on which Wedmore is set. The first village along the way is **Meare**, once the site of two lake villages which excavation has shown were inhabited for about 500 years until the second century AD.

In Saxon times Meare was an island on the edge of a large marsh, the home to fisherfolk, a way of life which persisted for centuries: in the 14th century the Glastonbury Abbot had a **Fish House** built here, fishermen living on the ground floor and salting the fish they caught on the first floor. The house is now in the care of English Heritage and can be visited. The key is available from Manor House Farm which stands on the site of a house to which Abbot Michael of Glastonbury retired in 1252.

From Westhay minor roads head west, cutting an angular path across the Levels to East Huntspill, but we head north over Westhay Bridge and between Westhay and Tadham Moors to reach Wedmore. Westhay Moor is more accessible than most of the Levels' areas and is a National Nature Reserve. Cetti's, sedge and reed warblers nest here and, it is hoped, they will soon be joined by the marsh harrier and the very rare bittern and bearded tit. The moor is also an important area for the hobby. Both otter and mink are found here, as are many dragon and damselflies and a full complement of marsh plants.

It was at **Wedmore** that, after inflicting a final defeat on them at Eddington near Chippenham, a peace treaty was agreed between Alfred and the Danish king Guthrum. Under the treaty Guthrum agreed to be baptised as a Christian and to accept Danish authority only over eastern England, leaving the rest under the kingship of Alfred and his heirs. It was an important treaty – though not one destined to be taken very seriously for very long – which begs the question of why Wedmore? It seems likely that Alfred had a residence of some sort at Mudgley, a short distance to the south-east and for a

Peat Moor Centre

Close to Meare is **Westhay** where the Sweet Track was discovered in 1973. The track, which is not open to the public, ran south towards Shapwick.

Beside the road that now links the two villages, the **Peat Moors Centre** recreates life in the lake villages. There is a reconstruction of the Sweet Track and of other, later, tracks, and of Iron Age canoes and coracles. There are Iron Age huts as well as reconstructions of an iron smelter and forge, pottery kiln and pole lathe. The site also has good collections illustrating all aspects of lake village life. Altogether a fascinating centre.

baptism a church was needed: there had probably been a church at Wedmore since the seventh century.

Today's church dates from the 12th and 13th centuries. It is large and so occasionally termed the 'Cathedral of the Moor'. Inside there is a Victorian window depicting Alfred burning the cakes. Look, too, for the Jacobean pulpit and the early 16th-century painting of St Christopher. There are also some interesting monuments, particularly that of Capt Thomas Hodges which notes his death at the Siege of Antwerp, in 1583, and that only his heart was returned to Wedmore.

Close to the church is the old village cross, with a plain shaft and lantern head. It dates from the 14th century, the figures in the lantern having been eroded down the years.

Legend has it that after Monmouth's rebellion Judge Jeffreys ordered a local doctor to be hanged from the cross after discovering that he had bound the wounds of, and comforted, a rebel. As with many stories of the Bloody Assize the truth of this tale is hard to judge.

But it is definitely true that in 1799 the educationalist Hannah More founded a Sunday School in Pilcorn Street.

Around Wedmore

To the north-west of Wedmore, the last section of the Levels, lying beneath the southern Mendip edge, is dotted with small villages. Near **Chapel Allerton** the Ashton windmill stands where there is known to have been a mill since 1317. The present mill dates from the 18th century when a mill of 1549 was rebuilt. It ground flour until 1927 and was restored in the 1970s. The church at **Badgworth** is dedicated to St Congar, a sixth-century Welsh missionary whose name is also remembered in Congresbury to the north. Badgworth Court is a fine early Georgian mansion.

At **Diddisham** the record of the Christmas feast the lord of the minor gave for his tenants notes that the food was washed down by 45 gallons of ale. Given the size of the manor that seems to be about a gallon for every man, woman and child. **Weare** can offer nothing to compete in terms of excess, but the church does have an interesting feature – communion rails of alabaster complete with alabaster angels.

Heading west from Wedmore the B3139 reaches **Mark** where terracotta lions – brought from Belgium by a Victorian vicar – guard the entrance to the church. The road then crosses Mark Causeway across the low-lying Mark Moor.

Coombes Somerset Cider

Just off the causeway is **Coombes Somerset Cider** where the cider making process can be observed. There is a small museum of cider making and cider can be sampled and bought. The site has a children's play area and a tearoom.

Beyond the causeway the B3139 splits, roads, heading west to Highbridge and south over Bason Bridge (crossing the River Brue, heading west to Highbridge and to reach East Huntspill, from where footpaths explore more accessible sections of the Levels.

Glastonbury to Bridgwater: the Polden Hills

From Glastonbury the A39, heading south-west, soon reaches **Street**, famous as the home of the Clarks shoe factory and Millfield School.

The town is named for the medieval causeway which linked it to Glastonbury – the Abbey 'owned' the town – though there is evidence of a settlement here in pre-Saxon times. St Gildas, the sixth century Celtic saint whose book *Concerning the Ruin and Conquest of Britain* details the loss of post-Roman Britain to the Saxons, was once a resident. St Gildas is thought to have written his book on Steep Holm, from where he could view the loss of Celtic Britain in relative safety (and mounting fury at the incompetence he saw in the Celtic kings). But Steep Holm was later attacked and the saint is thought to have fled to Street where he founded a church.

In the early 1800s Arthur Clothier opened a tannery at the town soon taking on, as an apprentice, Cyrus Clark, the son of a local Quaker. Clothier made Clark a partner in 1821, but in 1825 Cyrus formed his own company, together with his brother James, making rugs and slippers from sheepskin. This was the start of the C and J Clark business which has made the Clark name famous for fine shoes.

As Quakers, the Clarks were concerned with the welfare of their workers: they built houses for them and endowed Street with many buildings. Of these the most notable was Crispin Hall (named for the patron saint of shoemakers) which houses exhibitions, concerts etc.

The old shoe factory is now a **Shoe Museum** which explores the history of the shoe from Roman to present times.

The Clark benevolence to the town still continues: in 1993 the Clarks village was opened, a series of units where well-known companies – including famous fashion designers – offer goods at factory prices. One other Clark's building is also worthy of mention. In 1889 W S Clark, the son of James Clark, built a mansion to the east of the town centre. In 1935 the building became an independent school, Millfield, famous for its sporting ex-scholars.

Another traditional industry is illustrated in Middle Leigh where **Hecks Cider** offers sampling and buying. There is also a small cider museum.

From Street the A39 heads west – to the north of the road is Sharpham Park where Henry Fielding, author of *Tom Jones*, was born in 1707 – following the line of the Polden Hills, a leafy east-west ridge separating King's Sedge Moor from the northern Levels. **Ashcott** is the first Polden village, built of the blue lias rock which forms the hills. The Duke of Monmouth camped just south of the village before the Battle of Sedgemoor.

Shapwick, the next village, has an interesting church which houses several memorials to members of the Bull family who lived in the manor house close to the church. It is claimed that John Bull, the personification of England, was an early member of this family.

• The Battle of Sedgemoor •

James, Duke of Monmouth, was the eldest son of Charles II by his Welsh mistress, Lucy Walter. The Duke was in Holland, as a guest of William, Prince of Orange, when his father died and his uncle became king as James II. As James II was William's father-in-law, and hated the Duke, William ordered Monmouth out of Holland. This action appears to have been the spur to Monmouth's ambition and he decided on a rebellion, sparked from the largely Protestant West Country where, he believed, he would be supported against Catholic James.

On 11 June 1685 Monmouth landed at Lyme Regis in Dorset. With him he had just 82 men, but his hopes for an army were raised when the cry 'Monmouth and a Protestant religion' went up around his dark green standard. The Duke, encouraged by his reception, signed a declaration that he was rightful king and that James had poisoned Charles II to obtain the throne. In four days Monmouth's army had increased to 1,000 men and 150 horse, and with these he set out for Taunton.

By 24 June he had reached Pensford, south of Bristol, and on the 26 June a skirmish at Norton St Philip left 80 royal troops dead and Monmouth a temporary victor. By now his army numbered 3,500 men, with 500 horse, but it became nervous after summer rain left the men cold and sodden. Instead of advancing, the Duke retreated. On 6 July on Sedgemoor, Monmouth's army met the royal army and was utterly defeated: such a devastation that the rebellion was over.

Monmouth fled to Dorset where he was captured near Horton. He was taken to London, arriving there on 13 July. There he began bargaining for his life, asking the King for forgiveness, offering to change religion, and swearing that he had not read the declaration accusing James of poisoning Charles II, before he had signed it. Finally he complained of a cold in the head. The reaction to the latter was swift: he was assured that a good cure for that was coming shortly.

As a strong believer in astrology, Monmouth next remembered that an Italian astrologer had once told him that if he could outlive St Swithin's Day, 15 July, he would survive the year. But the king ordered his immediate execution and set the date for 15 July itself. Despairingly Monmouth tried to have the date put back, but to no avail, and he mounted the scaffold knowing that he would now not outlive St Swithin's Day.

The Civil War's First Casualties

A thousand years after St Gildas had watched the Saxon advance is despair, Street had a much closer view of another major conflict. On 4 August 1642 a small force of Royalists riding south from Wells under the command of Sir John Stawell met a Parliamentarian force at Marshalls Elm, to the south of Street. In the ensuing skirmish the Royalists, despite being outnumbered 6 to 1, put the Roundheads to flight, killing seven of them and wounding another 20 or so. These were the first casualties, and first deaths, of the Civil War.

The large, red-faced farmer in top hat and boots first appeared in a satirical work by John Arbuthnot in 1712, but, of course, he had to be based on someone.

To the north of the village, Shapwick Heath is a National Nature Reserve set up to protect marshland and hay meadows. The Reserve lies close to the Peat Moors Centre (see above)

On each side of the Polden ridge there are villages laid out along the spring line. To the north are **Catcott** where the church has inscriptions from Titus exhorting the old to aid the young; **Edington**, which some claim to be the site of King Alfred's great victory over the Danes (which most experts place at Edington, Wiltshire); **Chilton Polden**, where Chilton Priory, never a religious house having been built in the 1830s by William Stradling an eccentric antiquarian and collector, was once the home of Katherine Maltwood, discoverer of the Glastonbury Zodiac; **Cossington**, where an elm stump is preserved in concrete – it is said that the Duke of Monmouth sheltered and John Wesley preached, beneath the tree; and **Woolavington**, where the church has a blocked Norman doorway, the north door, in which stands the Hody stone claimed to commemorate John Hody, a 15th-century Chief Justice.

To the south are **Greinton**, the original home of the Clarks of Street; **Moorlinch**, where the church has a 14th-century effigy of a lady with fragments of its original vivid paint and the **Moorlynch Vineyard** offers vineyard tours and wine tasting – there is also a licensed restaurant; **Sutton Mallet**, once owned by Robert Knight, cashier of the South Sea Company – when the Company's bubble' burst in 1720, Knight fled his estate with funds he had embezzled; **Stawell**, with some surprising Georgian houses; and **Bawdrip**, a picturesque cluster of buildings around a fine church.

At the end of the Poldens is **Puriton**, most notable for the vast Royal Ordnance Factory which dominates it.

King's Sedge Moor

To the south of the Polden Hills, bounded by the uplands of Ham and the Currys, lies King's Sedge Moor, the most famous of the Levels' fens. The fen is drained by King's Sedgemoor Drain, a wide, arrow-straight rhine which imposes itself on the visitor who takes the A361 south from the Poldens.

Viewing the Drain

Stop at the little car park by Greylake Bridge where the huge sluice that controls the Drain can be seen, and the waterway followed (on its southern side) for miles in both directions. Viewing the Drain from the bridge is like looking along a railway line as it disappears to the horizon.

Beyond Greylake there is a junction of main roads. To the right, the A372 leads to **Middlezoy**, the first of the 'zoy' villages. The name is Saxon, deriving from *sow ig*, marsh island which became *sowi* or *sowey* in the records of Glastonbury Abbey. The name referred to raised, fertile islands set in the marsh, Middlezoy being the middle one of these. The high point of the 'island' is occupied by Holy Cross Church, a fine 14th-century building with a good rood screen and some 16th-century stained glass.

The next 'zoy' village, the western one, is also the most famous. On the north-western edge of **Westonzoyland** a monument marks the site of the Battle of Sedgemoor, the last full-scale battle fought on British soil. The monument, raised to the memory of all who died, was erected in 1928.

Not far from the monument the steam-powered pumping station, built in the 1830s to aid the drainage of the moor, can be visited. There are regular 'steam' days, but even when the station is not steaming the exhibits are worth a visit.

Elsewhere, the large village is worth a short tour. The church has an excellent, tall tower (30m – 100ft – high) and an effigy of a kneeling priest thought to date from about 1300.

Chedzoy is the last of the 'zoy' villages, probably named for its Saxon owner. The King's army camped close to the village before the Battle of Sedgemoor. A vicar of the village church was Dr Walter Raleigh, a nephew of the more famous Sir Walter. During the Civil War the staunchly Royalist Raleigh was turned out of his house, imprisoned and then murdered.

A turn left at the A372/A361 junction follows the A372 across the fen to the base of **Turn Hill**. Where the main road turns sharp right, go left, climbing the hill and bearing right to reach access to the National Trust land on the hill crest. The view of King's Sedge Moor from here is superb. To the east of Turn Hill is picturesque **High Ham** close to which is the **Heaven's Gate Farm**, a National Animal Welfare Trust site which is home to retired horses and donkeys, pot-bellied pigs and pet animals. There is a picnic area and tea shop.

To the south-east of the village is the **Stembridge Tower Mill** – often called **Thatch Cap** – the last thatched windmill remaining in England. It was built in 1822 and used until 1910. The now-restored mill, ideally sited to catch the prevailing south-westerlies sweeping across the Levels and rising over the hill, is now in the care of the National Trust.

To the south is **Low Ham** close to which a third century AD Roman villa was excavated.

• King Alfred •

Alfred was born at Wantage, Berkshire, in 848, the fourth son of King Aethelwulf of Wessex. With little chance of becoming king, Alfred was educated, probably in preparation for life in the church, learning to read and write and going on two pilgrimages to Rome. But after the death of his father, Alfred's two eldest brothers died after relatively short reigns and then the third brother, Ethelred, died, probably from wounds received in battle against the Danes.

Ethelred had a young son, but with the Danes set to invade the Wessex, noblemen chose Alfred as king as he was already battle-hardened. Alfred fought five battles against the Danes in 871, but still had to pay a huge sum to secure Wessex from further invasion.

The bribe gained Wessex four years: in 873 the Danes invaded again, outflanking Alfred's army to reach Devon. Two years of continuous warfare followed, but then in January 878 as Alfred was celebrating Twelfth Night at Chippenham the Danes attacked. Alfred was lucky to escape, and with a small band of men took refuge on a small island in the Somerset Levels – Athelney, the Isle of Atheling (Isle of the Prince). It was here, legend has it, that, while he was lost in thought in a cowherd's hut, he let cakes burn in the oven, incurring the wrath of the cowherd's wife who failed to recognise him.

In the summer of 878 Alfred led his army from the Levels and won a famous victory over the Danes at Edington – probably the village in Wiltshire, though some historians prefer the Edington on the northern flank of the Polden Hills. The victory secured Wessex from invasion for six years by which time Alfred had built a navy and fortresses along his kingdom's borders. Though there were a series of Danish attacks right up until Alfred's death in 899, Wessex was free of Danish rule from the time he left his Somerset base.

In about 888 King Alfred founded on abbey at Athelney as a memorial to the part the 'island' had played in the defeat of the Danes. Though built for such a laudable reason, the abbey was plagued by bad luck. Two French monks attempted to kill the abbot, aiming to put his body in the house of a local prostitute to add humiliation to murder (and cover their own involvement). But the abbot survived their attack and was able to identify them: they were tortured and executed.

After Alfred's death the abbey was sacked by the Danes, then, after refounding, it lost two abbots to Black Death. A later Abbot supported Perkin Warbeck's rebellion and was lucky to escape with a hefty fine. Then, after the Dissolution, the abbey was plundered of its stone and fitments to such an extent that nothing now remains above ground level. The Alfred monument stands at the crossing point of the abbey church.

Othery to Creech St Michael

Othery, the village close to the A372/A361, is the 'other sowi'. Most visitors to the Levels merely see the village from the main road: it is more picturesque away from the road. The church has some 15th-century stained glass and a framed cope from the same period.

South-east of Othery, reached by a minor road across North Moor, is **Aller**. In the church here the defaced effigy of a medieval knight is claimed to be John Aller who, legend has it, saved the neighbourhood by killing a dragon which was sucking the milk from the cows and destroying crops with its fiery breath. John Aller is said to have covered himself in pitch as protection against the dragon's breath and killed it with a spear.

South-west from Othery, along the main road is **Burrow Mump**, a Glastonbury Tor like mound, also topped by a ruined church tower. It is likely that the Mump was used as a look-out by King Alfred when he was at nearby Athelbury, though excavations have revealed no definitive evidence. During the Civil War the Mump was definitely held by a small group of Royalists after the battle at Langport. By then St Michael's Church was already a century old at least. Despite several attempts to raise money for restoration work, the church remains ruinous.

Beyond the Mump, to the left of the main road, is an excellent **basket and craft centre** where local willow canes and other natural materials from around the world are woven into baskets, furniture and other items. Further on, Alfred's Monument at **Athelney** can be seen off to the left. Athelney can be reached by a minor road from Lyng. The monument – erected in 1801 on the site of Athelney Abbey – lies on

A sluice gate on the King's Sedgemoor Drain

private land, but it is intended to provide public access.

To the south of Athelney a finger of lias rock pokes out into the Somerset Levels. The villages here are worth exploring, but first we head north of the A361 to North Newton, a pretty village close to which runs the **Bridgwater and Taunton Canal.**

The canal was to have formed part of the Grand Western Canal whose sponsors saw a waterway connecting Bristol to the English Channel, avoiding the journey around Land's End, a trip made hazardous by Atlantic storms, Cornish rocks and French pirates. The canal started at the Parrett Estuary and was completed through Bridgwater and Taunton to Tiverton. But money and enthusiasm ran out and the section to Exeter and the Exe estuary was never completed. The canal as cut is still filled and can be explored by boat or towpath.

An excellent starting point is the canal centre at **Maunsel,** just south of North Newton. Maunsel is also the centre of the Somerset Space walk. Here there is a scale model of the sun, with exact scale models of the planets at scaled distances along the canal towpaths (towards both Bridgwater and Taunton). Pluto is 8km (5 miles) along the towpaths.

Stoke St Gregory lies south of Athelney and has a number of farmhouses dating from the 16th and 17th centuries. The most interesting is Slough Farm, an early Tudor moated manor house at the northern edge of the village.

On Shrove Tuesday the pupils of the local school contribute an egg for egg-shackling. The eggs are placed in a large sieve which is shaken. The owner of the last uncracked egg wins a prize.

A little way south-west of the village the **Willows and Wetlands Visitor Centre** has exhibits on the history and wildlife of the Somerset Levels, a museum of willow craft and a shop selling locally-made, willow cane baskets and furniture.

Some would argue that **Creech St Michael** is more a Taunton Deane than a Levels' village, and it has certainly become a dormitory village for Taunton in recent years. But it has the feel of the Levels, and despite the recent expansion, it is still very picturesque close to the River Tone. The church, dating

North Curry

North Curry, the next village, has a large, elegant church with an ornate porch and an octagonal tower. Not surprisingly it, too, is sometimes called the Cathedral of the Moor.

The village was once the scene of one of Somerset's more flamboyant festivals which sadly ceased in the 1860s. Known as Reeve's Feast, the festival took place at Christmas, with the locals eating a vast mince pie and then drinking as much ale as they could consume while two 1lb candles burned. It is said that during the reign of King John the mince pie was made in his effigy. Now a 1lb candle is a very large amount of wax and two could burn for a long, long time. It is likely that the feast stopped because of the size of the ale bill and the locals' hangovers.

mostly from the 13th century, is very pretty and must be one of the few in Britain to have had a vicar who regularly took part in organised fights and was eventually removed from office for unlawful violence.

Around Somerton

A Saxon farm, probably called the *sumortun*, the summer settlement, was established by the River Cary soon after the Saxons had occupied the Levels. Gradually it became an important local centre, the local folk calling themselves the Somersaetas. This name has given us Somerset, the original settlement now being called **Somerton.**

The town's importance to the kings of Wessex led to its being fortified, though the town's old (and unsustainable) claim to have been the 'capital of Wessex' has now been dropped in favour of the correct claim to have been a 'royal town of Wessex'. The town has expanded in recent times, but its old centre, the Market Square and the streets surrounding it, have retained their character, making Somerton one of the pleasantest towns in the county.

The Market Square is a delight – an elegant cross, a dignified war memorial and the church tower peeping over the buildings at its edge. The Market (or Butter) Cross, an octagonal, embattled, arcaded building was erected in 1673 with cash raised by public subscription. Close by is the old Town Hall which dates from the early 18th century. The Square is also home to the Red Lion, a splendid old coaching inn, one of several in the town. On the north side of the Square is St Michael and All Angels' Church which dates, in part, from the 13th century.

Close by, there are fine old buildings in Cow Square – named because the market became so large that it outgrew Market Square – and New Street. In front of Old Hall in Cow Square is an old cattle trough. In West Street (which, not surprisingly, heads west from Market Square) are the single-storey Hext Almshouses built in 1626 for eight poor men. Also in West Street the **London Cigarette Card Company** has a showroom where cards can be admired and bought. There are over 2,500 sets of cards on show here.

Presidential Ancestors

Since 1926 the church at **Barton St David** has had a plaque recalling Henry Adams, born in the village in 1583, whose descendants include the second and sixth Presidents of the USA, John Adams and John Quincy Adams respectively.

To the east of Somerton are a collection of attractive villages close to the A37, the Roman Fosse Way. **Kingweston** has a large, but unadorned, Georgian House built by the Dickinsons, Bristol sugar and slave merchants. Monuments to the family take up considerable space in the nearby church (which has a very pretty octagonal spire).

There is also a claim to fame at **Keinton Mandeville**, to the south, where the actor Sir Henry Irving was born in 1838. Irving was then John Henry Brodribb, son of a village shopkeeper.

Martock

South again is **Charlton Adam**, where, to the east of the church, there is a fine Elizabethan house known as The Abbey. The name is incorrect: the building was once the rectory, but there was never a monastic house here. To the north of nearby **Charlton Mackrell** a Roman villa has been excavated, one of several discovered locally, an indication of the importance of Fosse Way.

Two villas have also been excavated near **Kingsdon**, to the south. The church here is a very attractive building: one of its vicars, Peter Hansell, held the office for 62 years until his death at the age of 91. This apparent devotion to duty was not always to the fore however: he was required to take seven years out at one stage, retiring to a retreat in France after having been suspended for 'immoral behaviour' with one of the village ladies.

To the east of Kingdon is **Lytes Cary**. This charming manor house dates, in part, from the 15th century when the Great Hall was built by the Lyte family. Significant additions were made in Tudor times, and there have been small changes several times since, though the essential character of the house has been maintained. After the Lytes were forced to sell, the house was owned by the Dickinsons of Kingweston: it has been in the care of the National Trust since 1948. The house is furnished in period style and set in gardens which owe much to Henry Lyte who, in the late-16th century, translated a Dutch garden book *Niewe Herball*. In his translation Lyte added references to several local types of fruit, including the Somerton pear.

Somerton to Martock.

From Somerton the B3165 heads south, soon crossing the A372 – or, rather, zig-zagging across it – to reach **Long Sutton**, picturesque village, its houses set around an old-fashioned green. At the northern end of the village there is a Quaker meeting house, built in 1717, Long Sutton having been a local Quaker centre. The village church is late-15th century and has a very good wooden pulpit.

Beyond Long Sutton the road crosses the River Yeo and soon reaches **Martock** a superb village of Hamstone houses strung out along the main road. Do find the time to stroll down Church Street from the Market House to the Craft Centre.

The Market House was built in 1750 and with its arcaded ground floor – once a butchers' shambles – is a delightful Georgian building. Close by is the Market Cross, locally called the Pinnacle. The cross, a slender Doric column, is a replacement, the original having been felled by a lorry.

Looking south down Church Street, the Manor House is to the left, an impressive building, originally erected in 1679 but rebuilt after fire destroyed it exactly 200 years later. Now walk down Church Street. To the left there are fine old houses and the George Inn, Martock's oldest, dating from the early 17th century. Also on the left is the **Treasurer's House**, the oldest inhabited house in the county, the Great Hall dating from the late-13th century, and the remainder only a century or so newer. The house is so called because the treasurer of Wells Cathedral was rector of Martock. The house is now owned by the National Trust and is open to the public on a limited basis.

Opposite the Treasurer's House is the church, its site and splendour reflecting the stewardship of the Wells treasurer. Inside there is a very old (probably 14th-century) effigy of a lady, but it is the roof which holds the attention, a magnificent panelled work: it is said to consist of 768 individual panels.

Continue along Church Street, rounding the bend to reach the Court House, on the right. Built in the 15th century, the house became Martock's Grammar School in 1661. Pupils were originally required to talk only in Latin – not only in school, but to each other out of school. The school closed in the 1860s: the house is now privately owned and not open to the public.

The walk can be extended by continuing along Church Street and then Water Street to reach Hurst and, to the right, the gallery of the **Somerset Guild of Craftsmen**. Here, as well as a showroom for the guild's members, there are demonstrations and master classes, guided visits and talks, and regular exhibitions of craftwork, including the annual Craftsperson Award show.

Langport to South Petherton

Despite its name, and the fact that the Somerset Levels were once submerged **Langport** has no sea-based history. 'Port' probably means market in this context though as there was a quay on the River Parrett, with goods unloaded from boats from Bridgwater, that could be the basis. 'Long' probably meant no more than long – and the long main street is still a feature of the town. At its southern end this is Bow Street, but as you move north it becomes Cheapside, 'cheap' deriving from *ceping*, the Saxon for market.

As with all other Somerset towns Langport was a cloth centre in medieval times, its prosperity being sustained when the trade died by two local entrepreneurs, George Stuckey and Thomas Bagehot who operated barges on the River Parrett, a trade which was only ended by the coming of the railway. The prosperity Stuckey and Bagehot brought explains the array of fine Georgian buildings in Bow Street and Cheapside.

From Saxon times the town was defended by earth banks and these were reinforced during the Civil War when the town was held by Royalist troops. In July the Royalists were tempted east towards Long Sutton and utterly defeated by a Parliamentarian army under Col. Fairfax. Cromwell is said to have believed that the victory (which he called the Long Sutton Mercy) was as important as Naseby in the overall context of the War, and to reinforce the point had a ship in the Commonwealth navy named *Langport*.

The **Hanging Chapel**, on The Hill, which heads east from Cheapside, is the town's most famous landmark and sits over a gateway in the old fortifications (though the chapel/gateway preceded the Civil War by at least 250 years). The chapel has been town hall, museum and school (as well as a chapel), and is now a Freemasons' Lodge. It is often said that the name derives from its use as a gallows during Judge Jeffreys' Bloody Assizes, but there seems to

Stuckey's Bank and The Economist

George Stuckey and Thomas Bagehot built wharves on the River Parrett close to Bow Bridge and used barges to transfer goods to and from Bridgwater from where their fleet of East Indiamen sailed. Their company – the Somerset Trading Company – brought prosperity to Langport and also allowed them to follow their own interests. Stuckey set up Stuckey's Bank which issued its own bank notes. By the time Stuckey's was taken over in 1909 only the Bank of England had more notes in circulation.

Walter Bagehot, a descendant of Thomas, gained experience in the family business before becoming a journalist and economic thinker. He became editor of *The Economist* and also wrote several influential books – *Lombard Street, Economic Studies* and – the best known and still a recommended text for students of politics – *The English Constitution*. In the latter Bagehot noted that the rights of the sovereign in British government were now only those of consultation, encouragement and warning. He noted (a brave observation in the reign of Queen Victoria) that a monarch would be required to sign his/her own death warrant if told to by Parliament. Walter Bagehot is buried in the churchyard of All Saints' Church.

be no truth in this: indeed, there is some evidence that the name (probably deriving from the fact that it hangs in space) is a century older.

The walk to the Hanging Chapel passes All Saints' Church where the 15th- century east window has the figures of ten saints. One is Joseph of Arimathea, who is shown with two 'cruets', corresponding to an early version of the Glastonbury legend. In this, Joseph brought cruets of Christ's blood and sweat to England, the Holy Grail legend being a later addition.

Through the arch beneath the Hanging Chapel can be seen the tower of the church at **Huish Episcopi**. The latter part of the name refers to the ownership of the village by the Bishops of Bath and Wells. The church is mostly 14th-century, a major rebuilding being required at that time because of a fire. The fire reddened the stonework of the Norman south doorway, the oldest remaining part of the church. The marvellous tower was added in the 15th century. Inside, the east window of the south chapel was designed by Edward Burne-Jones and made by William Morris. Just north of the village is the hamlet of **Wagg**.

An ancient, local wassail song refers to the Girt (great, ie. big) dog of Langport and Katherine Maltwood, who discovered the Glastonbury Zodiac figures, claimed to have found the dog's outline in the country north of Langport. She placed the dog's tail at Wagg.

From Langport a minor road heads south, soon reaching **Muchelney**. The name means 'great island' in Saxon, and it was on this island, chosen for its security and tranquillity that an abbey was founded in the late seventh century, probably by King Ine. Despite its remoteness the abbey was sacked by Vikings and was refounded by Athelstan, grandson of King Alfred. The monks fished the local marshes, mainly for eels, and planted vineyards, but Muchelney was never a major house, being too often in the charge of old and/or incompetent abbots. After the dissolution it was held by several local families before passing to the State. It is now in the care of English Heritage.

Though nothing remains of the church but the foundations, the Abbot's House is remarkably well-preserved. The house dates from the late-15th century and includes the kitchen, on the ground floor, and the Abbot's parlour on the first floor. Part of the abbey cloisters is also well preserved. In summer the abbey is the venue for a programme of events. Across the Drayton road from the abbey is The Almonry, thought to have been the abbey guesthouse.

Across the Langport road from the abbey is the village church, a fine 15th-century building famous for its painted wagon roof. The paintings include angels in low cut (in one case very low cut) dresses. Across from the church is the thatched **Priest's House** where the medieval 'vicar' lived. The house dates from 1308

John Leach's Pottery

Just to the south of Muchelney, on the road to Kingsbury Episcopi, is the pottery of John Leach, grandson of the famous St Ives' potter Bernard Leach, and son of David Leach, another well-known potter.

when a vicar was first appointed, but has been refurbished since. The gothic doorway and windows are original. The house is now in the care of the National Trust.

Kingsbury Episcopi was firstly the king's, and then the bishop's, manor. The church, with its ornate tower, is very similar to that at Huish Episcopi – clearly the bishops were proud of their estates. On the green stands a much younger building, the village's old octagonal lock-up. Even such a utilitarian building has its ornate finish though, a ball finial.

Bearing right at the fork to head for Burrow Hill leads to Pass Vale Farm, home of the **Somerset Cider Brandy Company** and Burrow Hill Cider. The cider here is pressed from traditional apple types, fermented in oak barrels and sold draught from wooden barrels. Some cider is also distilled to create a Calvados-like cider brandy. An apple liqueur is also produced. The farm has a display of old copper stills and a shop.

Southwards, at **East Lambrook**, Manor Garden is a cottage-style garden created by the late Margery Fish. Mrs Fish was a pioneer of this form of garden and wrote many books on the topic. After her death in 1969 the garden was neglected, but has been faithfully restored by the house's present owners. The house itself is not open to the public, but the garden is.

South again is **South Petherton**, an attractive town, once an important market town. The church is worth visiting for its monuments, which include an early medieval effigy of a knight, several good brasses and the extraordinary work commemorating William Ashe. This has three kneeling figures and two children stood weatherhouse-like. The monument owes more to enthusiasm than craftsmanship, but is delightful.

Langport to Taunton

The A378 heads south-west from Langport, crossing the River Parrett and soon reaching, to the left, the **Langport and River Parrett Visitor Centre** which explores life on the Somerset Levels. There is information on the River Parrett Trail which follows the river (and detours through Langport), and cycles can be hired to explore the local area.

Curry Rivel, the first village on the main road, has a splendid green (to the north of the main road) with a huddle of thatched cottages and a lovely church. The church has some interesting monuments and eight panels, in the south window, engraved by Laurence Whistler. To the south-east of the village is **Drayton**, a picturesque village of late medieval cottages. From it a road heads south to **Midelney Manor**, an Elizabethan manor house with a beautiful walled garden and an 18th-century brick falcon mews.

To the south-west of Curry Rivel, to the north of the main road is **Burton Pynsent**, an Elizabethan mansion given by Sir William Pynsent to William Pitt the Elder (Earl of Chatham) whom he admired. Pitt used the house as a second home, extending it and raising a Tuscan column memorial (designed by Capability Brown) to Pynsent.

Further along the main road a sign points the way north to the RSPB's **West Sedgemoor Nature Reserve**, one of the largest wet meadow areas in Britain. In addition to waders and wildfowl the reserve is home to one of the largest heronries in the country.

Fivehead lies just off the main road, a pleasant village whose folk seemed to have prospered despite John Wesley's disparaging comment: when he preached here in 1785, Wesley claimed he had to speak 'exceeding plain' because of the 'stupid people (he had) to deal with'.

Further west, a minor road heads south from the A387 to **Curry Mallet** where the manor house in Higher Street, a 16th-century building, was extended by Clough Williams-Ellis, more famous for his mock village of Portmeirion in North Wales. The village church has several fine monuments, including one of Ralph Mighill, a former vicar who died in 1633, but still seems to be preaching a sermon.

The Hanging Chapel at Langport

Christabel Pyne and English History

Fivehead was once home to Hugh Pyne, a staunch Royalist whose daughter Christabel wet-nursed the baby who become Charles II and who also almost changed the course of English history. Christabel's husband was Sir Edmund Wyndham, the governor of Bridgwater. During the siege of the town Christabel spotted Oliver Cromwell among the Parliamentarians and aimed a musket at him, her shot killing the man stood beside him.

Beyond the turn to Curry Mallet the A387 runs below Crimson Hill to reach the A358 close to Taunton.

Langport to Ilminster

From Curry Rivel the B3168 heads south, crossing the River Isle and going through **Hambridge** where – in Earnshill House, to the west of the main village – the first recorded game of lawn tennis took place in 1873 between the inventor Maj Walter Clapton Wingfield and one of his hosts, the Combe family. Wingfield was a cousin of the Combes.

At Bowdens Farm, to the north of the village and the Isle bridge, Levels' eels are smoked in a tradition which can be traced back to the eel fisheries of Muchelney Abbey.

South again, **Barrington** lies off the B3168. The village is famous for its Court, but many visitors to that fine building miss the extremely attractive village that lies to its west. Be sure to wander along the main street with its thatched cottages, perhaps looking in at the church, which has a central, octagonal tower. **Barrington Court** is a lovely Ham-stone building in the traditional E-style of Elizabethan England. The Court is owned by the National Trust, but let to Stuart Interiors who make and sell reproduction furniture.

The grounds of Barrington Court, a series of themed, walled gardens, were designed by Gertrude Jekyll.

To the east of Barrington is **Shepton Beauchamp**, once the home of the young Jane Seymour who became Henry VIII's third wife. The village is another in which the ancient Shrove Tuesday tradition of egg-shackling is maintained by the village children (see Stoke St Gregory).

To the west of Barrington are two villages named for their position on the River Isle. **Isle Abbots** has a fine church, built by Muchelney Abbey which owned the estate – hence the name. **Isle Brewers** is famous for Siamese twins born there in 1861. The twin girls, Aquila and Priscilla, were exhibited at local fairs for money, which seems in poor taste, but was mild in comparison to the fact that after they had died they were stuffed and continued to be exhibited.

The Levels' Coast

Geologically, **Brean Down** is formed from the same rock as the high

Mendips, but the River Axe cuts off the Down from the Mendips' western tip, making it more sensible (from the point of view of visiting) to place it in the Somerset Levels. The huge, cliff-sided, whale-backed ridge of the Down is so clearly a natural defensive structure that it comes as no surprise that finds have been made here from the Bronze Age, the Iron Age and the Roman era.

The Roman remains are of a fourth-century temple which seems to have been followed by a Christian church: certainly there are seventh-century Christian burials, and the dedication of the church in Brean village to the sixth-century Irish saint St Bridget argues for a very early Celtic foundation.

Then, after being largely ignored for a thousand years, the Down was pressed into service for the defence of the Bristol Channel, a fort being built near its seaward tip in 1867. The fort was armed with seven cannon and occupied until 1900 when its magazine exploded causing extensive damage. The cause of the explosion seems to have been suicide or madness by one of the fort's gunners who, it is thought, fired a rifle into the magazine while running amok stark naked. The gunner was killed in the blast.

The partially renovated fort served as a café, but was re-occupied during the 1939-45 War. It is now a ruin. The Down is owned by the National Trust and is a nature reserve, particularly for its seabirds.

Brean, with its extensive, but muddy, sands was the site of the first Pontin's holiday camp after the 1939-45 War and is still a holiday centre with numerous caravan and apartment sites (one of which is still a Pontin's Holiday Club), and a matching set of leisure attractions for the visitor.

At the Down end of the Coast Road, the **Tropical Bird Garden** has a large collection of parrots. At the other end of the Coast Road, the **Brean Leisure Park** has a collection of rides and other attractions, including water slides, aimed at children, a golf course and the Farmer's Tavern where there are regular cabaret evenings and dances.

To the south of Brean is **Berrow**, a coastal village which is now attached to Burnham-on-Sea, a much larger holiday town. Inland from Berrow the **Animal Farm Country Park** has rare breeds and pets – children can bottle feed the lambs at the right time of year – and large play areas for younger children with rides, trampolines etc. There are picnic areas and a tearoom.

The birth of **Burnham-on-Sea** as a resort is attributed to the Rev David Davies, the local vicar who built a lighthouse in 1801 for the protection of local sailors. This was bought from him by Trinity House and he used the cash to build holiday villas near the church. Those were successful, but Davies' attempt to create a spa was less so. He sank several wells but succeeded only in discovering water which smelled, a contemporary description suggests, like a cross between a cesspool and horseradish.

The vicar was followed by other entrepreneurs who built a promenade and persuaded the railway to serve the town. The beach is sand and vast, and enlivened by Low Light, a Trinity House lighthouse on stilts, dating from 1832 and complementing the High Light just off the beach. To the south of the town, the **Apex Leisure and Wildlife Park** has wild areas where Cetti's warbler and other birds thrive, a BMX cycle track, children's play area and opportunities for fishing.

From Burnham/Berrow the B3140 heads inland to **Brent Knoll**, a village named for the hill that overlooks it. The village church is worth visiting for the carved bench ends which include three relating a moral tale. In the first are a fox in a bishop's mitre and pigs as monks; in the second the fox, now in the stocks, is guarded by a monkey; in the third the fox is hanged by a flock of geese. Many have interpreted the tale as an attack on the Abbot of Glastonbury, though quite why is unclear. Others have pointed out that Bishop Fox of Bath and Wells owned land here in the late fifteenth century. It could of course, just be a local, now lost, fable.

Brent Knoll

Brent Knoll is Somerset's best known feature to travellers on the M5, rearing up beside the motorway near the western edge of the Levels. The hill is topped by an Iron Age hill fort – which must have commanded the entire western Levels – and is the basis of several local legends.

One maintains that it was formed when a spadeful of earth flung over the Devil's shoulder as he excavated Cheddar Gorge fell short of the sea. Another claims that it is the Mount of Frogs where three giants lived. King Arthur sent Ider, a young knight to fight the giants, but followed close behind to ensure that no harm came to the young man. Unfortunately Arthur arrived too late, finding Ider dead from the wounds he had received while killing the giants.

On the other side of Brent Knoll is **East Brent**, where the church has an elegant spire, and Lympsham. To the north of Lympsham an inn beside the River Axe marks the point where the river was once crossed by a ferry.

South-east of Burnham is **Highbridge**, once infamous for the holiday traffic jams on the A38, but, since the building of the M5, a quieter place. To the south of the town, the **Alstone Wildlife Park** has a collection of owls, camels and a red deer herd, and a pets' corner. There is also a picnic area. From Huntspill, a little further south, a road crosses the M5 to reach New Road Farm where **Secret World** has a collection of farm animals, and wild animals rescued after accidents or having been abandoned. There is also an adventure playground for children.

Above: Secret World, near East Huntspill
Below: The Somerset Levels, including Glastonbury Tor, from Alfred's Tower

• The Bloody Assizes •

The most unpleasant aspect of Monmouth's Rebellion was the trial and sentencing of the captured rebels, and those who had offered tacit support, which followed it. The event has become known as the Bloody Assize, and Judge Jeffreys, the man who headed it, has become infamous, his name a byword for savagery.

George Jeffreys was born in Shrewsbury in 1644 or 1645. He went to Shrewsbury Grammar School and Paul's School, London. This was, and is, St Paul's, but the Puritans had dropped the 'St'. He went to Trinity College, Cambridge, in 1662, but did not finish his degree, being admitted to the Inner Temple in 1663 as a gifted lawyer. As a barrister he acquired a considerable reputation as a skilled cross-examiner and by 1671, at the age of about 26, he was Common Sarjeant of the City of London. In 1677 he was knighted and in 1678 he became Recorder of the City of London. In 1683 he was made Lord Chief Justice and, later, Lord Chancellor, being created Baron Jeffreys of Wem.

It was in the capacity of Lord Chief Justice that Jeffreys was chief judge at the Bloody Assizes. Jeffreys became a close ally of James II in his plan to convert England to Catholicism and sat as president of the Court of Ecclesiastical Commission (an odd fact as Jeffreys was both a staunch Anglican and far too clever not to have seen James for what he was, a sadistic bully). When James fell and William of Orange landed in Torbay, Jeffreys was imprisoned in the Tower. There, four months later in April 1689, he died.

Jeffreys was a man about whom, in later life and after his death, much was said and none of it complimentary. It was claimed that he was a womaniser, a frequenter of brothels, but he appears to have been a devoted family man, having six children by his first wife, Sarah, although after her death he had a less happy second marriage. He was said to have been a drunkard and he certainly did drink, although that was largely to lessen the appalling pain from his kidney stones. He was said to have gloated over the deaths of men he had condemned, to have executed them himself and to have claimed to have sent more men to their deaths than any judge since the Norman Conquest. None of this seems likely, but his reputation remains: 'Judge Jeffreys? He'll rip yer guts out and show them to yer aiderwards.'

All the ugly rumours were, of course, due to the Bloody Assizes. At each Assize, Jeffreys headed a five-man commission. They started in Winchester and the auguries were immediately bad. Alice Lisle, a widow of 70, was tried for harbouring a rebel, found guilty of treason and sentenced to be burned at the stake. Jeffreys, in as many words, for he was not actually allowed to do so, recommended that she ask the King for mercy. It can only be assumed that either the man was malevolent or mistaken, for when she did plead all Widow Lisle received was the mercy of being beheaded instead of burned.

Many men were executed as a result of the Assizes, but the figures, though horrific, are not actually as appalling as sometimes claimed. It is likely that, of the men who were found guilty, 480 were sentenced to death, 850 transported, 260 whipped or fined and 80 pardoned. Of those sentenced to die, not all were executed, some being reprieved, some dying of their wounds or disease before the execution could take place. The executions were dreadful, the procedure being the full, ugly sentence laid down in the Treason Act. A sheriff's warrant at Bath for 16 November is typical:

'I require you immediately on sight here of to erect a gallows in the most public place of your said city to hang the said traitors on, and that you provide halters to hang them with, a sufficient number of faggots to burn the bowels of four traitors and a furnace or cauldron to boil their heads and quarters, and salt to boil therewith, half a bushel to each traitor, and tar to tar them with and a sufficient number of spears and pole to fix and place their heads and quarters, and that you warn the owners of four oxen to be ready with a dray or wain and the said oxen at the time hereafter mentioned for execution, and yourselves together with a guard of 40 able men at the least, to be present on Wednesday morning next by 8 of the clock, to be aiding and assisting to me, or my deputy, to see the said rebels executed ... You are also to provide an axe and a cleaver for the quartering of the said rebels.'

At Ilchester the executions were carried out within sight of the prison so that the next man could watch the hanging and quartering of his predecessor and smell the boiling pots.

In 1685 Judge Jeffreys was a hero, at least to those outside the West Country, and to loyalists within it, and no great protest against the Assizes was heard until the fall of James II. That Jeffreys was largely responsible for the outcome of the assizes cannot be denied. That James II was the real culprit is also beyond doubt. Jeffreys was probably not as evil as he has been painted, but acted on the instructions of an evil superior. But, as the Nuremberg trials demonstrated, carrying out orders is not an acceptable excuse.

Barrington

Barrington Court (NT)
Barrington
Open: April – October, Daily except Friday 11am – 5.30pm.
☎ 01460 241938

Berrow

Animal Farm Country Park
Red Road
Berrow
Open: All year, daily 10am – 5.30pm (4.30pm from November – March).
☎ 01278 751628

Brean

Tropical Bird Garden
Brean Down
Open: April – October 9am – Dusk.
☎ 01278 751209

Burrowbridge

Somerset Levels Basket and Willow Centre
Lyng Road
Burrowbridge
Open: All year, Monday – Saturday 9am – 5.30pm. Open most Bank Holidays and some Sundays in summer.
☎ 01823 698688

Chapel Allerton

Ashton Windmill
Chapel Allerton
Open: Easter – September, Sundays and Bank Holidays 2.30 – 4.30pm. Also open on Wednesday from July – September, same times.
☎ 01934 712694/712260

Barrington Court is now owned by the National Trust

Charlton Mackrell

Lytes Cary (NT)
nr Kingsdon and Charlton Mackrell
Open: April – October, Monday, Wednesday and Saturday
2 – 6pm or dusk.
☎ 01985 843600
(NT Regional Office)

Drayton

Midelney Manor
Drayton
Open: By appointment only.
☎ 01485 251229

East Huntspill

Secret World
New Road Farm
East Huntspill
Open: February – December,
Daily 10am – 6pm or dusk.
☎ 01278 783250

East Lambrook

East Lambrook Manor Garden
Open: March – October,
Monday – Saturday 10am – 5pm.
☎ 01460 240328

East Pennard

Avalon Vineyard
The Drove
East Pennard
Open: June – August, Daily 2 – 6pm.
☎ 01749 860393

Fivehead

RSPB West Sedgemoor Nature Reserve
nr Fivehead
Open: All year, any reasonable time.
☎ 01458 252805

The Somerset Levels Basket and Crafts Centre, Burrow Bridge

Glastonbury

Chalice Well
Chilkwell Street
Glastonbury
Open: April – October,
Daily 10am – 6pm, November – March,
Daily 12noon – 4pm.
☎ 01458 831154

Glastonbury Abbey
Open: All year,
Daily (except Christmas Day)
9.30am – 6pm or dusk
Opens at 9am June – August and
10am December – February.
☎ 01458 832267

Rural Life Museum
Abbey Farm
Chilkwell Street
Glastonbury
Open: Easter – October, Monday – Friday 10am – 5pm, Saturday and Sunday 2 – 6pm, November – Easter, Monday – Friday 10am – 5pm, Saturday 11am – 4pm.
☎ 01458 831197

Tribunal/Local History Museum
9 High Street
Glastonbury
Open: Easter – September, Sunday – Thursday 10am – 5pm, Friday and Saturday 10am – 5.30pm, October – Easter, Sunday – Thursday 10am – 4pm.
☎ 01458 832954

Highbridge

Alstone Wildlife Park
Alstone Road
Highbridge
Open: Easter – October, Daily 10am – 6pm.
☎ 01278 782405

High Ham

Heaven's Gate Farm
West Henley
High Ham
Open: All year, Daily except Monday (but open on Bank Holiday Mondays) 11am – 3pm.
☎ 01458 252656

Stembridge Tower (Thatch Cap) Mill
High Ham
Open: Easter – September, Sunday, Monday and Wednesday 2 – 5pm.
☎ 01458 250818

Kingsbury Episcopi

Somerset Cider Brandy/ Burrow Hill Cider
Pass Vale Farm
Kingsbury Episcopi
Open: all year, Monday – Saturday 9am – 5pm.
☎ 01460 240782

Langport

Langport and River Parrett Visitor Centre
Westover
Langport
Open: April – September, Daily 10am – 6pm, October – March, Daily except Monday 10am – 4pm.
☎ 01458 250350

Mark

Coombes Somerset Cider
Japonica Farm
Mark
Open: All year, Monday – Saturday 9am – 6.30pm (6pm from October – April), Sunday 12noon – 3pm for cider sales only.
☎ 01278 641265

Martock

Somerset Guild of Craftsmen
Hurst Works (Yandle and Sons Ltd)
Martock
Open: All year, Monday – Saturday 9am – 5pm.
☎ 01935 825891

Treasurer's House (NT)
Church Street
Martock
Open: early April – late September, Sunday – Tuesday 2 – 5pm.
☎ 01935 825801

Meare

Abbot's Fish House
(English Heritage)
Meare
Open: At any reasonable time. Key available at Manor House Farm.

Peat Moors Centre
Shapwick Road
Westhay
Open: April – October, Daily 10am – 5pm, November – February – booked groups only.
☎ 01458 860697

Moorlinch

Moorlynch Vineyard
Moorlinch
Open: Easter week and May – September, Tuesday – Saturdays and Bank Holidays 10.30am – 5pm.
The vineyard's shop is open during the rest of the year, same times.
☎ 01458 210393

Muchelney

Muchelney Abbey
(English Heritage)
Muchelney
Open: April – October,
Daily 10am – 6pm or dusk.
☎ 01458 250664

Priest's House (NT)
Muchelney
Open: April – September, Sunday and Monday 2.30 – 5.30pm.
☎ 01458 252621

Somerton

London Cigarette Card Company Showroom
West Street
Somerton
Open: All year, Monday – Saturday 9.30am – 1pm, 2 – 5pm
(but closed on Wednesday and Saturday afternoon).
☎ 01458 273452

Stoke St Gregory

Willows and Wetlands Visitor Centre
(P H Coate and Son, Willow Craft Industry and Somerset Basketware)
Meare Green Court
Stoke St Gregory
Open: All year, Monday – Saturday 9am – 5pm
Guided tours of the willow yards and workshops, Monday – Friday 10am – 12noon and 2 – 4pm. No tours on Bank Holidays.
☎ 01823 490249

Street

Shoe Museum
High Street
Street
Open: All year, Monday – Friday 10am – 4.45pm, Saturday 10am – 5pm, Sunday 11am–5pm. Closed 25 December – 2 January.
☎ 01458 443131

WE Hecks (Cider and Cider Museum)
9 – 11 Middle Leigh
Street
Open: All year, Monday – Saturday 9am – 6pm, Sunday 10am – 12.30pm.
☎ 01458 442367

Westonzoyland

Pumping Station
Westonzoyland
Open: All year, Sundays 2 – 5pm.
Also open on Thursdays from June – August 2 – 8pm
Steam Days: April – October, first Sunday of each month.
☎ 01823 275795

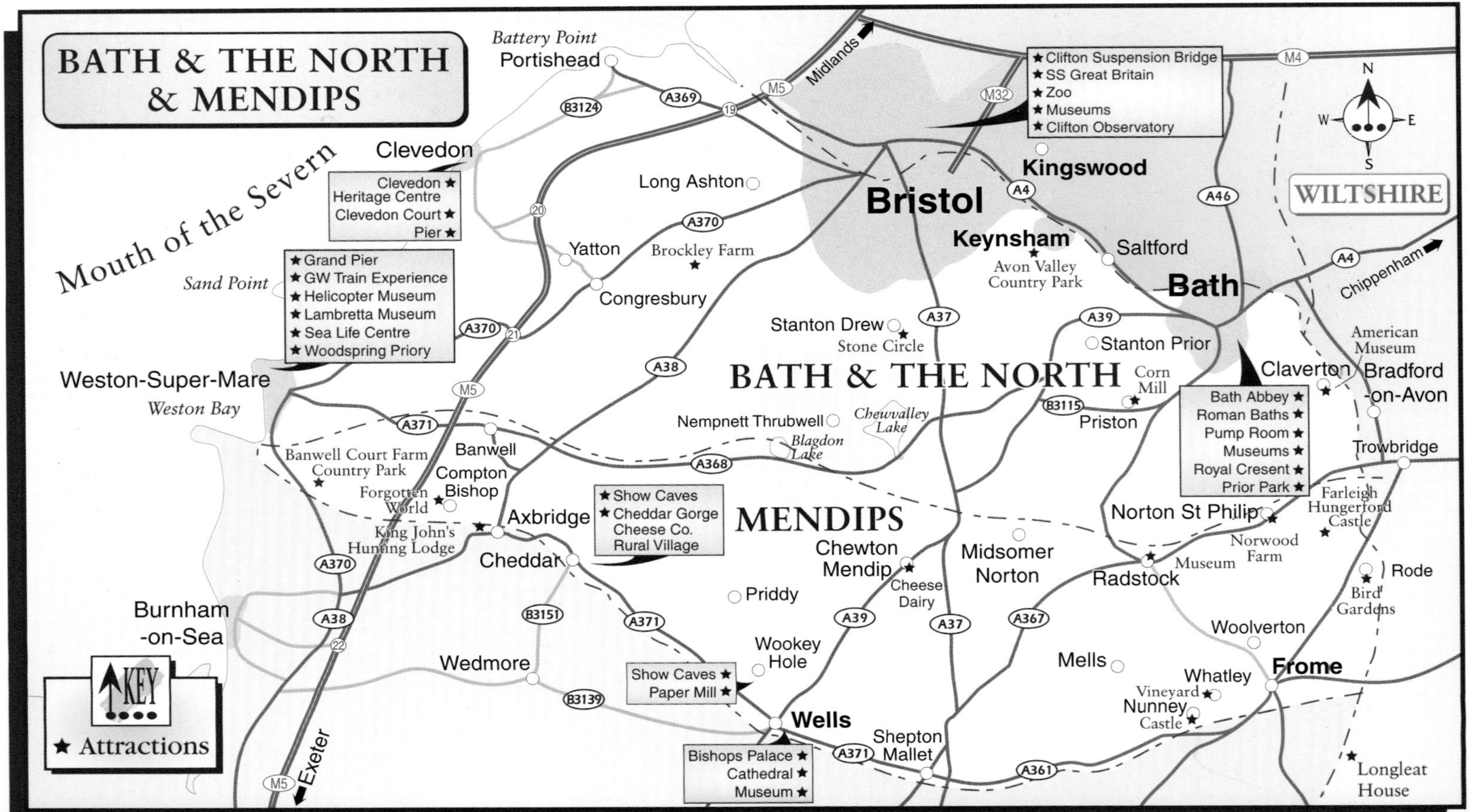
BATH & THE NORTH & MENDIPS
Battery Point
Portishead
Midlands
M5
M4
M32
Clifton Suspension Bridge
SS Great Britain
Zoo
Museums
Clifton Observatory
N
W
E
S
WILTSHIRE
B3124
A369
19
Clevedon
Clevedon Heritage Centre
Clevedon Court
Pier
Mouth of the Severn
Long Ashton
Bristol
Kingswood
A4
A46
20
A370
Yatton
Brockley Farm
Keynsham
Avon Valley Country Park
Saltford
Bath
Chippenham
Sand Point
Grand Pier
GW Train Experience
Helicopter Museum
Lambretta Museum
Sea Life Centre
Woodspring Priory
Congresbury
Stanton Drew
Stone Circle
A37
A39
Stanton Prior
21
A38
BATH & THE NORTH
Corn Mill
Claverton
American Museum
Bradford -on-Avon
Weston-Super-Mare
Weston Bay
A371
Nempnett Thrubwell
Chewvalley Lake
Blagdon Lake
B3115
Priston
Bath Abbey
Roman Baths
Pump Room
Museums
Royal Cresent
Prior Park
Trowbridge
Banwell Court Farm Country Park
Banwell
A368
Compton Bishop
Forgotten World
Show Caves
Cheddar Gorge Cheese Co.
Rural Village
MENDIPS
Axbridge
King John's Hunting Lodge
Norton St Philip
Farleigh Hungerford Castle
Norwood Farm
Cheddar
Chewton Mendip
Midsomer Norton
Radstock
Museum
Rode
Cheese Dairy
Bird Gardens
Burnham -on-Sea
Priddy
B3151
A367
Woolverton
Wookey Hole
Wedmore
Mells
Whatley
Frome
Show Caves
Paper Mill
Vineyard
Nunney Castle
KEY
Attractions
B3139
Wells
Shepton Mallet
22
Exeter
Bishops Palace
Cathedral
Museum
A361
Longleat House

6 The Mendips

The Great Hall (Chamber 2), Wookey Hole Caves

The northern edge of the Somerset Levels is defined by a ridge of high land stretching across the country from the sea to the Wiltshire borders. This high land is the Mendips. The ridge is formed of carboniferous limestone, a pale grey, pearly rock which forms attractive outcrops; but is easily dissolved by the action of water so that it is riddled with caves, making it one of Britain's foremost areas for the caver.

So famous is the area for its caves that it comes as a surprise to discover that the Mendips also has patches of Old Red Sandstone, an older rock exposed by uplifts and weathering. The sandstone is impermeable, allowing surface water to collect and flow – unlike the limestone areas where the water quickly disappears underground – and creating a different landscape with a quite different vegetation. Highland Mendip – Black Down – is sandstone, as is North Hill near Priddy, where the Priddy Pools are such a notable feature. Pen Hill, north of Wells and topped by a TV mast that is the Mendips' most obvious landmark, is sandstone too.

The extent of the Mendips is, largely, a matter of opinion. Brean Down and Brent Knoll are outliers of the hills, and eastwards, as the Wiltshire border is approached, the geology remains essentially the same, though the rocks of the Somerset coal field overlie the limestone. The western Mendips form an Area of Outstanding Natural Beauty (AONB), created to protect the magnificent limestone country. The western tip of the AONB lies west of the M5, as the hills descend towards the sea, though most people would see it as Crooks Peak, the hill which welcomes visitors on the M5 as they descend to the Levels.

The eastern edge is roughly defined by the A39. To the south the AONB is strictly accurate, following the Mendip edge, but northwards it covers an area of the plateau below the Mendip edge, including the Blagdon and Chew Valley Lakes. Here we adopt a more geology-based definition, including not only the AONB, but the country right up to the Wiltshire border and to the old boundary between Somerset and Avon. And we include Wells: if the Mendips had a capital it would be Wells.

Wells

Set at the resurgence of Mendip underground streams, Wells has been settled since Neolithic times, though it is with King Ine of Wessex, in about 700AD, that its recorded history begins. Ine is said to have been the patron of a church founded here by St Aldhelm: there was certainly a church here in 766 when Cynewulf, a later Wessex king, gave land to 'the minister by the Great Spring which they call Wells'. The spring – or, rather, springs as there are several – now bubble into an L-shaped pool to the east of the cathedral.

In 766 Wells was in the diocese of St Aldhelm's Sherborne, but in 909 the diocese was divided and the Minster church became a cathedral. Though an 11th-century bishop moved the see to Bath, the downgrading of Wells was to last little more than a century. Then, combined with Bath so that all later bishops were 'of Bath and Wells', Wells became a city again. It is England's smallest city, but one of incomparable beauty that should be explored at leisure. The cathedral and its associated buildings deserve a guide book of their own: here, the cathedral complex and the remainder of Wells are explored in a short tour that, hopefully, will encourage visitors to spend the time the city deserves.

The Cathedral and Bishop's Palace

The Saxon cathedral ran diagonally across the cloisters of the present building. Nothing remains of it above ground, though the font has been preserved. It stands in the south transept and is still used for baptisms, a usage that extends back over 1000 years.

The present cathedral was begun in about 1180 by Bishop Reginald of Bath and is one of the great Gothic works of Britain. The west face, with its truncated towers and dozens of niche statues was completed in 1250. Many, including Pevsner, claim that the front is the cathedral's least successful feature, its towers too short so that the whole does not have the soaring splendour of the Gothic interior. But others maintain it is magnificent, a masterpiece of the stonemason's art. Certainly it is the repository of the finest collection of 13th-century statuary in Britain, a collection of saints, bishops and knights.

The cathedral's central tower was also begun in the 13th century, but in 1313 another stage and a spire were added. Within 25 years the weight of these caused the lower stage to crack and the three scissors-arches were constructed to support the structure. This they were successful in doing, though there are some who maintain that, despite their elegance, the arches detract from the soaring lines of the interior. The upper tower stage and the spire were destroyed by fire in 1438. The tower was rebuilt to a height of over 55m (182 feet), the tallest in Somerset: the spire was not rebuilt.

In the 14th century, as well as the addition to the central tower, the eastern end of the cathedral was extended and the Lady Chapel added, as were the octagonal chapter house and the Vicar's Hall. In the following century the Chain Gate, arching across the road from the Chapter House, linked the Vicar's Hall to the Cathedral. The western and eastern ranges of cloisters were also added, the southern range completing the cloisters in the 16th century.

The building is one of the highlights of a tour of Wells, particularly when viewed from the traffic-free Cathedral Green that fronts the west front, or from across the pond fed by the Mendip springs. But the building is also filled with marvellous works of art and craftsmanship. There is medieval stained glass, including the North Quire window and the East window, each dated to the mid-14th century, and an array of fine tombs, these include those of Saxon bishops and that of Bishop Thomas Bekynton.

Bekynton was Bishop of Bath and Wells from 1443-65 and also Secretary to Henry VI. He was responsible for the building of the Chain Gate and several other cathedral features, and also built the New Works in the Market Place, feeding them with fresh water from the Mendip springs. Bekynton's tomb reflects his humanity, for although he lies in effigy in his rich bishop's vestments, beneath this image of the churchman there is a haggard cadaver. The tomb is protected by contemporary iron railings.

Special Clock

In the north transept is the cathedral's first clock, its 24 hour clock face believed to be the oldest in the world. (The clock itself is four or five years younger than that at Salisbury Cathedral, which is acknowledged as the world's first, but the Salisbury clock does not have a face). Close to the clock face the hours are struck by Jack Blandiver, a wooden quarter jack.

Near the north transept a stone staircase leads up to the Chapter House and the Chain Gate bridge – old, uneven steps, worn down by thousands of feet over hundreds of years.

Finally, after enjoying the stonework and vaulting of the cloisters, the cathedral library, above the east range, can be visited. It houses a priceless collection of books and manuscripts, some dating from the early 16th century, and some still chained in position.

Beside the cathedral is the Bishop's Palace, an old and moated site, surely Britain's most spectacular ecclesiastical palace. The palace is entered over a now-fixed drawbridge and through a 14th-century gatehouse. Beyond the gatehouse, immediately to the left, the out-of-bounds path leads to the 15th-century north wing built by Bishop Bekynton and still the private residence of the Bishop of Bath and Wells. Beside the residence is the public part of the palace (the 'Henderson Rooms', named for Edward Henderson, Bishop 1960-75, whose initiative opened them) which houses a portrait gallery of former bishops. Beside the Henderson Rooms is the Bishop's Chapel, dating from the 13th century.

Opposite the gatehouse is the remaining wall of the Great Hall, built in the 13th century, but abandoned in the 16th. Beyond the ruins are the South Lawn and Ramparts walk. Following the ramparts around the palace island leads to another moat bridge from where the Wells pool can be reached, crossing the weir that provides water to the moat.

To the left of the drawbridge as you enter, around the protruding wall of the gatehouse, is the famous bell and cord used by the mute swans who live in the moat to ring for food. The swans rang the bell for many years but then, replete with offerings from visitors, lost the habit (or skill). Recently they have been re-taught, though as visitor feeding is still a dependable food source the swan's ringing is somewhat erratic.

A walk around the City

The Cathedral and Bishop's Palace are both reached from the **Market Place** where a tour of Wells should start. The Tourist Information Office is here, on the southern side. On the north-west side are the New Works, Bishop Bekynton's houses for local residents. Nearby is a memorial

• Bishops of Wells •

Famous bishops whose portraits hang in the Bishop's Palace include Thomas Wolsey who, after his election as Cardinal, incurred Henry VIII's wrath for not securing the king's divorce from Catherine of Aragon and died on his way to the Tower, accused of treason.

Thomas Ken was another who incurred regal displeasure. After objecting to the inhuman treatment of Monmouth rebels, Ken (whose godliness was an inspiration to all who met him) was imprisoned with six other bishops for refusing to have James II's Declaration of Indulgence read in their churches.

Yet Ken was a firm believer in hereditary monarchy and refused to take the oath of allegiance to William III while James was still alive. For this he was forced to resign. Richard Kidder was perhaps the unluckiest bishop. He was killed, together with his wife, when a chimney fell through the roof of the palace during a storm in 1703.

The Bishop's Palace, Wells

to local athlete Mary Rand whose then world record for women's long jump won the gold medal at the 1964 Tokyo Olympics.

There are two eastern exits from the square: the Bishop's Eye leads to the Palace, while Penniless Porch, another work by Bishop Bekynton – the plaque explains the curious name – leads to Cathedral Green. Walk across the Green, with the cathedral's west front to your right, to reach the **Town Museum**, housed in the old cathedral chancellor's house. The museum has items on the history of the town and the geology of the Mendips, the latter including the original Witch of Wookey.

Bear right under the arch of Chain Gate to reach **Vicar's Close**, to the left. The Close was begun in 1363 and accommodated the bachelors who formed the cathedral choir.

Legend has it that the vicars – the choristers also acted as helpers to the canons and so were members of the cathedral – were brought here to end problems experienced when they were lodged in the town. There the closeness of ale houses and young ladies caused some to be late for, or to neglect, their duties.

The Close now comprises 28 houses, all still occupied by adult choristers and other cathedral workers.

Beyond the turning to Vicar's Close, St Andrew Street leads to **Liberty**, on the left. In medieval times the Liberty was the cathedral, bishop's palace and associated buildings, a city within the city. The present Liberty has a fine group of medieval buildings some incorporated into Wells Cathedral School. Liberty can be followed – turn left (East Liberty) from St Andrew Street, then first left (North Liberty): the school is to the right here – to Chamberlain Street.

Return to Chain Gate and walk ahead, passing the museum on your right to reach the Old Archdeaconry, dating from 1450, but with a 19th-century façade, and the Old Deanery, a fine 15th-century house. Ahead now is **Brown's Gate**, built by Bishop Bekynton and named for Richard Brown, a shoemaker who lived in the adjacent house in the 1550s.

Bear right (Sadler Street), then left into **Chamberlain Street**. Follow this past Union Street and Priest Row, to the left, to reach the **Bubwith Almshouses** built as single storey houses for 12 poor men and women in the early 15th century by Bishop Nicholas Bubwith. Close by are three later sets of almshouses – there is a fourth set (Harper's) in Chamberlain Street itself. Return to Priest Row and follow it, passing yet another set of almshouses – Llewellyn's, built in 1614 – and **St Cuthbert's Church**, Somerset's largest parish church. Inside is the monument of Henry Llewellyn who built the Priest Row almshouses.

At the end of Priest Row turn left along St Cuthbert Street which leads to **High Street**, its gutters running with Mendip spring water. Follow High Street to return to Market Place.

Wells to Cheddar: the Southern Mendip Edge

From Wells a minor road heads north-west to Wookey Hole, a hamlet famous for its cave, now the centre of a fascinating visitor complex – and not to be confused with the village of Wookey which lies to the west of

Wells. **Wookey** is really a Levels village, grouped around a fine late-12th-century church built by the bishops of Wells.

Wookey Hole has been known for thousands of years, the very obvious entrance, where the River Axe appears, having been created by underground streams sinking in the high Mendips (unlike other Mendip Caves which have required digging to expose their existence). Excavations have shown that the easily reached chambers were inhabited by Palaeolithic man as early as 30,000 BC.

Tools have been discovered, together with the bones of woolly rhinoceros, cave lion and bear, mammoth and hyenas, the latter having given their name to Hyena Den, a subsidiary chamber to the main chamber.

Occupation continued through the New Stone and Bronze Ages, and even through the Roman occupation of Britain.

A 15th-century document records men entering the cave purely for exploration, using torches made of 'sheeves of reed sedge' to light their way. The first three chambers were opened as a show cave many years ago, and in 1975 further chambers were opened after a tunnel was excavated to them. The accessible

The Witch of Wookey

William of Worcester, a servant of Sir John Fostolf, wrote the early account of Wookey Hole which mentions the use of reed torches, and goes on to describe chambers called the kitchen, the parlour and the oast (that is, the oast house). Worcester mentions that the entrance was guarded by the Porter, clearly a stalagmite in the shape of a man, and also mentions 'the figure of a woman clothed and spinning with a distaff held beneath her girdle'. This is the first reference to the Witch of Wookey, though that name was only applied to the stalagmite in the late 17th century.

Local legend tells of a young, beautiful woman who exploited the black arts, gradually turning into an ugly old witch embittered by her inability to recover her beauty. The witch, who lived in the cave, ruled the local neighbourhood by fear, making life miserable for anyone who crossed her. One day a young married couple, laughing in their happiness with each other, passed the cave, enraging the witch who used her skills to drive the young woman away, destroying the couple's marriage and happiness.

The heart-broken young man became a monk at Glastonbury Abbey where years later, the Abbot who had been asked for help by those living near the cave, gave him the task of confronting the witch. The young monk hurled holy water into the witch's face before she could weave spells around him: she was instantly turned to stone.

Interestingly, in the early 20th century, excavations in the cave revealed the skeletons of an old woman and two goats, suggesting that the cave had been inhabited in medieval times by a lonely old woman, perhaps the basis of the myth.

chambers are breathtakingly beautiful, the lighting having been organised to enhance the natural beauty of the flowstone formations and water pools.

From the early 15th century the River Axe, emerging from Wookey Hole, has been used to drive watermills, for fulling woollen cloth initially then, from about 1610, for paper making. The tradition of paper making is maintained in the Wookey Hole Visitors complex (which, since 1973, has been owned by Madame Tussauds). Visitors can try their hand at paper making. They can also visit the 'pier' where there is a working museum of traditional seaside entertainment, with penny arcade machines and a hall of mirrors. There is also a Victorian portrait studio and a museum of caves and caving. The complex also has a restaurant, licensed bar and picnic area, as well as gift shops.

Just west of Wookey Hole a car park gives access to the **Ebbor Gorge**, a short, but tight, cleft which is the most unspoilt of the Mendip gorges. The gorge was given to the National Trust in 1967 in memory of Sir Winston Churchill and is now

The "Vatman" making paper at Wookey Hole Paper Mill

The Cheddar Gorge Cheese Co., Cheddar

administered by the Nature Conservancy Council.

The minor road now passes a turn to Priddy (see below) then reaches the main A371. Turn right to reach **Westbury-sub-Mendip** which achieved fleeting notoriety in 1973 when Irish terrorists attempted to steal explosives from the quarry above the village. The centre of the village is dominated by a 14th-century cross, which has an elaborate, stepped, octagonal base and a plain shaft. Continue along the main road which bypasses the main section of the village of **Rodney Stoke** where the church has a superb collection of monuments of the Rodney family whose name the village bears. The finest is that of Sir Thomas Rodney who is shown in armour. In that of George Rodney his shroud-wrapped figure emerges from his coffin.

From close to Rodney Stoke, and from **Draycott,** the next village, roads head up on to the high Mendips. To the west of Draycott is Nyland Hill, an island in the Levels. The stone quarried close to the village is known as Draycott Marble as it polishes to a pearly grey lustre. Beyond Draycott the main road soon reaches Cheddar.

Cheddar

Cheddar is one of the best known places in Somerset, famous for its cheese, its caves, its strawberries and its gorge.

The lower reaches of the gorge have become 'touristy' over the years, the collection of souvenir shops and cafés gathering a congestion of people. Add a narrow road with streams of cars in both directions and you have a recipe for an over-done attraction. But for all that the lower gorge can be a monstrous place on a midsummer weekend, the town and gorge are still worth visiting. The history is interesting, and the scenery is magnificent.

The caves of the lower gorge have revealed evidence of human occupation since Palaeolithic times, but the town site was probably only settled in Roman times. The Mendips were a royal hunting forest in Saxon times and a palace was built here in the ninth century, beside which a village arose. Whether this was a true palace or merely a hunting lodge is not clear, but whichever purpose it served it was from this wooden building that, legend has it, King Edmund set out on his fateful hunt in 941.

St Dunstan and King Edmund

St Dunstan was when Abbot of Glastonbury, those jealous of the young abbot and his influence over Edmund's predecessor Athelstan persuaded the new king to get rid of him.

Edmund summoned Dunstan to Cheddar and dismissed him. The saddened Dunstan returned to Glastonbury and Edmund set out to hunt deer in the deep woods that then shrouded the Mendips. The king became separated from his party, pursuing his hounds who were chasing a lone stag. In blind terror the stag ran over the edge of the gorge which had been hidden from view by the trees, followed by the hounds. Edmund realised that he, too, would ride over the edge. In desperation he shouted that he would restore Dunstan to his position if his life was spared and miraculously his horse pulled up. Convinced that his life had been spared because of his promise, the king immediately re-instated the saint.

The truth of the story cannot be judged, but the existence of the palace has been proved by excavation: the post holes of the wooden building can be seen in front of the aptly named Kings of Wessex School.

The school lies in Station Road, a westward continuation of Bath Street leading off which is Lower North Street where the philanthropist Hannah More lived. Where Bath Street forms a Y-junction with Union Street and Church Street stands the village cross, a medieval cross now enclosed by a later, hexagonal, arcaded building. Church Street leads to St Andrew's Church, a fine early medieval building with a tall (34m – 110ft) tower. Union Street leads to **Cheddar Gorge**.

To the right in the Gorge is **Jacob's Ladder**, a somewhat unimaginatively named series of 274 steps which lead to an observation tower with a fine view of the lower gorge and the Somerset Levels. Just beyond, also to the right, is **Cox's Cave**. Gough's Cave is further on, also on the right.

Opening the Show Caves

In 1837 a local miller, George Cox, found the cave which bears his name by accident but, seeing the potential of the excellent flowstone formations, widened the entrance and opened the cave to the public.

Later in the century Cox's nephew Richard Gough found the larger system which now bears his name.

Excavations have shown that the caves, and others in the Gorge, were occupied from Palaeolithic times.

There is a small museum of finds and an illustration of the life of the times at **Gough's Cave**. Today the caves offer visitors a chance to see marvellous stalagmites and stalactites in safety, but for the more adventurous Gough's Cave offers an off-the-public way trip, supplying helmets, lights and boiler suits.

Beyond Gough's Cave the visitor is into unspoilt Gorge (apart from the road and car parks), soon reaching High Rock to the right. This is the Gorge's highest cliff, a near-vertical sheet of limestone. It was first climbed in a television spectacular involving Chris (now Sir Chris) Bonington taking a route which the team called *Coronation Street* in a seemingly thinly-veiled dig at their sponsors.

Today there are several routes on the wall, though visitors may not see climbers in action: Cheddar limestone is loosened by weathering and after accidents involving rocks dislodged by climbers there is a ban on climbing during the summer months. Beyond High Rock the Gorge continues in spectacular fashion, the road soon rounding Horseshoe Bend and climbing steeply, the cliffs reducing in height. After about 5km (3 miles) the top is reached on the Mendip plateau.

Cheddar Gorge

The exact origins of the sinuous, steep-sided Cheddar Gorge – Britain's deepest – is not well understood by geologists, a fact that has led to at least one fanciful suggestion. This maintains that the Gorge is the 'Lost Cave of Cheddar', that it was once roofed, having been created underground and exposed when the roof collapsed. Geologically this is extremely unlikely yet there is an intriguing 12th-century document which talks of a cave – it definitely states 'below the earth' – in which men could walk across 'land and streams, yet could never come to an end'.

The most likely explanation for the existence of such gorges is that they were formed by one of two materials (or by a combination of the two). The first suggests that after the Ice Age, frozen water in the fissures of the rock prevented water from seeping underground and allowed a surface flowing river to carve a valley. Such now-dry valleys are well-known, but in general do not create steep sided gorges. To explain that, it is conjectured that a drop in sea level or a local uplifting of the area caused a rapid flowing stream which carved a deep trench before it had time to lose its water to seepage.

Whatever the cause, the Gorge is one of the natural wonders of Britain, its cliffs rising to over 120m (about 400ft) at their highest and occasionally being almost vertical. The ledges and cracks in the steep cliffs are home to an extraordinary number of plants – over 300 have been recorded – one of which, the Cheddar Pink (*Dianthus gratianopolitanus*) is unique to the Gorge.

Wells to Cheddar: the Upland Route

Minor roads from Wells and Wookey Hole climb on to the Mendip plateau, soon reaching **Priddy**, once a lead mining centre and famous for its August fair. The sheep sold at the fair are held within the hurdles which form the

Continued on page 160...

Cheddar Cheese

It is known that cheese has been made in the area around Cheddar since the 11th century and the village itself was renowned for its cheese as early as 1586 when the traveller Camden noted its fame. At that time milk from local farmers was collected to make single large cheeses, so big that, as Camden noted they 'require more than a man's strength to set them on the table'. Eventually the mass production of cheese drove local makers out of business and today there is only one cheesemaker in Cheddar.

The special process that makes Cheddar cheese involves the repeated turning and squeezing of blocks of curd (created by adding a bacteria culture to heated milk, stirring, then adding fungal rennet and finally draining off the whey) to create a dough-like mass. Salt is then added and the cheese is allowed to cool. The salt preserves the cheese and expels the last of the moisture.

In a famous Somerset Court Case a few years ago the Showerings Company of Shepton Mallet were ordered to stop calling their Babycham a champagne perry as the French region of Champagne maintained a copyright on the name. Unfortunately when Cheddar attempted a similar move the European Union ruled that 'cheddaring' was a process and so could not be copyrighted. Cheddar cheese can therefore be made throughout the world.

The Cheddar Gorge Cheese Company is now Cheddar's only cheesemaker. They make cheese in grades from medium (which takes about 5 months to mature) to vintage (which takes a minimum of 14 months). Visitors can watch the process and sample (and buy, of course) the cheeses. The Company's site recreates a rural village, offering cider tasting – there is a small cider museum too – and a collection of local crafts from candle making to spinning. There is even a village stocks which visitors can try for size. The site also has a restaurant.

Cheddar Strawberries

Strawberry growing started in earnest at Cheddar and in the neighbouring villages at the foot of the Mendips in the late 19th century. The crop was harvested in early June and was usually first to market. This, together with the flavour of the Cheddar berries made the village famous throughout Britain. The trade offered local growers a good living for many decades but a series of changes has led to a decline. The first change was transport. The Cheddar berry was soft and when lorry transport replaced the railways, the rougher ride bruised the fruit. Rail was gentle but expensive and slow in comparison.

Chewton Cheese Dairy, Chewton Mendip

Next the building of the Cheddar reservoir – opened in 1937 – is said to have chilled the local soil making it unsuitable for strawberries (though the farms on the slopes survived). Then cheap air transport allowed Italian and Spanish berries to be imported cheaply, and earlier, than the Cheddar fruit. Lastly, the big supermarkets demanded a harder, redder fruit and Cheddar's softer, slightly paler berry lost out again, despite its superior taste. There are still some local growers and summer visitors will find strawberries available from roadside stalls, and some farms offering 'pick your own'.

picturesque bundle on the vast village green, a bundle which often baffles unknowing visitors. For cavers, Priddy is the capital of Mendip caving: the largest, most complex and most sought-after cave is Swildon's Hole, which lies to the east of the church at the top of the village.

Also to the east of the church, on North Hill, are **Priddy Nine Barrows**, a collection of Bronze Age round barrows. The local area abounds in prehistoric remains with several other groups of round and disc barrows.

To the north of North Hill and the B3135 are the most enigmatic of the sites. The **Priddy Circles** are three large earth rings – there is a fourth circle to the north, beyond the B3134 – set close together and aligned a few degrees off a north-south line. The circles are about 170m (around 180 yards) in diameter and differ from 'standard' henge sites in having ditches outside the banks. This configuration is normally associated with defensive structures, but there seems little likelihood that the circles were for defence rather than ritual.

Also east of Priddy, on the eastern flank of North Hill are the **Priddy Pools** (the largest occasionally called Waldegrave Pools) shallow ponds in the impermeable sandstone of the hill. The pools are a favourite with visitors, being home to newts, toads, dragonflies and other pond life.

Heading north-west from Priddy a minor road crosses the B3135 and then the B3371 (turn left on either to reach the top of Cheddar Gorge), then descends to Velvet Bottom before rising steeply to the little church at **Charterhouse**, named for a medieval Carthusian Monastery of which nothing now remains.

Turn right to reach a car park near the best remains of the Mendip lead industry and one of the finest short walks in the area.

The walk heads south from the car park, soon reaching the road in Velvet Bottom. Turn right then, soon, bear left along the obvious shallow valley – this is the real **Velvet Bottom**. The walk passes the remains of a lead furnace and further buddles, then a dam built to stop lead-rich water from the buddles leaching into Cheddar's water supply. The walk continues to Black Rock Gate near the top of Cheddar Gorge.

The dry valley of Velvet Bottom and the woodland at Black Rock are a nature reserve set up to protect lime-rich flowers including the delicate, white alpine pennycress and the equally delicate spring sandwort, and the butterflies that feed on them. The area is also famous (infamous?) for its adders.

Just beyond Charterhouse a turning on the left leads to a car park below a TV mast from where a short walk rises through heather to **Beacon Batch**, the highest point of the Mendips.

Turn left at Charterhouse to follow a minor road below highest Mendip. To the left is Long Wood, which has been here since Saxon times. At its western edge is Gorsey Bigbury a Bronze Age henge site. At the T-junction at the base of the hill, **Shipham** is to the right. The village was an important calamine (zinc ore) mining area in medieval times, the zinc being used in Bristol brass foundries. The village church has a memorial window to Hannah Mare who set up day and Sunday schools in the village in about 1790.

Turn left at the T-junction, descending a steep hill past the vast Callow Quarry to reach Cheddar.

Mendip Lead

Visitors who regularly walk the high Mendip plateau will be aware that in addition to swallets, the ground is occasionally disturbed by curious ditches, hollows and heaps.

This 'gruffy' ground, to give it its local name, is a reminder that the Mendips were once an important lead mining area. Within the limestone matrix were outcrops of galena (lead sulphide) in sufficient quantities to make it a workable ore. Small quantities of silver were also produced. In the western Mendips, around Shipham, there was also calamine (zinc carbonate) and this ore, too, was exploited.

The Romans were the first to exploit Mendip lead and to the north of the Charterhouse car park are the remains of a Roman settlement, a fort and an amphitheatre (though it takes a practised eye to discern the ridges that mark the sites). A road headed south from Charterhouse to the coast for the shipment of lead back to Rome. To the north of the car park are heaps of glassy black slag, the spoil from the furnaces, and a collection of water-filled pits. The latter were 'buddles' where excavated rock was washed to remove soil and light debris, concentrating the lead-bearing ore before firing.

After the Romans, lead was mined intermittently, then in earnest in the 17th century when most of the waste and remains at Charterhouse were created. Mendip lead was poor quality, its impurity level being too high for most uses, and chiefly found its way to the shot tower in Bristol. By the end of the 17th century the industry was in decline, but was revived 200 years later when Cornish tin-miners were used to re-smelt the medieval slag to extract more metal. The residue of this process was called slime, but looks similar to the untutored eye.

To maximise the output of the process the Victorians used condenser flues from their furnaces. These were horizontal chimneys along which the smoke travelled, lead condensing from the smoke on to the chimney walls. The lead was then scraped off by hand. Scraping was an appalling job, the chimney being choked with smoky air and lead fumes, and legend has it (though this is not verified) that boys from the Wells Workhouse were used. As lead poisoning is disabling at least and deadly if the lead concentration in the blood is high enough, whoever carried out the job was risking serious injury.

The Western Mendips

Heading westward from Cheddar the main A371 rounds Cheddar Reservoir to reach **Axbridge**, a lovely little town set at the foot of the Mendips. The town had an enclosing wall and a mint in Saxon times, its importance being reinforced by the Norman kings, particularly King John who granted it rights free of county interference. It is for this benevolence that a magnificent arcaded, timber-framed house in The Square is called **King John's Hunting Lodge**, though the building is actually late-15th century and so has no connection with the king. The Lodge is now owned by the National Trust and houses a museum of local history with an excellent collection on Mendip geology and archaeology.

Also in The Square is the fine Town Hall of the 1830s, while overlooking it, and reached by an imposing stone stairway is the church, an excellent late-14th-century building. Inside, the nave has an unusual 17th-century painted plaster ceiling and there are some good monuments. Away from The Square, there are some picturesque timber-framed buildings in High Street.

Crook Peak

Above Compton Bishop are Wavering Down and **Crook Peak**. The Peak is said to be named for its rocky summit which, from the north-west, is inclined, a little like a crooked finger. To visualise the suggestion that the peak looks like a shepherd's crook (as is sometimes claimed) requires a considerable effort of imagination.

The walk along **Wavering Down** to Crook Peak from a car park near the A38 at the eastern end of the Down is excellent and forms part of the West Mendip Way, a well-known walk linking Wells with Uphill, a distance of about 50km (30 miles).

To the west of Axbridge, across the A38, is **Compton Bishop**, an attractive little village nestling below the western tip of the Mendips. The church has a Norman font and some medieval stained glass.

To the west of Compton Bishop, near the Webbington Hotel/Country Club is **Forgotten World**, a Wheelwright and Romany Museum with a wheelwright's workshop illustrating the production of wooden cart wheels and a collection of items illustrating the life of Romany peoples. Gypsy pegs can be bought and palm and tarot readings can be requested. This is also a Flamenco Café.

On the northern side of Wavering Down is **Winscombe**, a busy town with a beautifully sited church. The church has superb medieval stained glass, one of the best collections in Somerset.

North-west is **Banwell**, its tight main street barely wide enough to take the A371. On the southern outskirts Banwell Castle is a Victorian folly – but a rather good one. Nearby are the remains of an Iron Age hill fort. Roman remains have also been excavated near the village. Above the village, to the south-west and now hidden in dense trees, is an octagonal tower topped by a spire which was built by a Bishop of Bath and Wells in the 1840s.

Just north of the village, the **Court Farm Country Park** has owl aviaries, farm animals and a pets' corner, as well as indoor and outdoor adventure play areas and free tractor rides. There is also a tearoom. To the west of Crook Peak, across the M5 motorway, is **Bleadon Hill** the final section of the Mendip AONB. It is named for the pleasant little village on its south-western flank. On its northern side is **Hutton** where Hutton Court, a 15th/16th century manor house has an embattled tower.

Right: The parish church, Axbridge

Below: The Rock of Ages, Burrington Combe

ROCK OF AGES
THIS ROCK DERIVES ITS NAME
FROM THE WELL KNOWN HYMN
WRITTEN ABOUT 1762 BY THE
REV A M TOPLADY
WHO WAS INSPIRED WHILST SHELTERING
IN THIS CLEFT DURING A STORM
Inscribed 1951

Plumley's Hole

Almost opposite the Rock of Ages another cave, Plumley's Hole, has been filled. It is said that the name belonged to that of the first man to be lowered, by rope, into the near vertical shaft. After investigating the cave the man was being hauled out.

At some point his progress stopped. His muffled cries were interpreted as his having become wedged and more men joined the hauling team. In fact Plumley's head had been caught behind a rock flake, but with his head pointing away from his companions he was unable to make them understand. When the hauling party finally brought him to the surface Plumley was dead, his neck broken.

The Northern Spring-Line Villages

The villages are best explored by taking the A368 eastward from Churchill, a hamlet on the A38. To the right of the road is the wooded northern flank of the Mendips. Here the ridge is topped by the vast Iron Age hill fort on Dolebury Warren. The fort is protected by a single rampart and ditch, the rampart still 6m (20ft) high in places which encloses over 10 hectares (25 acres).

The first right turn leads to **Burrington Combe**, less steep-sided than Cheddar Gorge but still an impressive cleft through the limestone.

The Combe is famous for the **Rock of Ages**, a 20m (70ft) high cliff split by a wide chimney which lies to the right, beyond the garden centre. Here in the 18th century the Rev Augustus Toplady, vicar of Blagdon, took shelter from a storm and was inspired to write the hymn of the name. The Combe is also famous for its caves, most of them short, but tight. One is easily seen by the visitor: Aveline's Hole, a little further up the Combe, on the left, has a huge entrance (belying the legend that it was discovered by men digging out a rabbit) – but be cautious it steepens inside. Here the skeletons of Palaeolithic men were discovered in the 19th century.

The second right turn from the A368 leads to **Burrington**, the pretty little village which names the Combe. The church here has some medieval stained glass. Continue along the main road, passing the village of **Rickford** where many of the Mendip underground streams have their resurgence, and continue uphill to **Blagdon**, a wonderfully sited village. From the road that climbs the hill above the village the view over the roofs and past the splendid church tower to Blagdon Lake is stunning. The tower, at 36m (117ft), is one of the tallest on the Mendips.

The road now continues past **Ubley**, where the church is of sandstone rather than limestone, and picturesque **Compton Martin** with its pond and fine church. Pevsner claims that Compton Martin has the finest Norman parish church in Somerset, and who would argue?

Next are the Harptree villages, **West Harptree** which has two fine early manor houses, and **East Harptree** where the church has a good medieval effigy tomb. From West Harptree a road descends to **Chew Valley Lake**, famous as a migration site for birds. The lake lies close to the road which is usually dotted with binocular-holding spotters.

The lake is home to numerous duck species (garganey nest regularly) and rare migratory species (little stints are regular callers). Ospreys and hobbies have also been seen.

The AONB deserts the Mendips to encompass Blagdon and Chew Valley Lakes and so includes **Nempnett Thrubwell** which lies close to them. There is little to see in this scattered hamlet – though the church has a Norman doorway – but who could resist a visit to the place with arguably the finest name in Britain?

On the eastern side of Chew Valley Lake are more pretty villages – Bishop Sutton, Hinton Blewett and Litton, then **Chewton Mendip**, set on the A39 which defines the eastern edge of the AONB. The village church has a lovely, and tall (38m – 126ft) tower, one of the best in the county and tallest on the Mendips, and several fine monuments.

An early skirmish of the Civil War was fought at the village when outriders of the armies seeking control of Bath clashed. Prince Maurice, one of the Royalist leaders, was wounded, but the main armies held off from a pitched battle when a thick mist descended.

Just to the south of the village, off the A39, at the **Chewton Cheese Dairy**, visitors can watch cheese being made by the 'cheddar' process, and buy the product, or view the owl collection and farm animals, the latter including longhorn cattle. There is also a restaurant and tea shop.

Shepton Mallet and Midsomer Norton

To the east of Wells the A371 bypasses **Dinder**, picturesquely set on the River Sheppey, then goes through **Croscombe** with its fine church to reach **Shepton Mallet**, a town whose name indicates the source of its wealth – this was a sheep town. The site was settled by the Romans (Fosse Way lies just to the east) and then seems to have been a metal working village, using lead brought from Charterhouse and Cornish tin to make pewterware. After the Conquest metal processing was replaced by cloth making, the town maintaining its prosperity when the industry failed, with a series of small industries. To the east of the town the Babycham deer of the Showerings plant tops the factory. The Showering family no longer owns the business but will always be associated with the town.

The town's main interest is concentrated at the centre, in the Market Place, which is dominated by the late-15th-century Market Cross erected by Walter Buckland as a memorial to his wife. The nearby covered wooden tables are The Shambles, once used by butchers for selling meat.

Close to the Market Place is the town church with its superb late-14th-century tower. Inside are a Saxon font and several good brasses, but the real treasure is the roof, constructed of 300 carved wooden panels held in place by 350 carved basses. Pevsner calls it the 'most glorious of all the wagon-roofs of England'. Beyond the church is HM

The Squealing Pig that almost ended a Siege

When the Civil War broke out, Nunney Castle was held by the Prater family, staunch supporters of the king. Col Richard Prater moved in a garrison of about 80 men and prepared to maintain a stronghold for the king in Somerset. His plan was soon put to the test when a small Parliamentarian force surrounded the castle.

To give the impression that the castle was well stocked with food and could hold out indefinitely, each morning Prater had the castle's only pig taken into one of the towers. The pig's ears and tail were pulled roughly causing it to squeal loudly: to the besieging force it sounded like another pig was being slaughtered for food. The ruse almost worked, the Parliamentarians losing heart.

But then Sir Thomas Fairfax arrived with his force. Fairfax was on his way to Bristol, but realised the significance of Nunney's castle. Unimpressed by the squealing pig he had his gunners bombard the castle walls by the entrance, making a large breach in it. The next day, before Fairfax could order his men into the breach, Prater surrendered.

Nunney Castle

Prison, built in 1627 (though largely rebuilt later) and claimed to be Britain's oldest working jail. The visible area of disturbed masonry was the site of the treadmill which prisoners turned to grind flour.

During the 1939-45 War the Prison was used to store valuable documents including the Domesday Book and Magna Carta.

To the south of the town, at the junction of main roads, is **Cannard's Grave**, a famous crossroads and inn. The name is a mystery, but is likely to refer to a suicide buried here many years ago. Suicides were often buried at crossroads as it was believed that their restless spirits, unable to work out which road to take, would remain at the junction, leaving the living in peace.

The A37 heads north from Shepton Mallet: fork right on the A367 to reach **Oakhill.** It is claimed that when, in 1889, the brewery here became a limited company the owners served a celebratory dinner for 25 people inside a brewing vat. The brewery is now long gone, destroy-ed by a fire. A right turn at Oakhill leads to pretty **Stoke St Michael**, close to which is Stoke Lane Slocker one of Mendip's most demanding caves, and **Leigh-on-Mendip.** Here the parish records note that in 1857 a parishioner took revenge on the vicar, for a perceived personal attack during a sermon on drunkenness, by filling a bull's bladder with the animal's blood and firing it at the vicar from a blunderbuss during the next service. The bladder found its target and the parishioner was given two years' hard labour.

North of Oakhill is **Stratton-on-the-Fosse**, claimed to have been the first place in Somerset where coal was mined in medieval times. To the east of the village is **Downside Abbey**, a Benedictine monastery with a fine nineteenth/early

Somerset Coal

Somerset Coal was laid down as thick layers of peat when acidic marshland covered the area at the end of the Carboniferous era of geological time. Compression then created the coal seams from the peat layers. It is known that the Romans took coal from the area, probably working deposits close to the surface and exporting it along Fosse Way. Later, in medieval times, the coal was worked in a small way to feed blacksmiths' forges.

Only in the 19th century did production accelerate, reaching a peak in the 1880s when Somerset coal, being bituminous, was highly prized for gas production and coking. As an indication of the importance of mining to the local area, the population of Radstock rose six-fold between 1801 and 1881. At its height the industry employed 6,000 men and raised over a million tons of coal annually. There are no longer any working mines in the county but the legacy is still visible in the grassed slag heaps.

Those wishing to explore the old coal field should head south from Radstock, passing Kilmersdon and continuing to Coleford and Vobster where the best of the industrial remains are to be found.

twentieth century church, the only part open to the public. Beyond Stratton the A367 follows the line of Roman Fosse Way, to Radstock, but we turn off to reach **Midsomer Norton** where, most unusually, the oldest building in town is the Roman Catholic Church, housed in a fifteenth century tithe barn. The town is also unusual in having a river flowing down the main street.

Radstock and the Coal Fields

Radstock was called 'really desperately ugly' by Pevsner, and while that may be harsh it is certainly true that picturesque Somerset seems a long way from this industrial, utilitarian town. There might seem to be little to detain the visitor, but a visit to the museum about 1.5km (1 mile) south of the centre, on the road through Haydon is worthwhile to understand a little more about this industrialised area of the county. The museum includes sections on the area's geology, mining history, the railways that moved the coal and local history.

Shepton Mallet to Frome

The A361 heads east from Shepton Mallet, soon reaching **Doulting** where St Aldhelm, Abbot of Malmesbury Abbey and first Bishop of Sherborne died in 709, close to a wooden church he had founded. The present village church is dedicated to the saint and probably stands on the site of his first church. The village is also famous for its stone, a pale brown limestone which is seen in many local churches and houses. There is still a working quarry to the north of the village.

The A361 now snakes through pleasant country to reach a turning on the left to **Nunney**, a truly delightful little village with an extraordinary castle. The castle consists of four round towers joined by short sections of wall standing on a small island within a moat. It looks quaint, but was clearly ill-suited to the role of war machine. It was built in the 1370s and had a Great Hall, a chapel and much else besides. Following the Civil War siege the castle was slighted (that is rendered useless as a fortress by being partially demolished). It is now in the care of English Heritage, its old walls home to pigeons, the moat home to ducks.

Beside the castle a bridge crosses the picturesque Nunney Brook. Cross this. A turn left reaches All Saints' Church, a 13th-century building with an interesting medieval wall painting and some good monuments. A turn right reaches the Market Place, close to which are some very attractive cottages.

North of Nunney a minor road passes **Whatley** where there is a vineyard and herb garden. Wines can be sampled and bought, while the walled herb garden, in the shape of a cross, is a secluded place. Continue north to one of Somerset's most picturesque villages. It is, though, a scattered village and a walk around it involves negotiating a complex maze of narrow lanes. To get the best

The Horners of Mells

Legend links Little Jack Horner, the nursery rhyme character, with a real John Horner who, in the 15th century, obtained Mells from the Abbots of Glastonbury.

The story is that the 'plum' that Jack Horner extracted from the 'pie' was the deed to Mells from a number of abbey deeds he, as steward of Glastonbury, was transporting to London. This libel is contradicted by the rhyme pre-dating the Horner purchase of Mells and the fact that John Horner paid a fair price in a strictly legal deal. But the legend persists.

The Horners lived in Mells Manor, the Elizabethan (though much rebuilt) mansion beside the church, but eventually moved to Mells Park using some stone from the partial demolition of the manor. The Mells Park house was rebuilt in the 1920s by Sir Edwin Lutyens for Reginald McKenna, Asquith's Chancellor of the Exchequer from 1915 to 1916. McKenna is buried in the churchyard.

from a visit, start at the church. The building itself is excellent, with a tall 16th-century tower, but is chiefly of interest for its monuments.

On the wall of the tower is one to Raymond Asquith, son of the Liberal Prime Minister, who was killed on the Somme in 1916. Asquith was married to Katherine Horner, sister of the last male of the Horner line. The lettering of the memorial is by Eric Gill. Opposite, the peacock tablet was the work of Edward Burne-Jones and commemorates Laura Lyttleton, a sister of Margot Asquith and wife of Alfred Lyttleton, cabinet minister and England cricketer.

The most famous monument is the equestrian statue of Edward Horner, the last male Horner, who was killed at Cambrai in 1917. The statue is by Sir Alfred Munnings on a plinth by Sir Edwin Lutyens. The church also has some medieval stained glass. This is in windows above the vestry and can be viewed with permission.

In the churchyard other famous Mells inhabitants lie buried. The headstones of Sir John and Lady Horner are by Lutyens, that of Mark Horner by Gill. Lutyens also designed the headstone of Reginald McKenna, a member of Asquith's government. Close to the Horner graves are those of Mgr Ronald Knox, the Roman Catholic priest/scholar, and Siegfried Sassoon, the war poet. On the north side of the church the yew avenue, leading to beautiful open country, was designed by Lutyens.

From the church follow New Street, built in the late 15th century by the Abbot of Glastonbury who owned the village. Turn left along High Street, soon reaching the War Memorial designed by Lutyens and continuing to the triangular stone 'mushroom' another work by Lutyens, erected as a memorial to

Left: Catherine Hill, Frome
Above: Nunney

Mark Horner. Bearing right from here follow the road beside the Mells Stream, passing delightful little cottages at regular intervals: it is best just to stroll, enjoying this most attractive of villages.

From Mells head east on minor roads to reach Frome.

Frome & Around

In Saxon times **Frome** was an important place: St Aldhelm built a monastic house here, a daughter house to his abbey at Malmesbury; Athelstan, King of Wessex, held a royal council here; and a later Wessex king, Edred, died in the town. A Norman king came too, but only as a guest of the town's new lord, Frome losing its earlier importance as the monastery was not refounded by the new rulers of England.

By the 14th century Frome was an important cloth making centre, growing its own dye stuffs, and cloth maintained the town's prosperity for several centuries. Although the industry was in decline by the 1800s the last mill did not close until the 1960s. Local entrepreneurs also set up successful small businesses – Singers cast bells and statues, the most famous being that of Boadicea on London's Embankment – and this light industry tradition has been maintained.

The town's Tourist Information Office occupies the Round Tower, an 18th century wool dryer, close to the River Frome. To explore the town start here. Turn right from the courtyard, then right again, soon reaching the main street into town. To the left, the triangular building was erected in 1868 as a gift to the town by a rich clothier. Originally a 'Literacy Institute' it now houses the **town museum** with collections illustrating local archaeology and history.

Turn right over the bridge. The building to the left, on an island formed by arms of the River Frome is the **Blue House**, built in 1728. The two wings were almshouses for old women, the central section a charity school for poor boys. The central façade has statues of an almswoman and boy. Continue along Market Place, then turn left up **Cheap Street** with its 17th-century houses and central leat. At the top of the street turn right to the steps.

To the left here is the entrance to the town church, marked by a Via Crucis. The **church** is almost certainly on the site of St Aldhelm's monastery. It has some interesting monuments and in the churchyard, on the east side of the church, is the dignified tomb of Thomas Ken, the Bishop of Bath and Wells forced to resign for refusing the oath of allegiance to William III.

At the top of the steps is **Gentle Street**, one of Frome's most charming streets. At the top turn right along Christchurch Street West. First right is Bath Street in which stands, to the left, the **Rock Lane Congregational Chapel**, built in 1707, a marvellous building, recently, and lovingly, restored.

Continued on page 174...

The Hungerfords of Farleigh

The Hungerford family seem to have been dangerous people to know. An early member and his son were executed for choosing the wrong side in the Wars of the Roses. Later Sir Edward Hungerford married a widow who was subsequently hanged for the murder of her first husband whose body she burnt at the castle.

Sir Edward's son, Walter, married three times and kept his third wife a prisoner for four years in a castle tower, feeding her so little that without food from villagers (who passed it through her window at night) she would have starved. Walter also persuaded the castle chaplain to make several abortive attempts to poison the prisoner. After his wife's release Walter was executed for alleged treason and incest with his daughter.

Another Walter was jailed for refusing to pay his wife's court costs when he divorced her. Later, during the Civil War, the castle was held by John Hungerford for the King, but attacked by Sir Edward Hungerford, his half-brother, and a Parliamentary army. Sir Edward was the victor. The half-brothers survived the war, but died soon after, succeeded to the estate by a third half-brother (who was Royalist) whose eldest son, another Sir Edward, was a Parliament man who tried, but failed, to marry Cromwell's daughter.

• Caves and Caving •

Cave Formation

Rainwater is slightly acidic due to dissolved carbon dioxide and dissolves carboniferous limestone, particularly along minute cracks and faults in the rock. In time this action results in the creation of depressions in the ground where the underlying rock is particularly susceptible to dissolution or where surface water collects. These depressions – called swallets in the western Mendips, slockers in the east – allow water in greater quantities to percolate into the rock. These streams carve out tunnels in the rock, choosing the weaker rock at natural joints – rifts as they are known to cavers. Sometimes the stream creates another depression underground and drops to a lower level leaving a high, dry passageway.

Occasionally the lower level may be close to the upper passage and the roof (or floor, depending on your point of view) collapses creating a high-ceilinged chamber. In such chambers, and also in the passages, water from the ceiling, loaded with the calcium carbonate it has absorbed in dissolving the rock, deposits the mineral as it slowly drips. Deposits of the mineral built up from the ceiling are stalactites, while those created on the floor below the drip point are stalagmites. Such flowstone formations vary in colour: usually they are pure white, but can be shades of red or pale blue if stained with iron or copper. The formations can form frozen waterfalls, huge basses or delicate straws.

Mendip Caving

Mendips' caves have, of course, been known from earliest times, but Palaeolithic man was keener on finding a dry, secure home than in having a fun time caving. Caving, that is exploring caves just for the fun of it, started in medieval times when lead miners broke into cave systems and explored them. Lamb Leer, one of Mendip's larger caves, began this way. But even in medieval times there were few men exploring, and those that were did not venture far. Only in the late-19th century did the sport of caving develop.

Mendip's pioneers were Herbert Balch, born in 1869 in Wells, and Dr Ernest Baker, also Somerset born in 1869. As a teenager Balch was fascinated by Wookey Hole and soon began to look for new caves, although he was not present when three of his friends made the first entry into Swildon's Hole – on 16 August 1901 – arguably Mendip's longest and most popular cave.

The exploration of Swildon's is a case study in British caving. Early trips were made in secret as the landowner disapproved. When he discovered what was going on he concreted a padlocked gate across the entrance, but the explorers found a key for the padlock and explored at night so as not to be seen crossing the fields to the entrance. The stream racing down the cave was diverted along canvas pipes to allow further exploration.

When a sump – a point at which a stream completely fills a passage, leaving no air gap, so that progress is only possible by diving (by breath holding if the sump is short, or bottled air if not) – was reached it was decided to blast a way past it using dynamite. The choice of a Sunday for the blasting was unfortunate: the sump lies almost directly under Priddy Church and it is said that the entire congregation rose 6 inches into the air, and were waiting for the cavers when they returned to the surface.

Most of Mendips' caves now enjoyed by weekend cavers were found by enthusiasts digging away in the bottom of swallets. Today there are caves for all grades of caver, from complete novices to those willing to free-dive the shorter sumps and to spend hours below ground.

Cave Diving

To many who do not understand the love of exploring underground passages the idea of crawling through narrow, pitch-black tunnels is horrific. In reality, of course, most caves are large and do not require excessive crawling through tight tunnels, but non-cavers are rarely convinced by such arguments.

Non-cavers reserve a special shudder when cave diving is mentioned, the idea of using bottled air to explore flooded tunnels adding several extra dimensions to the perceived horror. Here, though, reality and myth are closer together as many cavers also share the view that cave divers are madmen. Cave diving is a very exacting sport requiring not only extreme courage but a meticulous attention to detail. Flooded caves are often deep below the water level, requiring the same decompression times as normal diving, so air cylinders must be placed at strategic points along the intended route. The routes must be carefully marked with lines – mistakes in route finding are dangerous instantly. Even with all precautions taken the sport is still hazardous – any error is likely to lead to death, and deaths do occur.

The British cave diving record was established in Wookey Hole with divers pushing into a 25th chamber in a (probably forlorn) attempt to link Wookey Hole with Swildon's Hole near Priddy.

Continued from page 171

Continue along Christchurch Street West, turning fourth right down steep **Catherine Hill**, another fine street of 17th-century houses, this one steep and cobbled. Catherine Hill returns you to Market Place.

The A361 heads north-east from Frome, reaching **Beckington**, a village set awkwardly at a junction of main roads. As with Frome, this was once a cloth making centre, and still has a number of buildings from it s more prosperous past. At the southern end of the village Beckington Castle is a 16th-century mansion (and was never a castle) while nearby Beckington House is thought to be older.

The church tower is plain and sturdy, but this is not lack of ambition, rather a remarkable survival as it is Norman. Pevsner calls it 'the most ambitious Norman tower of any Somerset parish church'.

Thomas Bekynton, the famous Bishop of Bath and Wells was born in the village.

North of Beckington **Rode** is a quieter place. Here, too, there are attractive buildings, though the main interest lies in the **Bird Gardens** across the River Frome. The Gardens occupy Rode Manor, a 7 hectare (17 acre) site, and include hundreds of bird species, many tropical – including free flying macaws – but also including penguins. There is a pets' corner and a miniature steam railway. The site is also home to the national clematis collection with around 160 varieties. The site has a children's play area and a licensed café.

North again are two villages set on what was the border of 'new' Somerset and the artificial creation of Avon.

Norton St Philip was the furthest point reached by Monmouth's army during the rebellion of 1685. After heading north towards Bristol, and reaching Pensford on 24 June, Monmouth turned towards London. On 26 June he stopped at Norton St Philip and set a trap for a troop of the King's men who were heading towards him. The ambush was successful, Monmouth claiming 80 dead for 18 of his own men, but the skirmish clearly sapped his confidence. In atrocious weather he retreated to Frome: a week later his retreating army was caught at Sedgemoor. Although it seems no village men joined the rebellion, a dozen prisoners were hanged, drawn and quartered in the market place after the Bloody Assize.

Norton is a pretty village with many interesting houses, but the most interesting (if sad) item is the stone carved with two heads at the base of the church tower. These are claimed to be of the Fair Maids of Foscott, Siamese twins joined at the stomach whose existence was noted by Samuel Pepys. A century after the death of the twins it was recalled that 'one of them dying, the survivor was constrained to drag about her lifeless companion till death released her of her horrid burden'. Just north of the village, **Norwood Farm** is an organic farm which welcomes visitors, who can follow farm trails and view the rare breeds of farm animals.

The second village is **Farleigh Hungerford**, memorable for the remains of a castle built in the late-14th century by Sir Thomas Hungerford. The castle chapel has medieval wall paintings and stained glass, and the tomb of Sir Thomas. There is also a crypt with the lead coffins of other members of the family.

Above: The Miniature Steam Railway, Rode Bird Gardens

Axbridge

King John's Hunting Lodge (NT)
The Square
Axbridge
Open: Easter – September,
Daily 2 – 5pm.
☎ 01934 732012

Banwell

Court Farm Country park
Wolvershall Road
Banwell
Open: March – November, Daily except Monday 10am – 5.30pm, December – February, Daily except Monday 10.30 – 4.30pm. Open daily during school holidays and on Bank Holiday Mondays.
☎ 01934 822383

Cheddar

Cheddar Gorge Cheese Company Rural Village
Cheddar
Open: mid – March – October, Daily 10am – 5pm (open until 6pm May – September, but closes at 4pm in October).
☎ 01934 7428210

Cheddar Showcaves (Cox's Cave, Gough's Cave and Jacob's Ladder)
Open: Easter – September, Daily 10am–5pm, October – Easter, Daily 10.30am – 4.30pm. Closed Christmas Eve and Christmas Day.
☎ 01934 742343
Please note that adventure caving trips must be booked in advance

Chewton Mendip

Chewton Cheese Dairy
Chewton Mendip
Open: Cheese making, Daily except Thursday and Sunday 11am – 2.30pm.
Shop/restaurant,
Daily 9am – 4.30pm.
☎ 01761 241666

Compton Bishop

Forgotten World (Wheelwright and Romany Museum)
Webbington
nr Compton Bishop
Open: Easter – October, Wednesday – Sunday and Bank Holidays 10am – 6pm. Open daily in July and August, same times.
☎ 01934 750841

Farleigh Hungerford

Farleigh Hungerford Castle
(Engkish Heritage)
Open: April – September, daily 10am – 6pm, October, daily 10am – 5pm, November – March, Wednesday – Sunday 10am – 1pm & 2 – 4pm.
☎ 01225 754026

Frome

Frome Museum
1 North Parade
Open: February – December,
Wednesday – Saturday 10am – 4pm
☎ 01373 467271 for information.

Norton St Philip

Norwood Farm
Bath Road
Norton St Philip
Open: Two weeks before Easter – mid – September, Daily 10.30am – 6pm
☎ 01373 834356
Please note that dogs are not allowed.

Nunney

Nunney Castle (English Heritage)
Open: Any reasonable time.

Radstock

Radstock, Midsomer Norton and District Museum
Barton Meade House
Haydon
Radstock
Open: January – November, Saturday 10am – 4pm, Sundays and Bank Holidays (except Good Friday) 2 – 5pm.
☎ 01761 437722

Rode

Rode Bird Gardens
Rode
Open: May – September, Daily 10am – 6pm, October – April, Daily 10am – dusk. Closed Christmas Day.
☎ 01373 830326

Wells

Bishop's Palace
Wells
Open: Easter Saturday – October, Tuesday – Friday and Bank Holidays 10.30am – 6pm, Sunday 2 – 6pm. Open daily in August, times as above.
☎ 01749 678691

Cathedral
Open: April – June and September, Daily 7.15am – 7pm, July and August, Daily 7.15am – 8.30pm, October – March, Daily 7.15am – 6pm
Library: Open: Easter – September, Monday – Friday 2.30 – 4.30pm. Also open on Saturdays in July and August, same times.
☎ 01749 674483

Museum
9 Cathedral Green
Wells
Open: Easter – June, September and October, Daily 10am – 5.30pm, July and August, Daily 10am – 8pm, November and January – Easter, Wednesday – Sunday 11am – 4pm.
☎ 01749 673477

Wookey Hole Showcaves, Paper Mill etc
Open: All year except 17 – 25 December, Daily 9.30am – 5.30pm (10.30 – 4.30pm from November – March).
☎ 01749 672243

Whatley

Whatley Vineyard and Herb Garden
Whatley
Open: April – September, Wednesday – Sunday 11am – 1pm, 2 – 6pm.
☎ 10373 836467

7 Bath & North Somerset

The abbey from the Roman baths, Bath

When county boundaries were redrawn a few years ago the artificial county of Avon was created. The latest redrawing removed Avon from the map, but did not re-integrate old north Somerset, creating two new boroughs instead. Here we ignore the new geometry, exploring what was (and still is to many inhabitants) the northern part of the county, starting with its most famous city.

Bath

Bath's origins are steeped in mystery. It is likely that earliest man knew of the existence of the hot springs, although as the surrounding area is likely to have been a salt marsh, he may not have had a home here.

According to legend the town was built by Prince Bladud, descendent of refugees from Troy, and father of Shakespeare's King Lear. The poor prince contracted leprosy and was immediately banished from court to live out his days as a pig herder in the marshes. Inevitably one of the pigs also contracted leprosy but to Bladud's astonishment it was cured after taking a mud-bath near the hot springs. Bladud then tried the mud-bath himself and he, too, was cured, and allowed back to court. To commemorate this legendary founding of the city, about 2,800 years ago, there is a statue of Bladud at the Cross Bath.

The archaeological evidence of the founding of the city is more mundane. It is likely that the first town was Roman, *Aquæ Sulis* — the waters of the goddess Sulis — constructed in the first century AD. The Romans were undoubtedly tempted by the million or so litres (250,000 gallons) of water at 50°C (120°F) that rushes to the surface daily, and constructed a town around the public baths. The baths themselves are a minor wonder, with central heating in all rooms, a sauna and, of course, the pool, all fed by the hot waters.

When the Romans left, the town quickly decayed. The Saxon invaders, reaching here after the battle at Dyrham, to the north, could only wonder at the building. They were not great builders themselves and they believed the town was the work of giants, and haunted. Certainly the decaying buildings, the deep, warm pools, all overgrown, must have been ghostly.

Gradually the site became holy, probably fired by superstition and legend, and King Offa founded an abbey here. This became an important site, and King Edgar was crowned here, the first king of all Saxon England, in 973.

The abbot and the townspeople of medieval Bath knew of the hot waters and their medicinal purposes, for there are early references to people visiting the town to bathe in the waters. Indeed the visitors were a major source of income to the townspeople.

The bathers were subject to no regulations, however, and the baths became so unwholesome that people were reluctant to use them. In 1533 the chief bathers were those with 'lepre, pokkes, scabbes and great aches' and since there was no

• Beau Nash, King of Bath •

Richard Nash was born on 18th October 1674 in Swansea, the son of a Welsh gentleman and a mother who was the niece of the Royalist Colonel killed defending Pembroke against Cromwell. Richard was educated at Carmarthen School and then went to Jesus College, Oxford. There, as Oliver Goldsmith put it 'though much might be expected from his genius, nothing could be hoped from his industry'. Richard's problem was women, or, rather, his extreme delight in their company. He became so infatuated with one Oxford girl of dubious reputation that his tutor sent him home when he heard that the 17 year old Nash had proposed marriage.

Richard next joined the army, apparently because he believed that the uniform was a sure way to a girl's heart, but left because the hours and discipline were not to his taste. He then joined the Temple as a student, living a life that seemed almost beyond his means, a life typified by the suggestion that he 'preferred a bow from a lord to a dinner from a commoner'.

He was, by all accounts, well-mannered and friendly, and very compassionate. As an illustration of the latter, he once put in an expenses claim of £10 for 'making someone happy'. On being questioned, he said that he had been talking to a man who had said that £10 would make him happy and Nash had given him the money as an experiment. His employers, impressed, paid him the £10. Sadly, the result of the experiment is not known. In addition to these rather endearing habits, Richard also had an equally endearing farcical streak – he once rode a cow naked through a village for a bet.

It was probably the combination of being impressed with the upper-class and being eccentric in a way that would appeal to those same folk, that made Bath offer him the job of Master of Ceremonies (at first as the assistant to MC Capt Webster who was soon killed in a duel).

As MC Richard – by now known as 'Beau' to everyone because of his manner of dress – cleaned and lit the pump rooms, brought in a band, drew up a list of rules of behaviour and scrupulously enforced them. These rules applied to both the nobility and the sedan chairmen, waitresses etc. One of the rules was 'That all whisperers of lies and scandal be taken for their authors'. Beau might have been a womaniser and a gambler, but he was also fair and honest. His compassion for the less fortunate remained too: he set up a hospital in the town for poor folk who received no help from doctors, who were too busy peddling their potions to the rich.

Under Beau Nash Bath became the place, both to be and to be seen to be. His imagination helped the rich fill their time, his fairness and justice maintaining the city's reputation, and his wit keeping the place lively. Once when a (supposedly reformed) alcoholic came to dine with him (and others), the man drank too much wine and seemed intent on drinking much more. In response to Beau's aggravation, the man claimed that 'the company is so agreeable here that my resolution is quite gone'. Beau replied 'I ask your pardon sir, but I am sure that if your resolution is gone, it is time for you to go too'.

Beau is also credited with the invention of the riposte that has seen frequent use since: in reply to the suggestion by James Quin, a retired actor, that he had been overcharged in a shop, Beau replied that the shopkeeper had been acting on truly Christian principles because 'you were a stranger and they took you in'. (Interestingly, Quin is said to have responded with an even better line, claiming that had they really been Christians they would have clothed, rather than fleeced, him.)

In 1750, at 76, Beau Nash seemed to age suddenly and became that worst of all things in society, a bore. People began to avoid him, though he nevertheless continued as MC. By February 1760, in a wheelchair, with no teeth and most of his possessions sold to maintain his lifestyle (and very bitter about the fact) he was granted a 10 guineas per month pension by Bath Council. It was a very shabby way to treat the man who had brought prosperity to the town: in 56 years as MC, Nash had never received a day's pay, his income deriving from a percentage of gambling house profits (an income reduced by government legislation on the gaming house). Even this miserly pension was only paid for eleven months.

On 12 February 1761 Beau, insisting he was fine, but unable to stay awake, went to sleep. He never awoke. He was 86 and had lived through the reigns of seven monarchs. His last mistress, Juliana Popjoy, was so distressed at his death that she left the house and lived out her days in a hollow tree, an eccentricity of which Beau Nash would doubtless have approved.

Continued from page 181

the process he became rich, and his arrival in Bath, around 1710, was the start of Bath's rise to fame. It was Allen who saw the potential of the hot springs and bought the Combe Down quarries that supplied the stone for his architect, John Wood the Elder, who designed Allen's own house, near the abbey. All aspects of the postal service and the Royal Mail are covered in the museum.

Also to the left in Milsom Street is the Royal Photographic Society's **National Centre for Photography**. It has both an exhibition centre and a museum of photography.

Bear left along New Bond Street, then turn right into Northgate Street. Ahead is High Street and the **Guildhall**, a fine Georgian building of 1776 with what is widely regarded as the finest Adam-style interior in Britain.

The Banqueting Room on the first floor is magnificent. It is lit by a crystal chandelier of 1778 and hung with portraits of some of the famous people associated with Bath.

Turn left into Bridge Street. To the right at the end the **Victoria Art Gallery** houses, in addition to paintings, fine collections of glass and ceramics, and items of local interest. Many times during the year there are special exhibitions covering a range of subjects. Bridge Street leads to Pulteney Bridge, built in 1769 by Robert Adam. It is one of the few bridges with shops now surviving in Europe.

At the far end of Great Pulteney Street, beyond the bridge is the **Holburne Museum and Crafts Study Centre**, part of the University of Bath. This contains the collections of Sir Thomas Holburne: paintings, including works by Gainsborough, Stubbs and Turner; silver, one of the finest collections in Britain; porcelain and glass; bronzes and enamels. In addition to the set collections, there are special exhibitions during the year, and a Craft Study Centre for modern craftwork in metal and glass. Outside, the gardens are also of interest.

Turn right along Grand Parade. Bear right here, crossing to **Orange Grove**, named after the Prince of Orange. At its centre is an obelisk raised by Beau Nash to commemorate the Prince's visit to the city. Do not follow the Grove, which leads back to the Abbey, but continue south, bearing right along Terrace Walk and turning right into North Parade Passage. Here, and in nearby Old Lilliput Alley are some of Bath's oldest houses, built around 1500. **Sally Lunn's**, named after a Georgian pastrycook, is claimed to be the oldest. It has a restored Georgian kitchen and is an excellent coffee house, selling Sally Lunn's Buns, perhaps not as famous as Bath buns, but just as delicious.

The walk can be extended by continuing south along Grand Parade. Continue along Pierrepoint Street where, on the left, is the house Lord Nelson shared with Lady Hamilton. Ahead now, in Manvers Street, is the **Book Museum** where the history and considerable art of the craft of bookbinding are explained and displayed.

• The Other Places of Interest at Bath •

Away from the city centre there are three further museums. The **Bath Industrial Heritage Centre** (more often known as **Mr Bowler's Business**) is at the Camden Works, Julian Street, to the north of the Assembly Rooms: here the visitor can get away from the social elegance of Georgian Bath to discover how the ordinary city dweller lived in the 18th and 19th centuries. The works themselves are an exact reconstruction of a Victorian brass foundry and a Bath stone quarry face, with other exhibits illustrating different industries and lifestyles. Children will love the old plant for putting fizz in fizzy drinks: the drinks are on sale.

About 1 km (half a mile) north-east of the abbey, on the southern bank of the Avon, in Forester Road is the **Bath Boathouse**, a near perfect Victorian boathouse where punts can still be hired. For the less skilled there are also skiffs.

The **American Museum** at Claverton Manor, 3km (2 miles) east of the city centre, shows the history of North America from the time of the Pilgrim Fathers with period rooms containing fine examples of American furniture: exhibits deal with the opening of the West and with the Indians, and in the gardens there are several exhibits including a covered wagon. The gardens of the manor are also worth visiting.

Also near Claverton the **Pumping Station** of the Kennet and Avon Canal used a 5m (16ft) waterwheel to drive a pump which lifted water from the River Avon into the canal. The waterwheel was driven by the river. Now restored, the pump operates on certain summer days, but can be seen throughout the summer.

Finally, a bus or taxi is needed to visit Bath's most recently opened attraction, there being no parking at the National Trust's **Prior Park**. The 18th-century garden was landscaped by Capability Brown for Ralph Allen and has typical follies and a lake. The Park has been carefully restored and includes several miles of woodland walking. The views of Bath from the Park are breathtaking.

Left:The impressive abbey, Bath

Below: The beach and pier at Weston-Super-Mare

Opposite page: Street entertainers, Bath

Bath to Weston-super-Mare

South-west of Bath is a collection of attractive villages set in the fine country which leads to the **Chew Valley Lake**, though to tour through them all takes an effort of map reading as the main roads tend to head north towards Bath and Bristol.

South of Bath, **Hinton Charterhouse** is named for the Carthusian Priory (or Charterhouse) founded in the early-13th century. Legend has it that it was consecrated on the same day as Lacock Abbey so that the Countess of Salisbury, who founded both, could make a single journey between them. To the west, the church at **Wellow** has medieval wall paintings and an early-15th-century effigy of a priest.

Stoney Littleton Long Barrow

To the south of Wellow, above the Wellow Brook and reached by a track from the hamlet of **Stoney Littleton**, is a well-preserved long barrow.

Those barrows were the burial chambers of Neolithic man. A 'box' was created from upright stone slabs capped by another slab, the whole being earthed over to form the barrow. Often the earth mound has eroded away, leaving only the stone slabs, but here enough remains for an appreciation of the as-constructed form. The burial chamber beneath the mound is huge, over 15m (50ft) long, and has side chambers to accommodate a succession of burials.

Continue westwards through the larger village of Peasedown St John then head north to **Priston** where there is an ancient water mill still capable of grinding flour. The mill is on a working farm. Continue west to Farmborough, then on to **Clutton** where the church has an excellent 12th-century doorway. To the north is **Pensford**, once a cloth making town, then a centre for local coal mining and famous for the viaduct, built in 1873, that once took coal trains north to Bristol.

A short distance west of Stanton Drew is **Chew Magna**, a delightful village with high, wide pavements. It is easy to share the enthusiasm of Leland, the Elizabethan traveller, who claimed Chew was a 'pretty cloathing townelet'. The clothmaking has long gone, but the prettiness remains.

The church has a superb tower and a fine set of gargoyles. Inside there is a full-width wooden rood screen and several fine monuments one of which, is said to be of Sir John Hauteville, who threw the Stanton Drew stone. It consists of an effigy of a knight with some remarkable features. Firstly (and very unusually) it is of oak; secondly it is lying on its side, the head supported on the left hand; and thirdly the lion, which usually supports the feet, has been forced to stand on its hind legs to support the curious position of one of the feet. A further mystery is that the armour is 14th century, but the form of the work reflects the 16th century.

To the south of the church the 15th-century Tun Bridge crosses the River Chew. On its eastern side, over the parapet, there is a small trough.

Stanton Drew

Just north of Pensford the B3130 turns left from the A37: take this, soon reaching a turn on the left for **Stanton Drew**, close to which stands one of Britain's most important megalithic sites. The site consists of three stone circles, on private land (the site is in the care of English Heritage and can be visited) to the east of the church, three standing stones called The Cove in the garden of the local inn, and a single standing stone (called Hauteville's Quoit) to the north, beyond the River Chew.

The largest of the stone circles is about 120m (394ft) in diameter and consisted of 20-30 stones, many of which remain. Magnetic surveys have shown that originally there were nine concentric rings within the circle – presumably of wooden posts – and a broad enclosing ditch. The two smaller circles are 15m (49ft) and 20m (66ft) in diameter. There is some evidence to suggest that the site has alignments to critical sun and moon risings and settings, lending credence to the idea that here, as elsewhere, the site was rather more than ritualistic.

The recent rise in 'New Age' beliefs has enlivened the debate on such sites, but there is no doubting that the mute stones, and the site's enigmatic origins combine to create a powerful presence.

When plague or smallpox ravaged the village money and farm goods were exchanged in the trough to stop the infection spreading.

Close to Chew Magna is **Chew Stoke**, another picturesque place. When preparatory was work was being carried out for Chew Valley Lake the remains of a Roman villa were found. A Roman temple has also been discovered on Pagan's Hill to the north of the village.

West of the Chew villages lies Bristol Airport set high on a hill that seems to encourage fog, causing regular inconvenience to travellers. The runway runs east-west, its western edge overlooking a fine area of woodland that can be explored by a series of tracks. A minor road snakes through **Brockley Combe** in the northern section of the wood, while to the south **Goblin Combe,** which has several outcrops of limestone, is followed only by a path. In Brockley Combe, Brockley Mini Farm has farm animals, llamas and pets which can be viewed and fed. There is a children's play area and a tearoom.

The minor road through Brockley Combe meets the A370 at a T-junction. To the right the main road goes through Backwell, a satellite town of Bristol, then bypasses Long Ashton to reach Bristol itself. Before the River Avon is crossed a turn left reaches the **Ashton Court Estate.**

Ashton Court was built by the Smyth family, Bristol merchants, over a period of several hundred years, additions to the original medieval house giving it the longest façade in Somerset. The family also created a park – in part by knocking down some of the neighbouring village of Long Ashton – and a deer park. Now owned by Bristol City Council, the parkland is open to visitors and is the venue for the annual international balloon festival in August.

At this, dozens of hot air balloons – in shapes from the usual to the extraordinary – take off *en masse* in colourful displays spread over three days. On one evening there is a 'night glow' when the tethered balloons are lit by their burners, an awesome sight.

At the northern, top, end of the Ashton Court Estate it is just a short walk to Brunel's Suspension Bridge (see below) and to the forest walks in **Leigh Woods** which cloak the left-bank of the Avon Gorge. This lovely piece of woodland – astonishingly close to the centre of Bristol – is a nature reserve.

A left turn along the A370 at Brockley Combe leads to Weston-super-Mare.

The North Somerset Coast

Acres of sand, a Victorian pier, donkey rides, ice cream and candy floss – **Weston-super-Mare** has all the requirements of a traditional British seaside resort. It has also weathered the problems caused by cheap package tours to southern Spain rather better than most, being bright and clean rather than rundown and faded. There are new attractions set alongside the familiar favourites, and while Weston may not be everybody's idea of perfect happiness, it still has a particular appeal to great numbers and exploits its popularity to the full.

To look at today's Weston, with few buildings older than Victorian, it would be easy to suppose it is a modern invention, the 'super-Mare'

Above: Long Ashton Balloon festival by night

addition to the name an addition by the town fathers to further its cause in drawing visitors. In fact there was a Saxon settlement here, and the addition to the name was made by Glastonbury's abbot in medieval times to distinguish the Weston 'on sea' from all the other Westons in Somerset. But it is true that the town's growth was fuelled by the resort phenomenon: there were fewer than 200 people living here in the early-19th century – by the century's turn only Bath, of Somerset towns, was bigger.

Weston's first holiday home was built in about 1770 by the Rev William Leeves, vicar of Wrington, a village about 15km (10 miles) inland. The cottage – called The Old Thatched Cottage and very exactly dated at 1774 – stands on the sea front to the north of the Winter Gardens. Leeves was a friend of the Rev Wadham Piggot, whose family lived at Glebe House in nearby Grove Park. The Piggots had been in the habit of inviting friends to stay during the summer, so it might be claimed that they were the instigators of Weston holidays, but Leeves' modest cottage was definitely the first holiday home.

Close to the thatched cottage is the Royal Hotel, the first built in the town, in 1810. By then sea bathing had become a fashionable 'cure'. In 1790 a Dr Crane of Weymouth wrote *Cursory Observations on Sea Bathing*, extolling the virtues of not only bathing, but drinking sea water (at a rate of one pint per day). George III visited Weymouth soon after, using a bathing engine while a band on the beach played the National Anthem. Within a few years the gentry were arriving at resorts such as Weston creating a boom in the building of hotels and smart villas. Most of Weston's old town dates from this time, and from a second boom a few years later when the railway arrived allowing the Victorian middle classes to share the delights. Royal Crescent, near Grove Park, dates from this time.

To explore Weston it is really only necessary to walk along **Marine Parade**, the sea front.

At the southern end is a **miniature railway** where steam and diesel engines take passengers around an 800m (half a mile) track that encircles an 18 hole putting green. Heading north, train enthusiasts will also be interested in the **Great Weston Train Experience** in Clifton Road (which heads inland mid-way between the model yacht pond and the Tropicana) where there are four working layouts with trains modelling types from all over Europe. The models include a gravity operated freight marshalling yard, the only one of its kind in Britain.

The **Tropicana** was built as an open air pool in 1937 and was at that time, the largest of its type in Europe and included an Olympic standard 10m (33ft) diving platform). After a face-lift and name change it is still one of the town's most popular attractions. The **Sea Life Centre** beyond is a new venture, set on its own pier. Here many different sea habitats are recreated and stocked with thousands of sea creatures from octupuses to seahorses. The jelly fish display is particularly fascinating.

The Sea Life Centre is set at the heart of the beach's bathing area, the beach being divided into sections so that bathers are not at risk from water skiers and sailors.

The helicopter museum at Weston-Super-Mare

The Knightstone Baths

Knightstone was an island before the sea front road was extended northwards and excavations at that time, the 1820s, revealed the skeleton of a man over 2m (almost 7ft) tall. The origins of the man are unclear, but it has been suggested that he was pre-Roman, perhaps a Celtic leader from the hill fort on nearby Worlebury Hill. It is also suggested that the burial might be the reason for the name, though others contend that the island was where fishing boats were tied up at night – the night stone.

Whatever the origin of the name it was here, in 1831, that Dr Fox of Bristol built a Bath House for patients he sent down for a water cure. There were showers, hot and cold plunge baths and baths laced with sulphur, iodine and chlorine. Soon Weston was being prescribed as a cure for 'delicate children, especially from India, the anaemic and scrofulous, for convalescents and cases of neurasthenia, nervous breakdown, chronic albuminaria and chronic bronchitis'. Weston, it was claimed, had the lowest death rate of any British resort, which must have been a great comfort to visitors.

Weston Bay is very gently shelved and the tidal range of the Bristol Channel is 12m (40ft), the second highest in the world. Consequently low tide exposes vast areas of sand and mud.

Beyond the Tourist Information Centre, on the right, is the **Grand Pier**, built in 1904 as a berth for steamers, but soon taken over as an amusement area with all the traditional items. Video games have replaced the slot machines, but with its dodgems, big wheel and ghost train – together with ten-pin bowling and numerous fast food outlets – the pier still offers traditional seaside entertainment.

Inland from the pier is the town's floral clock (of course!) and museum. Museums in seaside resorts have a hard time competing with other attractions, but Weston's has responded well, creating **The Time Machine** which explores the history of the seaside holiday, as well as local history. There are also collections of toys and dolls. Close to the museum visitors who have not disposed of their long green 'Mod' anoraks will be interested in the **Lambretta Museum** which boasts one of each of the 61 models the factory produced.

Continuing along the promenade (Marine Parade has now become Royal Parade) the **Winter Gardens** and Pavilion stand across the road. The complex was raised in the 1920s

Where is the Sea?

It is a well-known local saying that when the tide is out the sea is only visible on a clear day, and it is true that at low tide the water is a very long way away, beyond mud flats that start where the sand ends.

as a centre for concerts, shows and dances. Go past **Knightstone** and the **Marine Lake**, created by building a causeway across a small bay, to reach **Birnbeck Pier**, the only one in Britain which links an off-shore island to the mainland. The pier was built in 1867 for steamer traffic and was the main arrival point for thousands of visitors from South Wales when seaside holidays came within reach of the working class.

Finally, before heading north along the coast, it is worth travelling inland to see the **International Helicopter Museum** beside the A371 at Weston Airport. The museum, the only one of its kind in the world has more than 70 machines from all over the world, many of them very rare prototypes. Helicopter pleasure flights are available at certain times.

Weston to Portishead

North of Weston, beyond Worlebury Hill, is Sand Bay, defined at its northern edge by the low rise of Middle Hope. On the eastern side of Middle Hope are the remains of **Woodspring Priory**, a small house for Augustinian Canons founded in the early-13th century by a grandson of one of Thomas à Becket's murderers to atone for his ancestor's crime. The priory church, the outline of the cloisters and a barn survive and are open to the public.

No road follows the coast to the north of the Priory, though a succession of minor roads head inland from the main A370 which links Weston to Bristol. The next coast town is Clevedon.

Clevedon is another resort town, growing up in the first decades of the 19th century as a rival to Weston. Here, too, there are fine period houses and a pier, but Clevedon has never matched Weston's success, lacking a sandy beach and the colossal entrepreneurial enthusiasm of the larger town. Clevedon remains a genteel place, gently turning up its nose at its brash neighbour.

Literary Visitors

In its earliest years Clevedon was beloved of artists and writers. Coleridge and Southey, Tennyson and Thackeray all stayed – Coleridge was on honeymoon – and the tradition was maintained, Sir John Betjeman enjoying his visits to a 'beautiful haven of quiet'.

The sea front walks – there are really two, the front being split by the large pool in Salthouse Bay – are excellent, with gardens and views of the rocky coast. For children there is a fine play area and a miniature railway.

The **pier** was built in 1867 and is a masterpiece of Victorian elegance, a more graceful and delicate structure than Weston's, with a delightful pagoda at its seaward end. Sadly in 1970 part of the pier collapsed during a statutory load test. Only in 1989 was it reopened, though full restoration was not completed until May 1998. Today it is open for walkers and fishermen, and as an embarkation point for Bristol Channel steamers. Close by, the **Clevedon Heritage Centre** explores the town's history.

On the east side of the town, set below the wooded hill of The Warren is **Clevedon Court**, built in

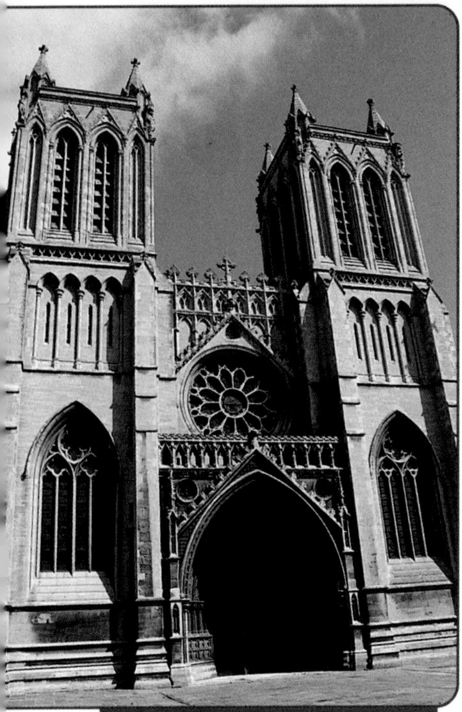

The Cathedral at Bristol

about 1320 and one of very few survivals (in complete form) from that time. The house also incorporates sections of older buildings: the east kitchen is believed to be 13th century. The builder, Sir John de Clevedon, included a chapel in the house rather than constructing a separate church and as it was dedicated to St Peter, the patron saint of fishermen, had a window constructed of delicate tracery, a replica of a fishing net.

The house eventually passed to the Elton family who were responsible for the creation of Elton Ware, colourful earthenware: there is a museum of the pottery in the Court.

The house is set at the base of the hillside which has been terraced to produce fine gardens. There is also excellent parkland at the hill base. The house is now owned by the National Trust and is open to visitors.

From Clevedon a fine walk follows the coast past Lodge Point and Walton Bay to **Portishead**, now a dormitory town for Bristol, where there is an open air swimming pool and boating lake.

Bath to Bristol

Visitors with time to spare could travel from Bath to Bristol along the new Railway Path, a walking/cycling path which follows the trackbed of the old Midland Railway, producing a traffic-free 20km (12 mile) route. The journey is enlivened by a series of sculptures which have turned the path into an outdoor, linear art gallery.

But following the path misses the **Avon Valley Country Park**, set close to the A4 near Keynsham. Here there are rare breeds of farm animals – and a few more exotic animals too – a boating/fishing lake and adventure playground.

Bristol

As with Bath, Bristol could sensibly fill a guide book on its own, with an exploration of its history – particularly the prosperity the slave trade brought it, a story which is only being fully detailed now – its architecture and its artistic and cultural life.

When the county of Somerset extended as far north as the River Avon, Bristol was its own county borough, its boundaries extending south of the river. Even if the strictest definition of Somerset was used, only a fraction of Bristol – and almost

• Selected Visitor Sites in Bristol •

Arnolfini Arts Centre: A gallery of contemporary art housed in a Victorian tea warehouse.

Blaise Castle House Museum: A museum of 18th-century life housed in a period mansion. The mansion stands in 400 acres of fine parkland and close to Blaise hamlet, nine picturesque cottages built in 1809 and now owned by the National Trust.

Bristol Industrial Museum: The city's industrial heritage with exhibits on road transport, railways, the port of Bristol and the city's aerospace industry (from the Blenheim to Concorde).

Bristol Zoo Gardens: Wide collection of animals in beautiful grounds. Interesting features include a nocturnal house and gorilla island.

Cabot Tower: Built in 1897 to commemorate the 400th anniversary of John Cabot's voyage to America. Cabot sailed from Bristol in the *Matthew*, a replica of which can be seen near the SS *Great Britain*.

City Museum and Art Gallery: The museum has collections on archaeology, Egyptology and natural history, as well as local history. The art gallery has a good collection of European paintings, chiefly 18th and 19th centuries, together with Bristol made porcelain, glass and pottery.

Continued on page 197...

The SS Great Britain and spire of St Mary Redcliffe, Bristol

none of its historic centre – would lie within the county. Yet few visitors to northern Somerset will ignore the city, if only to make use of its endless possibilities for shopping and dining. Here we very briefly look at the heart of the city, and include a section on the visitor attractions it has to offer.

Close to an arm of the river – the so-called Floating Harbour, separated from the river by a lock, so allowing it to remain full at all times – is **Bristol Cathedral**, founded as an Augustinian Abbey in 1140 and given cathedral status in 1542. It is widely acknowledged that the cathedral's Chapter House is one of the finest Norman buildings in England. Beside the Cathedral is the Norman gateway of the original Abbey. Outside the Cathedral is **College Green** with the 1950s Council House, seat of local government, topped by two gilded unicorns.

Beside the Green, runs **Park Street** at the top of which is the **University Tower**. The tower is 65m (215ft) tall and was completed in 1925, the gift to the university of the Wills Family, the tobacco magnates.

Climbing Park Street, **Harvey's Wine Museum** is off right, the **Georgian House** off left. At the top of Park Street the **City Museum and Art Gallery** lies just beyond the Tower. To the left, beside Blackwells Bookshop, a road leads to the late-18th-century Berkeley Square and **Brandon Hill**, with its excellent gardens and the tall **Cabot Tower**. From the Tower, or even from the Hill, there is a view of the **SS *Great Britain***. and the ***Matthew***. To the left of the ship (as viewed from Brandon Hill), a little further along the river, is the **Industrial Museum**.

Turning right at the top of Park Street takes the visitor along Park Row. Soon, to the right, **Red Lodge** is passed. Bear right down Lower Park Row and cross the road to reach the top of **Christmas Steps**, constructed in 1669 by a local wine merchant to prevent further accidents on a steep, slippery path down to what was then the River Frome. The river, which empties into the Floating Harbour, now lies beneath The Centre (so-called because it was the Tramway Centre in the days of trams, not because it was the centre of the city).

Descend the Steps to reach Colston Avenue and the northern end of The Centre. Cross the road, the 'island' and another road and bear left to reach **St John's Gate**, Bristol's only surviving medieval gateway. The seated figures are Belinus and Brennus, legendary founders of the city. Go through the gate and follow Broad Street to Corn Street, the banking heart of old Bristol.

Hard Cash

The **Nails** – four bronze pedestals – outside the Corn Exchange (opposite Broad Street) are 17th century trading tables. Such tables are the origin of the expression 'cash on the nail'.

Behind the Corn Exchange is the city's covered market and the Tourist Information Centre in the old St Nicholas Church.

Bearing left from Broad Street (along Wine Street) leads to **Castle Park**, the site of Bristol's Norman castle – of which only fragments of the keep survive. The ruined church is St Peter's, traditionally the city's

• Selected Visitor Sites in Bristol •

Continued from page 195

Clifton Observatory and Camera Obscura:
The observatory is a tunnel leading to a viewpoint in the cliff above the River Avon, close to the Suspension Bridge.The camera obscura gives a panoramic view of the city.

Clifton Suspension Bridge Visitor Centre:
The story of the design and building of the famous bridge.

Exploratory:
Britain's biggest, and arguably best, hands-on science exploratory housed in Brunel's original GWR terminus.

Georgian House:
A merchant's town house, built in 1791. Furnished in period style.

Harvey's Wine Cellars:
Housed in the former head office of the wine merchants famous for Harvey's Bristol Cream sherry. There is a wine museum, wine shop, glass gallery and a superb restaurant.

John Wesley's Chapel:
The world's oldest Methodist building, founded by John Wesley in 1739. He lived here while in Bristol and his brother Charles lived here for a year.

Red Lodge:
Built in 1590 and now the city's only surviving Tudor interior.

SS *Great Britain*/The Matthew:
The world's first ocean-going, propeller-driven iron ship. Designed by I K Brunel, the ship sailed from 1843 to 1886. Until 1937 she was a floating warehouse in the Falkland Islands and was then abandoned. Brought back to Bristol in 1970 and now almost fully restored. The ship was in the news again in 1998 when its owners produced a promotional pamphlet in which the well-known photograph of Brunel had had the cigar air-brushed from his lips. Not wanting to create a bad role model said the owners. PC gone mad responded critics.

Beside the *Great Britain* is a replica of the *Matthew* which was built in Bristol and traced John Cabot's journey to the New World before returning to the city.

The site also includes the **Maritime Heritage Centre** which explores the history of Bristol shipbuilding.

Above: **Park Street and the University Tower, Bristol**
Below: **Clifton Suspension Bridge**

oldest and claimed to be on Saxon foundations. It was gutted by fire a fter a bombing raid in November 1940.

Steps near St Nicholas' Church lead down to Baldwin Street. Cross and follow Queen Charlotte Street ahead, soon reaching the **Llandoger Trow Inn**, the best timber-framed house in the city. The inn dates from the 1660s and is named for the 'trows', a particular form of sailing barge, that unloaded on the nearby quay having sailed from the River Wye and South Wales. The barges were named for Llandogo, a ship-building village on the Wye.

To the right is **King Street**, a very old street in which stands the Theatre Royal. Continue along Queen Charlotte Street and on through **Queen Square**, built around 1700 and named for Queen Anne when she visited the city in 1702. Bear left over the river to reach **St Mary Redcliffe Church** famously called 'the fairest, goodliest' church in England by Elizabeth I. The church is breath-taking beautiful, set off by its huge – 89m (292ft) – spire.

The Cabot Tower, Brandon Hill, Bristol

Reverse the route to Queen Square and cross it to reach Prince Street. To the left from here is the **Arnolfini Arts Centre**. Turn right to regain The Centre, bearing left past Neptune's Statue and the Watershed shopping complex beside the harbour to reach the bottom of Park Street. The Cathedral is just beyond the Swallow Royal Hotel.

This short tour misses the most famous of Bristol's landmarks, the one that actually crosses the River Avon and so has a foot in Somerset. The **Clifton Suspension Bridge** was the dream of William Vick, a wealthy city merchant (explaining the curious Latin inscription on the towers) who gave money in 1752 for its construction. Only in 1829 had the bequest earned enough interest for there to be any chance of building the bridge. A design competition was organised and was won by Isambard Kingdom Brunel the famed engineer of the GWR (who also built Bristol's Temple Meads Station and the SS *Great Britain*). Work started in 1836, but halted in 1840 when the money ran out. Brunel died in 1858, and only in 1861 did work recommence. The bridge was completed in 1864. The bridge was, and is, a marvel of engineering and quite beautiful.

Bath

American Museum
Claverton Manor
Claverton
Open: Museum: Easter to November, daily (except Monday) 2 – 5pm.
Gardens: Easter to November, daily (except Monday) 1 – 6pm (open at 12noon on Saturday and Sunday).
☎ 01225 460503

Assembly Rooms and Costume Museum
Bennett Street
Open: all year, Monday – Saturday 10am – 5pm, Sunday 11am – 5pm.
☎ 01225 477789

Bath Abbey
Open: Easter – November, Monday – Saturday 9am – 6pm, Sunday 1.30 – 2.30pm and 4.30 – 5.30pm.
November – Easter, Monday – Saturday 9am – 4.30pm, Sunday 1.30 – 2.30pm and 4.30 – 5.30pm.
☎ 01225 422462
The Heritage Vaults are open all year Monday – Saturday 10m – 4pm.
(☎ 01225 422462)

Bath Boathouse
Forester Road
Open: April – September, daily 10am – 6pm.
☎ 01225 466407

Book Museum
Manvers Street
Open: all year, Monday – Friday 9am – 1pm and 2 – 5.30pm, Saturday 9.30am – 1pm.
☎ 01225 466000

Buildings of Bath Museum and British Folk Art Centre
Huntingdon's Chapel
The Vineyards, The Paragon
Open: Mid – February to November Tuesday – Sunday and Bank Holiday Monday 10.30am – 5pm.
☎ 01225 333895

Claverton Pumping Station
Ferry Lane
Claverton
Open: Easter – late October, Sundays and Bank Holidays 10am – 5pm.
Pumping on certain days only.
☎ 0117 986 7536

Costume Fashion Research Centre
4 The Circus
Open: all year by appointment only.
☎ 01225 477752

Georgian Garden
Gravel Walk
Open: May – October, Monday – Friday 9am – 4.30pm.
☎ 01225 477752

Guildhall
High Street
Open: all year, Monday – Friday 9am – 5pm unless being used for a special function.
☎ 01225 477724

Herschel House & Museum
19 New King Street
Open: March to October, daily 2 – 5pm; November to February, Saturday and Sunday 2 – 5pm.
☎ 01225 311342

Holburne Museum & Crafts Study Centre
Great Pulteney Street
Open: mid – February to mid – December, Monday – Saturday 11am – 5pm, Sunday 2.30 – 5.30pm. Closed on Mondays until Easter.
☎ 01225 466669

Mr Bowler's Business
(Bath Industrial Heritage Centre)
Camden Works
Julian Road
Open: Easter to October, daily 10am – 5pm; November to Easter, Saturday and Sunday 10am – 5pm.
☎ 01225 318348

Museum of East Asian Art
12 Bennett Street
Open: April to October, Monday – Saturday 10am – 6pm, Sunday 10am – 5pm; November to March, Monday – Saturday 10am – 5pm. Sunday 12noon – 5pm.
☎ 01225 464640

No. 1 Royal Crescent
Open: Mid – February to October, Tuesday – Sunday and Bank Holiday and Bath Festival Mondays 10.30am – 5pm; November, Tuesday – Sunday 10.30am – 4pm.
☎ 01225 428126

Postal Museum
8 Broad Street
Open: all year, Monday – Saturday 11am – 5pm, Sunday 2 – 5pm.
☎ 01225 460333

Prior Park (NT)
Ralph Allen Drive
Open: all year daily except Tuesday 12noon – 5.30 or dusk.
Disabled visitors should ring to reserve one of the three disabled parking bays. There is no parking for other visitors who must arrive by bus or taxi.
☎ 01225 833422

Roman Baths & Museum
(☎01225 461111)

Pump Room
(☎01225 477738)
Open: April to September, Monday – Saturday 9am – 6pm; October to March, daily 9.30am – 5pm.

Royal Photographic Society National Centre for Photography
The Octagon
Milsom Street
Open: all year,
daily 9.30am – 5.30pm.
☎ 01225 462841

Sally Lunn's
4 North Parade Passage
Open: all year Museum: Monday – Saturday 10am – 6pm, Sunday 12noon – 6pm.
Teashop: Monday – Saturday 10am – 11pm, Sunday 12noon – 11pm.
☎ 01225 461634

Victoria Art Gallery
Bridge Street
Open: all year, Tuesday – Friday 10am – 5.30pm, Saturday 10am – 5pm.
Closed Bank Holidays.
☎ 01225 461111

BRISTOL

Arnolfini Arts Centre
16 Narrow Quay
Open: All year, Daily 9am – 5pm.
☎ 01179 299191

Blaise Castle House Museum
Henbury Road
Henbury
Open: All year, Tuesday – Sunday
10am – 1pm, 2 – 5pm.
☎ 01179 506789

Bristol Industrial Museum
Princes Wharf
Wapping Road
Open: April – October, Saturday – Wednesday 10am – 5pm,
November – March, Saturday and Sunday 10am – 5pm.
☎ 01179 251470

Bristol Zoo Gardens
Clifton Down
Clifton
Open: All year, Daily 9am – 5.30pm
(closes at 4.30pm
November – March).
☎ 01179 738951

Cabot Tower
Brandon Hill
Open: All year, Daily 8am – dusk
City Museum and Art Gallery
Queens Road
Open: All year, Daily 10am – 5pm.
☎ 01179 251470

Clifton Observatory and Camera Obscura
Clifton Down
Clifton
Open: All year, Daily 11am – 6pm
(closes at 4pm November – March).
☎ 01179 741242

Conkey's Tavern, The American Museum

Above: Clevedon Court
Below: Helicopter Museum, Weston-Super-Mare

Clifton Suspension Bridge Visitor Centre
Bridge House
Sion Place
Clifton
Open: April – September, Monday – Saturday 10am – 6pm, Sunday 10am – 4pm, October – March, times vary – ring beforehand.
☎ 01179 744664

The Exploratory
Old Station
Temple Meads
Open: All year, Daily 10am – 5pm.
☎ 01179 079000

Georgian House
7 Great George Street
Open: April – October, Saturday – Wednesday 10am – 5pm.
☎ 01179 211362

Harvey's Wine Cellars
12 Denmark Street
Open: All year, Monday – Saturday 10am – 5pm. Closed on Bank Holidays.
☎ 01179 275036

John Wesley's Chapel
36 The Horsefair
Open: All year, Monday – Saturday 10am – 1pm, 2 – 4pm. Closed on Bank Holidays and Wednesday November – March.
☎ 01179 264740

Red Lodge
Park Row
Open: April – October, Saturday – Wednesday 10am – 5pm.
☎ 01179 211360

SS Great Britain/The Matthew/ Maritime Heritage Centre
Great Western Dock
Gas Ferry Road
Open: April–October, Daily 10am – 5.30pm, November – March, Daily 10am – 4.30pm.
☎ 01179 260680

Brockley Coombe
Brockley Mini Farm
Brockley Coombe
Open: Easter – September, Daily 10am – 5pm.
☎ 01934 862639

CLEVEDON

Clevedon Heritage Centre
4 The Beach
Open: 9am – 5pm.
☎ 01275 341196

Clevedon Court (NT)
Tickenham Road
Open: April – September, Wednesday, Thursday, Sunday and Bank Holiday Mondays 2 – 5pm.
☎ 01275 872257

The Pier
Clevedon
Open: All year, Daily 9am – 5pm, but closed Wednesday from November – March.
☎ 01275 878846

Keynsham

Avon Valley Country Park
Pixash Lane,
Bath Road
Keynsham
Open: April – October, Daily except Monday 10am – 6pm. Open on Bank Holiday Mondays and all Mondays in August.
☎ 01179 864929

Priston

Corn Mill
Priston
Open: Bank Holiday Sunday and Monday 11am – 5.30pm and Thursdays in August 2.15 – 5pm.
☎ 01225 423894

Stanton Drew

Stanton Drew Stone Circles
(English Heritage)
Open: Any reasonable time.

Weston–super–Mare

Grand Pier
Marine Parade
Open: mid – March – April and October, Monday–Friday 10am – 5.30pm, Saturday and Sunday 10am – 7pm. May and September, Daily 10am – 7pm, June – august, Daily 10am – 10.15pm.
☎ 01934 620238

The Great Weston Train Experience
Clifton Road
Open: May – September, Daily 10.30am – 4.30pm, October – April, Thursday – Saturday 10.30am – 4.30pm.
☎ 01934 629717

International Helicopter Museum
Locking Moor Road
Open: April – October, Daily 10am – 6pm, November – March, Wednesday – Sunday 10am – 4pm.
☎ 01934 635227

Lambretta Museum
77 Alfred Street
Open: All year, Daily 10am – 5.30pm (but closes at 12.30pm on Wednesday).
☎ 01934 614614

Sea Life Centre
Marine Parade
Open: April – October, Daily 10am – 6pm, October – April, subject to change: please ring for details.
☎ 01934 641603

The Time Machine (North Somerset Museum)
Burlington Street
Open: All year, Daily 10am – 5pm (4pm November – February).
☎ 01934 621028

Weston Miniature Railway
Marine Parade
Open: Spring Bank Holiday – mid – September, Daily 10.30am – 6pm (weather permitting).
☎ 01934 643510

Woodspring Priory
Open: All year, Daily 10am – dusk.
☎ 01934 512728

LANDMARK
Publishing Ltd

Other Landmark Visitors Guides to Britain
'Pack 2 months into 2 weeks'

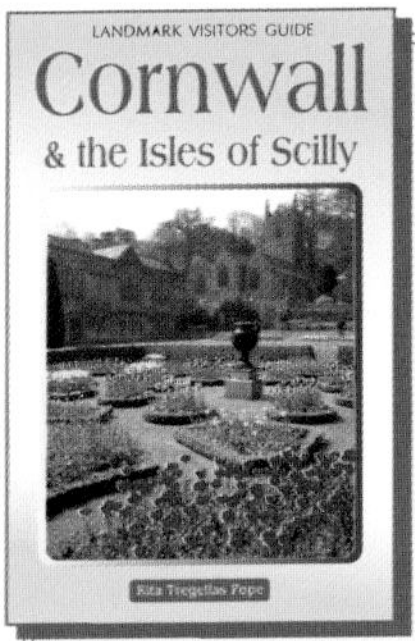

Cornwall & the Isles of Scilly
ISBN:
1 901522 09 1
256pp, Full colour,
£9.99

West Cornwall
ISBN:
1 901522 24 5
96pp, Full colour,
£4.95

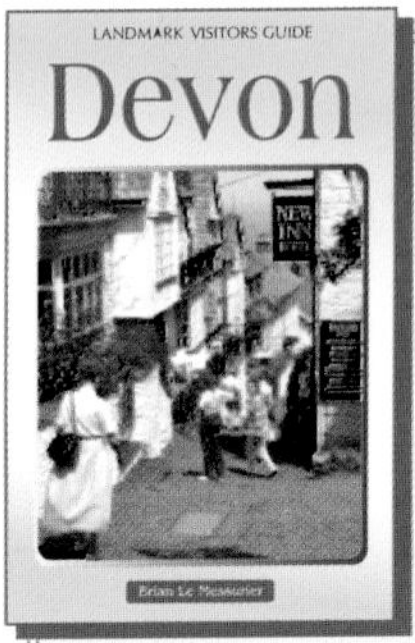

Devon
ISBN:
1 901522 42 3
224pp, Full colour,
£9.95

South Devon
ISBN:
1 901522 52 0
96pp, Full colour,
£4.95

Peak District
ISBN:
1 901522 25 3
240pp, Full colour,
£9.99

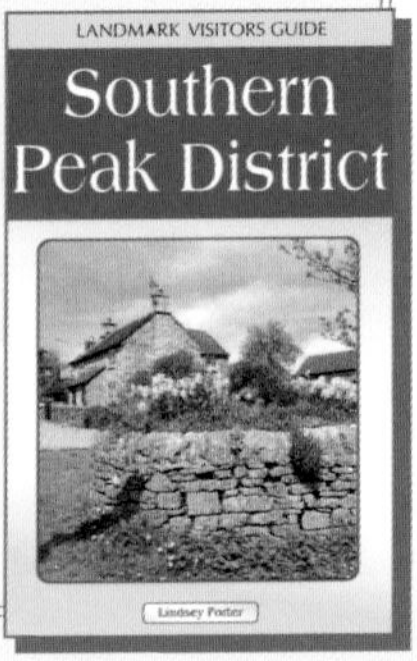

Southern Peak District
ISBN:
1 901522 27 X
96pp, Full colour,
£4.95

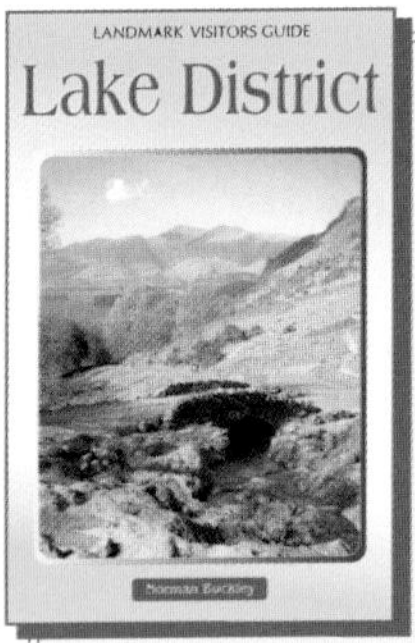

Lake District
ISBN:
1 901522 38 5
224pp, Full colour,
£9.95

Southern Lakeland
ISBN:
1 901522 53 9
96pp, Full colour,
£4.95

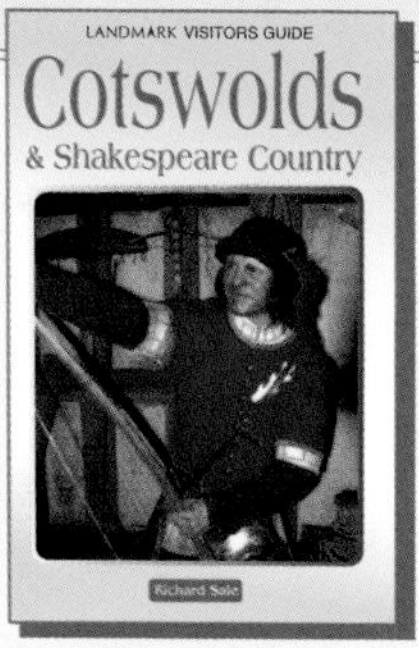

Cotswolds
ISBN: 1 901522 12 1
224pp, Full colour, £9.99

Dorset
ISBN: 1 901522 46 6
224pp, Full colour, £9.95

East Anglia
ISBN: 1 901522 58 X
224pp, Full colour, £9.95

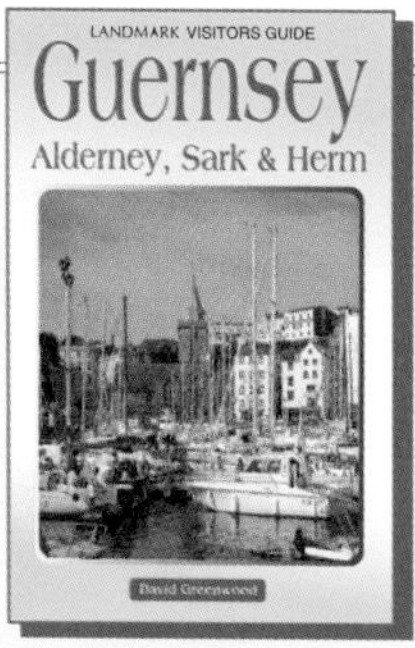

Guernsey
ISBN: 1 901522 48 2
224pp, Full colour, £9.95

Hampshire
ISBN: 1 901522 14 8
224pp, Full colour, £9.95

Harrogate
ISBN: 1 901522 55 5
96pp, Full colour, £4.95

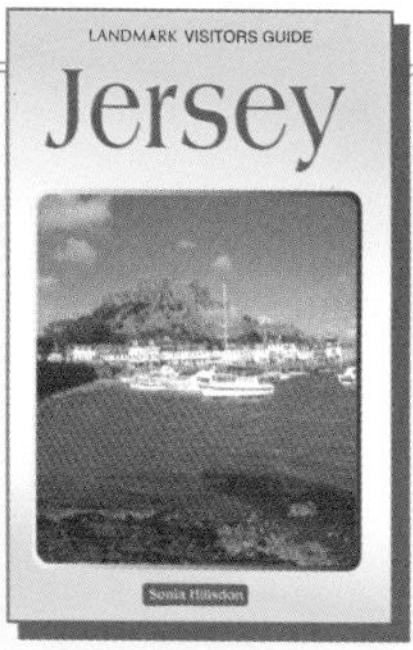

Jersey
ISBN: 1 901522 47 4
224pp, Full colour, £9.99

Scotland
ISBN: 1 901522 18 0
288pp, Full colour, £11.95

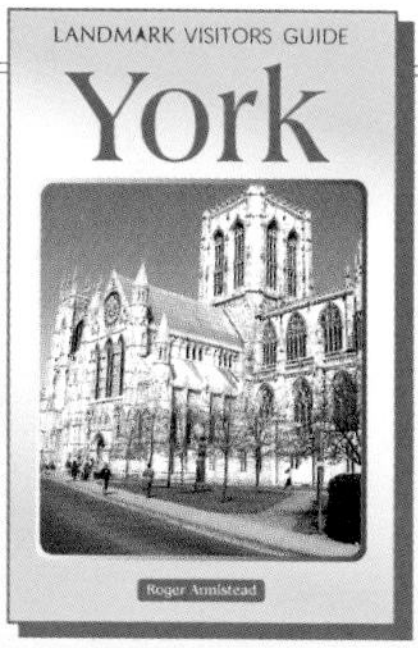

York
ISBN: 1 901522 56 3
96pp, Full colour, £4.95

Landmark Publishing
Waterloo House, 12 Compton, Ashbourne, Derbyshire DE6 IDA England
Tel: 01335 347349 Fax: 01335 347303 e-mail: landmark@clara.net

For all our Foreign titles see page 223

ATTRACTIONS FOR CHILDREN

Some of the theme parks/fun parks for children are mentioned in the main texts. Below a list of all the main parks is gathered together for convenience.

Brean Leisure Park
Cross Road
Brean Sand
Open: Easter-May, Saturday and Sunday 11am-6pm, June-September, daily 11am-6pm
☎ 01278 751595

The park has indoor and outdoor pools with rides and slides and a fun fair, The same site has an 18-hole golf course and regular cabarets.

Jungle Jungle
4 Artillery Road
Lufton Trading Estate
Yeovil
Open: all year,
daily 9.30am-5.30pm
☎ 01935 433833

The site is an indoor adventure playground aimed at children up to the age of 12.

Kidscove
Searle Crescent
Weston-super-Mare
Open: all year, daily 10am-7pm
☎ 01934 417411

Aimed at younger children – there is a toddlers' section – with ball pools, net climbs etc.

Little Terrors
Unit 4, Rawlings Mill
South Parade
Frome
Open: Somerset Term Time, Monday-Friday 11.30am-7pm, Saturday and Sunday 10am-7pm; Somerset School Holidays, daily 10am-7pm
☎ 01373 453670

Indoor adventure play area with ball pool, aerial runways etc

Monkeys
Tweentown
Cheddar
Open: Somerset Term Time, Monday-Friday 3.30-5.30pm, Saturday and Sunday 10.30am-5.30pm; Somerset School Holidays, daily 10.30am-5.30pm
☎ 01934 742270/712304

Ball pools, bouncy castle etc for children up to age 12.

Somerwest World
Minehead
Open: late April-October, daily 10am-midnight
☎ 01643 703331 Ext 5123

Minehead's Butlins, open to day trippers to enjoy the rides and shows.

In addition to the above, Weston-super-Mare and Minehead have all sorts of entertainments for children, as have the larger towns such as Bath and Bristol.

CRAFT AND ART CENTRES

Many of the towns and villages of Somerset have thriving craft centres and art galleries. Some of the more traditional and interesting are mentioned in the text, but a more complete list is given below. In general all these outlets are open shop hours, though they are also open on Sundays.

Somerset Guild of Craftsmen
The Visitor Centre
Dunster
☎ 01643 821235

Somerset Guild of Craftsmen Gallery
Yandle and Sons, Hurst Works
Martock
☎ 01935 825891

Art Benattar Craft
31 Market Square
Crewkerne
☎ 01460 77780

Black Swan Guild Centre/Art Centre
2 Bridge Street
Frome
☎ 01373 473980

Clevedon Craft Centre
Moor Lane
Clevedon
☎ 01275 342114

David Brown Pottery
Highway Cottage
Merriott
☎ 01460 75655

Douglas and Jennie Phillips
The Pottery
Queen Camel
Nr Yeovil
☎ 01935 850753

English Hurdle
Curload
Stoke St Gregory
☎ 01823 698859

John Leach
Muchelney Pottery
☎ 01458 250324

Martin Pettinger
Williton Pottery
☎ 01984 632150

Michael Cooper's Studio
Clarks Village
Street
☎ 01458 445742

Michael Gaitskell
Mill Pottery
Wootton Courtenay
☎ 01643 841297

Moobles Design (Handmade Furniture)
Higher Farm
Wayford
☎ 01460 731666

Quantock Pottery and Gallery
West Bagborough
☎ 01823 433057

Shakespeare Glassworks
Foundry Road, Riverside Place
Taunton
☎ 01823 333422

Simonsbath Pottery and Craft Gallery
Simonsbath
☎ 01643 831443

Somerset Countryware
Smocklands Farmhouse
Drayton
Langport
☎ 01458 251640

Somerset Levels Basket and Craft Centre
Lyng Road
Burrowbridge
☎ 01823 698688

Village Pottery
Clarks Village
Street
☎ 01458 443889

Willow Craft Industry and Basketware (Willows and Wetland Visitor Centre)
P H Coate and Son
Meare Court Green
Stoke St Gregory
☎ 01823 490249

NATURE RESERVES

There are many nature reserves within the county. Some of the most important are mentioned in the text. For full details of the reserves, contact:

English Nature
Roughmoor
Bishop's Hull
Taunton TA1 5AA
☎ 01823 283211

Somerset Wildlife Trust
Fyne Court
Broomfield TA5 2EQ
☎ 01823 451587

Royal Society for the Protection of Birds
South-West Office
10 Richmond Road
Exeter EX4 4JA
☎ 01392 432691

PASTIMES

Balloon Flights

Hot air balloon flights are available from:

Bristol Balloons
Winterstoke Road
Bristol BS3 2NT
☎ 0117 963 7858

Canal Trips

Boat trips are available on the Bridgwater and Taunton Canal. Details are available at the Canal Centre at Maunsel.

Cheese Making

The following sites (both mentioned in the text) offer the visitor the chance to see 'real' Cheddar cheese being made:

Cheddar Gorge Cheese Company Rural Village
☎ 01934 742810

Chewton Cheese Dairy
Chewton Mendip
☎ 01761 241666

Steamer Trips

The *Waverley*, the last sea-going paddle steamer in the world, and the *Balmoral*, a conventional pleasure cruise ship, make trips in the Bristol Channel, occasionally visiting Lundy Island. The ships sail from Bristol, Clevedon, Weston-super-Mare, Minehead and Ilfracombe in North Devon. Details of sailings are available from:

Waverley Excursions Ltd
Gwalia Buildings
Barry Docks CF62 5QR
☎ 01446 720656

Wildlife Safaris

Land Rover safaris of Exmoor are available from:

Moorland Wildlife Safari
The Tantivy
Fore Street
Dulverton
☎ 01398 323465

SPORTS

The main towns, particularly Bath, Taunton, Yeovil and, of course, Bristol have sports centres with swimming pools, squash and tennis courts etc.

Activity Centres

Black Rock (climbing, caving, canoeing, mountain biking)
16 St Andrews Road
Cheddar
☎ 01934 744389

Country Wide Weekends
(climbing, caving, canoeing, mountain biking)
Broadway House
Cheddar
☎ 01934 743775

Mill on the Brue
(all outdoor sports and activities, including water sports)
Trendle Farm
Bruton
☎ 01749 812307

Millfield Holiday Village
(all outdoor sports and activities, including water sports)
Street
☎ 01458 445823

Cycling

As might be imagined, the Somerset Levels are ideal for cycling, with flat roads meandering through delightful country. Somerset County Council publishes leaflets on four suggested tours of the Levels, each taking about a day. In addition, South Somerset District Council publishes leaflets on a further five tours. The leaflets are available from the local Tourist Information Offices. Yeovil Tourist Information Office also has details of a 160km (100 mile) route that explores the whole of South Somerset. There are also Mendip cycle routes (again details from local Tourist Information Offices) but here the cyclist has to be prepared for uphill work.

Fishing

Somerset's reservoirs are controlled by Wessex Water who publish a brochure on the fishing and sporting possibilities at each site. This is available from Tourist Information Offices or from:

Wessex Water
Wessex House
Passage Street
Bristol BS2 0JQ
☎ 0117 975 7788

Details on rod licences etc for the county's rivers are available from Tourist Information Offices or the Exmoor National Park Visitor Centres.

Golf

(Full Courses, Approach Courses and Driving Ranges)

Ashton Course Estate Golf Course
Long Ashton
Bristol
☎ 0117 973 8508

Bath Golf Club
North Road
Bath
☎ 01225 425182/463834

Brean Leisure Park
Brean Sand
☎ 01278 751595

Bristol and Clifton Golf Club
Beggar Bush Lane
Failand
☎ 01275 393474/393117/
393031

Burnham and Berrow Golf Club
Christopher Way
Burnham-on-Sea
☎ 01278 785760/784545/
783137

Cannington College Golf Course
Cannington
☎ 01278 655050

Chedington Court Golf Club
Holts Farm
South Perrott
☎ 01935 891413

Clevedon Golf Club
Castle Road
Walton St Mary
☎ 01275 874057/873140/874704/340578

Enmore Park Golf Club
Enmore
☎ 0101278 671481/671519/671740/671244

Entry Hill Golf Club
Entry Hill, Coombe Down
Bath
☎ 01225 834248

Farrington Golf Club
Marsh Lane
Farrington Gurney
☎ 01761 241274

Fosseway Golf Club
Charlton Lane
Midsomer Norton
☎ 01761 412214

Frome Golf Centre
Critchill Manor, Nunney Road
Frome
☎ 01373 453410

Golf Driving Range
Wolvershill Road
Banwell
☎ 01934 823382

Isle of Wedmore Golf Club
Wedmore
☎ 01934 713649

Kingsdown Golf Club
Kingsdown
Bath
☎ 01225 742530/743472

Lansdown Golf Club
Lansdown
Bath
☎ 01225 422138/425007/420242

Long Ashton Golf Club
Long Ashton
☎ 01275 392229/392265/392316

Long Sutton Golf Club
Long Sutton
☎ 01458 241017

Mendip Golf Club
Gurney Slade
☎ 01749 840570/840793

Mendip Spring Golf Club
Honeyhall Lane
Congresbury
☎ 01934 852322/853337

Minehead and West Somerset Golf Club
The Warren
Minehead
☎ 01643 702057

Oake Manor Golf Club
Oak
☎ 01823 461992/461993/461995

Orchardleigh Golf Club
Frome
☎ 01373 454200

Portishead Approach Golf Club
Nore Road
Portishead
☎ 01275 844951

Saltford Golf Club
Golf Club Lane
Saltford
☎ 01225 873220/872043

Tall Pines Golf Club
Cooks Bridle Path, Downside
Backwell
☎ 01275 472076

Taunton and Pickeridge Golf Club
Corfe
☎ 01823 421537/421240

Taunton Vale Golf Club
Creech Heathfield
☎ 01823 412220/412880

Tickenham Golf Club
Clevedon Road
Tickenham
☎ 01275 856626

Vivary Golf Club
Vivary Park
Taunton
☎ 01823 289274

Wells Golf Club
East Harrington Road
Wells
☎ 01749 672868/675005/
679059

Weston Golf Centre
Weston Links
Hutton Moor
☎ 01934 613423

Weston-super-Mare Golf Club
Uphill Road North
Weston-super-Mare
☎ 01934 626968

Wheathill Golf Club
Priory Farm, Wheathill
Lydford on Fosse, Somerton
☎ 01963 240667

Wincanton Golf Course (9 hole)
The Racecourse
Wincanton
☎ 01963 34606

**Windwhistle Golf,
Squash and Country Club**
Cricket St Thomas
☎ 01460 30231

**Woodspring Golf and
Country Club**
Yanley Lane
Long Ashton
☎ 01275 394378

Worlebury Golf Club
Worlebury Hill Road
Worlebury
☎ 01934 625789/623214/
418473

Yeovil Golf Club
Sherborne Road
Yeovil
☎ 01935 475949/422965

Riding

There are a number of riding schools and trekking centres in the county, especially on Exmoor, the Quantocks and Mendips. Details of these can be obtained from local Tourist Information Offices. Camel trekking is also available at:

Bridgwater Camel Co
Orchard Farm
Plainsfield
Over Stowey
☎ 01278 733186

Skiing

Avon Ski Centre
Lyncombe Lodge
Churchill
☎ 01934 852828/852335

Yeovil Ski Centre
Addlewell
Yeovil
☎ 01935 421702

SPORTS CENTRES

Backwell Leisure Centre
Farleigh Road
Backwell
☎ 01275 463726

Bath Sports and Leisure Centre
North Parade Road
Bath
☎ 01225 462563/462565

Bucklers Mead Sports Centre
1 St John's Road
Yeovil
☎ 01935 431716

Chew Valley Sports Centre
Chew Lane
Chew Magna
☎ 01275 333375

Chilton Trinity Sports Centre
Chilton Trinity School
☎ 01278 429119

Churchill Sports Centre
Churchill Green
☎ 01934 852303

Culverhay Sports Centre
Rush Hill
Bath
☎ 01225 480882

East Bridgwater Sports Centre
Parkway
Bridgwater
☎ 01278 456087

Frome Leisure Centre
Princess Anne Road
Frome
☎ 01373 465446

Glastonbury Leisure Centre
St Dunstan's Community School,
Wells Road
Glastonbury
☎ 01458 830090

Goldenstones
Brunswick Square
Yeovil
☎ 01935 74166

Gordano Sports Centre
St Mary's Road
Portishead
☎ 01275 843942

Huish Episcopi Sports Centre
Huish Episcopi School,
Wincanton Road
Langport
☎ 01458 251055

Hutton Moor Leisure Centre
Hutton, near Weston-super-Mare
☎ 01934 635347

Keynsham Leisure Centre
Temple Street
Keynsham
☎ 0117 986 1274

King Alfred Sports Centre
Burnham Road
Highbridge
☎ 01278 251055

Kings of Wessex Leisure Centre
Station Road
Cheddar
☎ 01934 744939

Parish Wharf Leisure Centre
Harbour Road
Portishead
☎ 01275 848494

Preston Sports Centre
Monks Dale
Yeovil
☎ 01935 412137

Scotch Horn Leisure Centre
Brockway
Nailsea
☎ 01275 856965

South Wansdyke Sports Centre
Rackvernal Road
Midsomer Norton
☎ 01761 415522

Strode Sports Centre
Strode Road
Clevedon
☎ 01275 879242

Tor Leisure Centre
Glastonbury
☎ 01458 832393

Wellington Sports Centre
Corams Lane
Wellington
☎ 01823 663010

Wells Leisure Centre
Charter Way
Wells
☎ 01749 670055

Yeovil Recreation Centre
Mudford Road
Yeovil
☎ 01935 411120

There are also several centres in Bristol

SWIMMING POOLS

Aquasplash
Seaward Way
Minehead
☎ 01643 708000

Burnham Pool
Berrow Road
Burnham-on-Sea
☎ 01278 785909/794764

Crewkerne Aqua Centre
South Street
Crewkerne
☎ 01460 77665

Greenbank Swimming Pool
Wilfrid Road
Street
☎ 01458 442468

Knights Templar First School
Liddymore Road
Watchet
☎ 01984 633429

Paulton Swimming Pool
Plumptre Road
Paulton
☎ 01761 412849

Portishead Open Air Swimming Pool
Esplanade Road
Portishead
☎ 01275 843454

Sedgemoor Splash
Mount Street
Bridgwater
☎ 01278 425636

Taunton Swimming Pool
Station Road
Taunton
☎ 01823 284108

Tropicana
Marine Parade
Weston-super-Mare
☎ 01934 626581

Shepton Mallet Outdoor Swimming Pool
Shaftsgate Avenue
Shepton Mallet
☎ 01749 342126

Solarsense
The Old Mill, Mead Lane
Saltford
☎ 01225 874299

Strode Swimming Pool
Strode Road
Street
☎ 01458 443918

There are also several pools in Bristol

WATER SPORTS

Somerset's reservoirs are controlled by Wessex Water who pub-lish a brochure on the sporting possibilities at each site. This is available from Tourist Information Offices or from:

Wessex Water
Wessex House
Passage Street
Bristol BS2 0JQ
☎ 0117 975 7788

The Middlemoor Water Park, near Bridgwater (☎ 01278 685578) also offers jet and water skiing.

TOURIST INFORMATION OFFICES

The main office for information is:

Somerset Tourism
Somerset Visitor Centre
Sedgemoor Services
M5 Motorway (South)
Axbridge BS26 2UF
☎ 01934 750833

Other main offices can be found at:

Bath
Abbey Chambers
☎ 01255 477101

Bridgwater
(Easter-September only)
50 High Street
☎ 01278 427652

Bristol
St Nicholas Church
St Nicholas Street
☎ 0117 926 0767

Burnham-on-Sea
South Esplanade
☎ 01278 787852

Chard
The Guildhall
Fore Street
☎ 01460 67463

Cheddar
(Easter-September only)
The Gorge
☎ 01934 744071

Frome
The Round Tower
Justice Lane
☎ 01373 467271

Glastonbury
The Tribunal
9 High Street
☎ 01458 832954

Gordano
Service Area, Junction 19 of M5
☎ 01275 375516

Minehead
17 Friday Street
☎ 01643 702624

Podimore
(Easter-September only)
Service Area, A303 near Yeovil
☎ 01935 841302

Taunton
The Library
Paul Street
☎ 01823 336344

Wells
Town Hall
Market Place
☎ 01749 672552

Weston-super-Mare
Beach Lawns
☎ 01934 888800

Yeovil
Petters House
Petters Way
☎ 01935 471279

The main information centre for the Exmoor National Park is at:

Exmoor National Park Authority
Exmoor House
Dulverton TA22 9HL
☎ 01398 323665

There are National Park Visitor Centres at:

County Gate
(Easter-September)
A39 near Countisbury
☎ 01598 741321

Dulverton
Fore Street
(Easter-October only)
☎ 01398 323841

Dunster
Dunster Steep
(Easter-October only)
☎ 01643 821835

There are also offices in Devon at Combe Martin
(☎ 01271 883319)
and Lynmouth
(☎01598 752509)

TRAVEL AND ACCOMMODATION

Somerset is easily reached, the M5 motorway traversing the county from north to south.

The county has an abundance of accommodation ranging from plain and simple hotels to luxury class hotels. Lists are available from the Tourist Information Offices.

WALKING

The Exmoor National Park has a regular programme of guided walks on the moor. Details are available from the Visitor Centres.

• Index •

• Index •

LANDMARK
Publishing Ltd

VISITORS GUIDES

* Practical guides for the independent visitor
* Written in the form of touring itineraries
* Full colour illustrations and maps
* Detailed Landmark FactFile of practical information
* Landmark Visitors Guides highlight all the interesting places you will want to see, so ensuring that you make the most of your visit

1. *Europe*

Bruges
Burgundy & Beaujolais
Cracow
Dordogne
Italian Lakes
Madeira
Iceland
Provence
Riga
Tallinn
Vilnius

2. *Other Titles*

Antigua & Barbuda
Bermuda
Dominican Republic
India: Goa
India: Kerala & The South
New Zealand
Florida Keys
Florida: Gulf Coast
Orlando & Central Florida
The Gambia
The Virgin Islands
Sri Lanca
St Lucia

Landmark Publishing
Waterloo House, 12 Compton,
Ashbourne, Derbyshire
DE6 IDA England
Tel: 01335 347349 Fax: 01335 347303
e-mail: landmark@clara.net

For all our UK titles see page 206

Published By
Landmark Publishing Ltd
Waterloo House, 12 Compton, Ashbourne,
Derbyshire DE6 1DA England
Tel: 01335 347349 e-mail: landmark@clara.net

1st Edition
ISBN 901 522 40 7

British Library Cataloguing in Publication Data: a catalogue record
for this book is available from the British Library.

Print: UIC Printing & Packaging Pte Ltd, Singapore
Cartography: James Allsopp
Designed by: James Allsopp

Cover Pictures

Front cover: The cathedral and Bishop's Palace, Wells
Back cover top: Remains of the abbey church, Glastonbury
Back cover bottom: The miniature Steam Railway,
Rode Bird Gardens

Picture Credits

Haynes Motor Museum: P95, **Secret World:** P139B,
Wookey Hole Caves, Marketing Dept: P147 & P154,
Chewton Cheese Dairy: P159, **Rode Bird Gardens:** Back Cover B
& P175, **Nicholas Sale:** P190, **American Museum:** P202,
Lindsey Porter: Cover, Back Cover T, 6, 11T, 11B, 15, 18, 19, 22L,
22B, 23, 27T, 27B, 30B, 31, 33, 34T, 34B, 38, 42T, 42B, 47, 50,
51, 54, 59, 62B, 63B, 94, 142, 155, 163T.
All other pictures are supplied by the author